REMEMBER THE FUTURE
(THE PROPHECIES OF NOSTRADAMUS)

by

Victor Baines
Holographic Books

REMEMBER THE FUTURE
(THE PROPHECIES OF NOSTRADAMUS)

by

VICTOR BAINES

HOLOGRAPHIC BOOKS
P.O. Box 101862
Fort Worth, Texas 76185
U.S.A.

THE NOSTRADAMUS SOCIETY OF AMERICA
http://www.NostradamusUSA.com

Cover Art by Keith Lymon

Printed in the United States of America

Special thanks to Shere, Alice, Liz, John, Jim, Phil, H.P.D., Chris, David, Vicki, Paul, Mike, Grayson, Tom, Curtis, Patti, Bob, T.S., Stuart, Ironman, Larry, Helen, Humena, Barbara, Robert and everyone else who provided assistance and inspiration during the creation of this literary project.

Copyright © 2001 by Victor Baines

Library of Congress Cataloging in Publication Data

Card Catalog #93-078753

Baines, Victor

REMEMBER THE FUTURE
(THE PROPHECIES OF NOSTRADAMUS)

1. Nostradamus, 1503-1566
2. Prophecy
3. Futurism

ISBN# 0-9631740-2-9

Some of the contents of this book are speculative in nature, and it is not the intent of the author (or publisher) of this literary work to advocate (or denounce) any particular nation, race, religion, special point of view, or position, in this book. We support the rights of freedom of speech, freedom of religion, and freedom of the press. The information presented in this book is intended to be educational in its scope and nature. The author and publisher shall have neither liability nor responsibility to any person, persons, or entity, with respect to any loss or damages caused, or alleged to be caused, directly or indirectly, by the information contained in this book.

All rights reserved. This copyright is protected under the Berne Copyright Convention, the Universal Copyright Convention, and the PanAmerican Copyright Convention. No part of this book may be reproduced, stored in a retrieval system, or transmitted in any form or by any means, electronic, mechanical, photocopying, recording, or otherwise, without prior express written consent of the publisher.

All plagiarizers and copyright infringers will be liable for civil damages under Title 17 U.S.C. 502, 503, 504, and 505 and possibly subject to criminal penalties under title 18 U.S.C. 2319.

*Dedicated in memory of Michel de Nostredame,
physician, astrologer, humanitarian, prophet.*

The souls of people, on their way to Earth-life, pass through a room full of lights; each takes a taper--often only a spark--to guide it in the dim country of this world. But some souls, by rare fortune, are detained longer--and have time to grasp a handful of tapers, which they weave into a torch. These are the torch-bearers of humanity--its poets, seers, and saints, who lead and lift the race out of darkness, toward the light. They are the law-givers and saviours, the light-bringers, way-showers and truth-tellers, and without them, humanity would lose its way in the dark.

--Plato

All I saw hast kept safe in a written record, here thy worth and eminent endowments come to proof.

--Dante (The Divine Comedy, Canto II)

When I was young I went to school for knowledge. But did I lose wisdom? Knowledge cuts the world into many pieces. Wisdom attempts to make the world whole.

--Shaman of the Macuna Tribe, Amazon Basin

Nothing is certain but the unforeseen.

--an ancient Chinese philosopher

Up, flee away o'er field and fen!
And let this dark, mysterious tome
from Nostradamus' very pen
suffice to guide you as you roam.

--Goethe, Faust (I, 1)

The input of the people determines the outcome of their democracy.

--Victor Baines

The input of the people determines the outcome of their democracy.

--Victor Baines

We have grasped the mystery of the atom and rejected the Sermon on the Mount. The world has achieved brilliance without wisdom; power without conscience. Ours is a world of nuclear giants, and ethical infants. We know more about war than we know about peace, more about killing than we know about living.

--General Omar Bradley, former Chairperson,
U.S. Joint Chief's of Staff

Humanity, as never before, is spilt into two apparently irreconcilable halves. Psychological rule says that when an inner situation is not made conscious, it happens outside, as fate. That is to say, when the individual remains divided and has not become conscious of his inner contradictions, the world must perforce act out the conflict and be torn into opposite halves.

--Dr. Carl Jung, Swiss psychiatrist

Woe is to you who cannot read the signs of the times.

--St. Luke

Give peace a chance!

--John Lennon, 1969

Noah's peers thought that he was losing his mind, and then, *the rain* began to fall.

--Victor Baines

TABLE OF CONTENTS

	PAGE
PROLOGUE	8
INTRODUCTION	9
THE BIOGRAPHY OF NOSTRADAMUS	10
ABOUT THE QUATRAINS	13
HYPOTHETICAL CHRONOLOGY OF THE FUTURE	20
GLOSSARY (PREFACE & QUATRAINS)	26
THE PREFACE TO "THE CENTURIES"	29
PROPHECY, SPIRITUALITY, DIVINITY	38
THE NAPOLEONIC ERA	40
ADOLF HITLER AND WORLD WAR II	53
CENTURY I	73
CENTURY II	80
CENTURY III	92
CENTURY IV	101
CENTURY V	106
CENTURY VI	117
CENTURY VII	124
CENTURY VIII	127
CENTURY IX	131
CENTURY X	138
THE NEW CITY (AMERICA?)	143
THE KENNEDY BROTHERS	147
THE UNITED KINGDOM	151
THE THIRD ANTICHRIST	156
THE CATHOLIC CHURCH	161
THE ASTROLOGICAL QUATRAINS	168
EARTH CHANGES	187
THE EPISTLE TO KING HENRY II AND SUB-GLOSSARY	192
IN CONCLUSION	212
ADDENDUM	214
INDEX TO THE QUATRAINS	216
BIBLIOGRAPHY & ACKNOWLEDGEMENTS	222

PROLOGUE

Thunder rumbled in the distance. Pondering the weight of my endeavor, I asked myself am I on the right track with this Nostradamus book? Taking a break from my research, I stepped out onto my balcony to view the splendor of an oncoming spring storm.

Looking up toward the heavens, a huge bolt of lightening thrust downward from the nocturnal sky, reaching its abrupt end some 50 feet above my head. Before I heard the thunder, the tip of the lightening bolt fragmented into smaller rays. The loud clap of thunder, which quickly followed, stood my hair on its end. After my adrenalin subsided, I realized that I had narrowly missed being struck by Zeus' folly!

The revelation then dawned upon me that "yes", I most certainly was on the right track with this book. Refocusing my thoughts, I anxiously returned indoors to rejoin my pen and paper. Sitting near the light of a candle, that illuminated from atop the visage of an angel, the words flowed through my pen like a cresting river.

INTRODUCTION

In May of 1791, during the passionate and emotional days of the French revolution, some drunken French soldiers became hell-bent on robbing the grave of Michel Nostradamus. Legend had it that whoever opened the grave of Nostradamus, and drank wine from his skull, would inherit his magical powers.

After much digging, the soldiers gathered around his grave and opened the casket lid. Much to their surprise they saw a metal plaque dated May, 1791. They gasped with amazement -- the plaque had to have been put there at the time of Nostradamus' death in 1566! After one of the soldiers drunk wine from his skull, they tossed Nostradamus' remains about the grave yard in a fit of intoxicated madness.

Hours later, the soldier who had drunk the wine from Nostradamus' skull was shot and killed by opposing troops. These grave robbing soldiers were apparently unaware that Nostradamus foresaw this event 217 years earlier. And they were further unaware that Nostradamus predicted that the robber of his grave would be struck down and killed.

Amazing you say? How else would one describe such an event foreseen by Nostradamus 217 years earlier? Incredible?

One of Nostradamus' first prophetic acts as a young man was when he fell to the ground in front of a young Catholic friar and kissed his feet while pronouncing him "Pope!" In 1585 this friar was anointed Pope Sextus V, nineteen years after Nostradamus' death. Unbelievable you might say?

Nostradamus has been credited with foreseeing many significant events over the centuries. He foresaw the accidental death of King Henry II of France in 1559; the splitting of the Catholic Church; the French Revolution and the storming of the Bastille; the rise of Napoleon and Hitler; the assassinations of John and Robert Kennedy; space travel; the Holocaust and the creation of Israel; the American landing on the Moon; Operation Desert Storm; and hundreds of other events.

Since its first publication in 1568, the only book which has out sold *The Prophecies* has been *The Holy Bible*. As we approach the end of one millennium and the beginning of another, public interest in *The Prophecies* is as strong and popular as ever. Nostradamus stated that as time passed, people would continue to see his writings as relevant and attach special significance to them.

This abridged version of *The Prophecies* contains the Epistle to King Henry II of France, the Preface (Nostradamus' letter to his son Caesar), and the Prohecies deemed significant to the past, and the approaching future.

The two glossaries contained in this book consist of various words, allusions, and geographic locations. Familiarizing yourself with these glossaries should make your reading easier. One glossary pertains to the quatrains and the Preface, the other pertains to the Epistle.

With the exception of the quatrains contained in the chapters of Century One through Ten, all the other quatrains have been chaptered as per the general subject matter of their contents.

THE BIOGRAPHY OF NOSTRADAMUS

Michel de Nostredame (Michael of Our Lady), whose latinized name was *Nostradamus*, was born on December 14th, 1503, 11 years after Christopher Columbus discovered the New World. Nostradamus' home town of St. Rémy de Provence, was located in France. His family, who was of Jewish decent, converted from Judaism to Catholicism when Nostradamus was still a young boy.

Some historians suggest that Nostradamus was a descendent of the lost Jewish tribe of Issacher, a tribe that was noted to be knowledgeable in astrology and the mystical arts. As a child, Nostradamus was apparently influenced by occult Jewish literature. Nostradamus' ancestors on his mother's side were men skilled in mathematics and medicine. His father, James, was a notary. Nostradamus' great-grandfather inspired him to study astrology and the celestial sciences when he was very young. It was then that Nostradamus was introduced to Latin, Greek and Hebrew. Later he was sent to Avignon, France, to study medicine.

In 1522, at the age of nineteen, Nostradamus decided to study medicine and enrolled at Mont Pellier (the most famous school of medicine in France). He graduated with a bachelor degree and was soon licensed to practice medicine. As a healer, he was active in treating the victims of the "Black Plague" and developed unique and effective methods of treatment which helped to lessen the suffering of many people.

At 26, Nostradamus returned to Mont Pellier to obtain his Doctor's degree. The academic skill he displayed while working towards his doctorate won him praise and admiration from the whole college. He was recruited as an instructor after his graduation and taught for about a year.

Upon leaving Mont Pellier, Nostradamus passed through Agen while returning to Toulouse and married a young woman. It was at this time Nostradamus is believed to have been reintroduced to mystical and ancient books of knowledge. Sadly, both Nostradamus' wife and their two children were struck by disease and died. As if to add insult to injury, in 1538 Nostradamus was falsely accused of heresy by Church officials, due to an innocent comment he made one day about a church statue. This was unjust because Nostradamus was a spiritual and religious man.

One misconception led to another, and the infamous agents of the Spanish Inquisition (the repressive European religious establishment of that era) sought his arrest. Wishing to avert the wrath of tainted religious extremists, Nostradamus left his home in France and wandered through Italy, avoiding arrest by the Inquisitors. Nostradamus did as he wished during this period traveling, making new friends, and constructing astrological charts for people.

Over time, circumstances reversed with the Inquisitors. And after traveling through Italy and France for six years, Nostradamus returned to his native turf where he was employed by the city of Aix in 1546. For a period of three years he again fought the plague. His services were viewed as invaluable by both his patients and his peers. Nostradamus later moved to Salon de Croux, married for a second time, and started a new family. It was during this period of his life that he acquainted himself with the apothecaries and healers of the area in order to include them in his book *Traite des Fardmens*, the world's first medical directory, which listed the names, location and specialties of physicians and healers practicing in Europe.

By 1555 Nostradamus had finished the first phase of his book that would contain his prophecies. Upon its publication, Nostradamus' fame quickly spread throughout Europe. This first version of his prophecies contained over 300 predictions. His book became very popular among the literate and educated Europeans of the day, so much so that the French Queen, Catherine de' Medici, summoned Nostradamus to her court in Paris. He and the Queen became close personal friends, and they discussed his quatrain predicting the death of her husband -- King Henri II of France. It was during that era that Nostradamus was appointed as the personal physician and royal advisor to Henry II. Later, he also advised the French Kings Francis II and Charles IX.

Nostradamus was called to Paris by the Queen a second time and was asked to draw astrological horoscopes for the royal children. In 1557, when he was told that the Justices of Paris were again asking about his magical practices, he hurriedly returned to Salon.

On June 28, 1559, quatrain # 1-35 which predicted the accidental death of an "old lion" (an allusion to Henri -- the King of France) came true. Some people were upset with Nostradamus, others amazed. His fame grew even more. Nostradamus remained in Salon for a number of years, and continued to work on his writings. He was visited by many people of nobility and distinction during those days.

In 1565-66, Nostradamus' health began to be troubled with gout and arthritis. His health continued to worsen and he wrote his will on June 17, 1566. On July 1st, Nostradamus sent for the local Catholic priest and requested that his last rites be administered to him, telling his close friend Chavigny that he would not live to see the next day.

As Nostradamus prophesied, he was found dead in the morning, and was buried in one of the walls of the Church of the Cordeliers, in Salon. After the incident with the revolutionary soldiers described in the Introduction, the old prophet's remains were reburied at the Church of St. Laurent in Salon, France.

In the words of James Chavingy, his friend and understudy, Michel Nostradamus was described as a good man.

> "He was a little under medium height, of robust body, nimble and vigorous. He had a large and open forehead, a straight and even nose, gray eyes which were generally pleasant, but which blazed when he was angry. By nature he was taciturn, thinking much and saying little, though speaking very well in the proper time and place. He slept only four to five hours per night. He praised and loved freedom of speech, and showed himself joyous and facetious, as well as biting, in his joking. He approved of the ceremonies of the Roman Church and held to the Catholic faith and religion. I do not want to forget to say

that he engaged willingly in fasts, prayers, alms, and patience; he abhorred vice and chastised it severely. I can remember his giving to the poor, towards whom he was very liberal and charitable."

After his death, his son Caesar gathered the remaining prophecies which had been unpublished up to that point, and published them in 1568, two years after Nostradamus passed away.

ABOUT THE QUATRAINS

One thing is certain, Nostradamus apparently took the good times for granted because he seldom wrote about them. Therefore, the majority of the quatrains which comprise the complete prophecies of Nostradamus deal with war, famine, plague, social conflict, revolution, earthquakes, flooding and other calamitous events.

Nostradamus referred to the ten chapters of his famous book *The Centuries* as "centuries," although they have nothing to do with one hundred-year cycles. Each of the centuries (or chapters) included in the complete prophecies of Nostradamus contain 100 quatrains, except for Century VII which has 42, for a total of 942 prophecies. Nostradamus intentionally confused the chronological order of his *quatrains* (a four line prophetic stanza which constitutes one of his prophecies) as a way to make the interpretation of future events slightly more difficult.

To understand what Nostradamus was trying to say, the theory of *less can be more* was utilized in this book. Thus, after a detailed examination of all his quatrains, most of the ones which appeared to have not yet been fulfilled, were separated from the ones which seemed to have already occurred.

These unfulfilled quatrains are the major focus of this work, especially the ones which make references to natural disasters and future military conflicts involving N.A.T.O. countries (European and North American nations who are members of the North Atlantic Treaty Organization).

This book also contains the quatrains which appear to apply to the times of Napoleon Bonaparte and Adolf Hitler (Nostradamus' first and second so-called antichrists). Some quatrains which appear to have been fulfilled in the recent past are also included in this work. In these recently fulfilled quatrains, as well as in the quatrains pertaining to Napoleon and Hitler, Nostradamus appears to have accurately forecasted various events which have now come to pass.

The prophetic French text used in this book was borrowed from the 1568 edition of *The Centuries,* published by the Frenchman, Benoit Reigaud. Care was taken to stay as literal as possible in the English translations located to the right of the original quatrains, which are composed mostly of old French, but also include Provençal, Latin, Greek (and a few English words). The quatrain number is located in the center of the page and the author's interpretation of the quatrain is located just beneath the French text and English translation.

The interpretations of some quatrains are very specific, others more general in nature. The clearly stated quatrains speak for themselves, requiring little interpretation. Most quatrains, however, require a detailed examination.

Some readers might be shocked by the perceived content of some quatrains, for in many ways Nostradamus' quatrains read like a book of a 1001 future disasters. Yet in an effort to remain unbiased, even the most unpleasant predictions were analyzed in detail.

Bearing this fact in mind it is hoped that readers will realize that the author intends no offense to any particular nation, religion, or specific group of people, in this work. It can easily be said that Nostradamus included enough unpleasant predictions to go around for everyone, regardless of their national origin or personal beliefs. Nostradamus apologized in the Epistle for being unable to please all the people, in all the regions of the world, in regard to the content of his predictions.

It is challenging to be 100% unbiased toward anything, considering that we are all creatures of our societal (and environmental) programming and conditioning. Nevertheless, a concerted effort was made on behalf of the author to remain neutral and unbiased while examining and interpreting Nostradamus' writings.

Over the past 400 years, the interpretations of almost every commentator on Nostradamus' prophecies appears to have been influenced by the events of the century in which they were living and writing. For example, nineteenth-century commentators were tempted to apply "nineteenth-century" interpretations to certain quatrains, while twentieth-century commentators might be influenced in their interpretations, by the events of their own times. Taking this temptation into consideration, precautions were taken to not let this rule of thumb effect the author's personal interpretations in this book.

Nostradamus stated in the Epistle, that as time goes on, he perceived his prophecies to "carry more weight". This is interesting and seemingly correct, especially considering that as time passes, with a little hindsight, we can see the past from a clearer perspective.

In the Preface (a letter dedicated to his son Caesar) Nostradamus stated that his prophetic quatrains were "covered with a veil cloud, but are clear enough to be comprehended by men of good intelligence."

Thus, considering the magnitude (and ramifications) of the events prophesied in most quatrains, my interpretations of the prophecies were written in a uniquely definitive style, addressing key words and phrases contained in the quatrains. Utilizing this definitive method of interpretation assures that every phrase is scrutinized, so that nothing is overlooked.

Some quatrains were written in a manner that suggests a chronology of time from the beginning of the quatrain to its end. The first line or two of this type of quatrain may pertain to one given period of time, while the lines following it may apply to a time frame later than the lines before it. While this chronological rule does not apply to all quatrains, it seems to apply to some.

The majority of the quatrains pertain to the geographical regions of France, Europe, the Mediterranean, North Africa, the Middle East, and Asia. A few quatrains pertain to the New World, one pertains to the Moon, and a couple of others make references to outer space.

The phrases Nostradamus may have used as allusions to the United States of America include "the Eagle, the three brothers, the New City, Arethusa, l'Americh, and the younger in the land of Britany." The word "Hesperia" (the lands of the West) appears to be an allusion to the geographical region of the New World.

Nostradamus' writing style is more like that of a reporter, rather than a judge. Occasionally, however, he lets his personal feelings be known in a subtle manner by the choice of his words.

It should be noted that most of the quatrains appear to be written as if Nostradamus had already "seen" them occur, as if his visions and predictions were part of history, instead of as yet to be verified future events.

To many people's amazement, Nostradamus wrote the proper sirnames of several of history's greatest men in his quatrains. This includes men like Charles DeGaulle (French general and president), Francisco Franco (revolutionary and Chief of Spain), Primo de Rivera (Franco's rival during the Spanish Revolution of the 1930's), Joseph Montgolfier (Frenchman and inventor of the modern balloon) and Louis Pasteur (the renowned French chemist and inventor of pasteurization).

As if he were teasing us, Nostradamus used the name "Hister" in several quatrains, which appears to suggest Adolf "Hitler". He also used an anagram "Pau, Nay, Loron" which suggests "Napaulon Roy" (or in English -- Napaulon King) as an allusion to Napoleon Bonaparte.

Nostradamus wrote dozens of quatrains describing events which occur during the times of his three so-called antichrists (two of which have come and gone). The third antichrist is yet to arrive.

As used in the context of this book, we can define antichrist as an "individual" who is an enemy of Christ, an antagonist of his teachings, and someone more warlike than peaceful. Although Nostradamus made several references to the antichrists in his quatrains, it is in the Epistle that Nostradamus goes into greater detail describing the three antichrists (see paragraphs #45, #46, and #55 in the Epistle).

Though Nostradamus failed to clearly state the names of his three antichrists, the personification of at least two of his antichrists becomes apparent if we penetrate his literary camouflage. Thus, Nostradamus never plainly stated that Napoleon and Hitler were the first and second antichrists. However, if we personify Nostradamus' allusions to the antichrists mentioned in paragraphs #45 and #46 in the Epistle, it becomes apparent that Napoleon and Hitler were the two individuals he was referring to.

Nostradamus' first two antichrists entranced large masses of people by their speech and maliciously vexed the citizens of other nations (both Christian and non-Christian nations). These so-called antichrists seemed to have little regard for peace and were perceived as heroes by most of their fellow countrymen. Among other things, Napoleon and Hitler were clever manipulators who succeeded in mesmerizing the population of their own countries first, followed by the mesmerization of weaker individuals who led other nations, enticing them to ally themselves with the given antichrist.

As evidenced by history, these two men maintained absolute control over powerful military forces, which they utilized as a tool to manipulate others. Nostradamus' antichrists appear to trouble the Vatican and whichever pope is seated during the reign of the given antichrist.

Ironically, Nostradamus' first two antichrists were from traditional nations of Christianity; France and Germany. Napoleon was the lesser of the antichrists, Hitler was incomparably worse than Napoleon, and the third antichrist will be more horrific than either of the previous two.

Since Nostradamus suggests that Napoleon and Hitler were the first and second antichrists of modern European history, quatrains which deal with their respective eras were included in this book as a way to see, in retrospect, if what he had prophesied about them was indeed historically accurate.

The name and geographical domain of the yet-to-arrive third antichrist remains somewhat of a mystery and is a topic of great interest among Nostradamus commentators. But according to this author's research, the allusion Nostradamus may have used as a reference to the third antichrist is the name "Selin". It appears that Selin will be a Muslim leader of an Asian nation located east of the Black Sea.

In the Preface, Nostradamus states that his prophecies are "perpetual vaticinations from the 16th century, to the year 3797" (when perhaps humanity or the world as we know it comes to an end). He refers to this event as *the final conflagration* (a great destruction by fire). Nostradamus states that during the years preceding the final conflagration the Earth will be bombarded by burning stones from the heavens (suggesting a massive meteor shower or asteroid strike). If Nostradamus is correct, this would indicate that mankind has approximately 1800 years remaining before meeting his "final" doom.

This seems to suggest that no matter how horrible or disastrous any particular future earth change or war might be, humanity will endure the great suffering and will continue to move forward into the future. A possible exception to this concept might be the catastrophic events around the year 3797.

The idea of global doom at the change of a millennium is a concept rooted in medieval Christian folklore which evolved in Europe shortly after the year 1000 A.D. Apparently, devout Christians of that era faithfully anticipated the end of the world due to their misinterpretation of a particular line from the Holy Bible. Much to their amazement, the end of the world never occurred!

Readers should not confuse this age-old superstitious notion with any direct quote from Nostradamus. The idea that Nostradamus said the world was going to end around the year 2000 is merely a myth and not based in fact, as per the writings of Nostradamus.

It is common for people in Western societies to associate the word "prophecy" with religious matters. However, the word has several connotations. It is imperative to realize this fact so as not to mistakenly confuse the prophecies of Nostradamus with the prophecies contained in the Holy Bible, the Koran, the Bhagavad-Gita, or any other book of religion. Though Nostradamus was a Christian, his book *The Centuries* is not classified as a religious work by orthodox theologians.

According to the Catholic Church, of which Nostradamus was a member, any prophecy other than the prophecy of Christ is considered to be a *personal prophecy*. Therefore, the prophecies of Nostradamus are considered to be personal prophecies, as defined by Catholicism. Though Nostradamus states that devine inspiration compelled him as a prophet and he references Biblical texts in the Preface and Epistle, the author has purposely avoided analyzing *The Centuries* from a Biblical perspective. Analyzing the writings of Nostradamus from a Biblical perspective is a matter for theologians and would require another book in itself.

Nostradamus stated in his Incantation of the Law Against Inept Critics, "may those who read this verse think upon it profoundly, let the profane and ignorant herd keep away. And far away all astrologers, idiots and barbarians, may he who does otherwise be subject to the sacred rite."

Considering that Nostradamus was himself an astrologer, this warning might have applied to the astrologers of the Third Reich, or to any other astrologers, who had (have, or may someday have) an ill intent toward his prophetic writings.

Dr. Carl Jung, the renowned Swiss physician and founder of the analytical discipline of psychology that bears his name, stated that Nostradamus must have been familiar with Alchemy, since that was an art used mainly by physicians in the Renaissance days.

He suggests that Nostradamus probably had read the classics of Alchemy like the *Turba philosophorum, Allegorical super librum Turbae,* the *Allegoriae sapientum supra librum Turbae XXIX distinctions,* together with the *Aenigmata ex Visione Arislei* and *In Turbam philosophorum exercitationes*. Nostradamus apparently utilized various principles of alchemy and ancient mystical knowledge, which he combined with astrological calculations, as the method he used to "see" into the future.

In his book *Aion*, Dr. Jung stated that "the course of our religious history, as well as an essential part of our psychic development, could have been predicted more or less accurately, both as regards time and content, from the precession of the equinoxes through the constellation of Pisces." By making this statement Dr. Jung, in essence, seems to consider astrology as a valid predictive science (or "fine art" depending upon your point of view).

This is interesting since Nostradamus was a noted astrologer and integrated astrological positions and terminology into some of his quatrains. Presumably, Nostradamus included astrological positions (called transits) in some quatrains, as a way to provide potential dates for the fulfillment of various prophesied events. He also used astrological terminology as a means to help describe certain aspects of some of the characters and situations contained in his quatrains.

In addition to alchemy, astrology, and Kabalistic mysticism, Nostradamus may have utilized *astral travel* as one of the methods he used to see into the future. Astral travel consists of one's spiritual body temporarily leaving one's physical body (via meditation or the dream state) allowing one to travel forward or backward in time, while perceiving events both near and far. Recently the phrase *remote viewing* has been used to describe the activity of astral travel.

According to astral travelers many secrets of the future can be perceived in this out-of-body state. Although this ability is not fully understood by modern science, astral travelers (and people who have lived through near death experiences) testify to the existence of the spiritual realm beyond our physical existence.

It should be noted that the interpretations arrived at in this book have nothing to do with *channeling* (the process of inviting the spirit of a deceased person to speak through the voice of a living medium) as utilized by one interpreter of Nostradamus' predictions. Although channeling might indeed prove to be valid in some situations, common sense should tell us that this unverifiable process also leaves open the possibility for misinformation on each end of the spectrum (both in the spiritual realm and on the material plane).

The literal method of interpretation was utilized in this book in the attempt to assure that we focused upon what Nostradamus himself wrote, exempting our interpretations from those who take greater liberties in interpreting his prophecies. Due to the magnitude of most of the events prophesied in the quatrains, a common sense approach in deciphering them seemed imperative.

In spiritual defense against anyone who chooses to maliciously slander his prophecies (as in the case of Nazi Propaganda Minister Joseph Goebbels), Nostradamus stated in his Epistle ". . . there are some who would attribute to me that which is not mine at all. The eternal God, alone, who is the thorough searcher of human hearts, pious, just and merciful, is the true judge, and it is to him I pray to defend me from the calumny of evil men."

A case could be made for the perceived validity of many of Nostradamus' prophecies. Though a few of his predictions have seemed to fail, the majority of his predictions have already been shown to bear a remarkable likeness to recorded history.

Detractors of Nostradamus argue that the validity of any given prediction is all a matter of interpretation and several possible interpretations could be made for any quatrain. Though this idea might at first appear to have some merit, Nostradamus states in the Epistle that ". . . such secrets should not be bared except in enigmatic sentences having, however, only one sense and meaning, and nothing ambiguous or amphibological inserted."

Since Nostradamus stated that his quatrains have only one intended meaning, the challenge presented to any interpreter of his prophecies is to accurately determine the "exact" meaning that Nostradamus intended for any given quatrain. This presents a challenge to interpreters of his prophecies, since this is the most important parameter every interpreter must take into consideration while deciphering the quatrains. Thus, the issue of validity regarding the quatrains is actually a matter to be determined by the intelligence of the interpreter.

The bottom line regarding Nostradamus' predictions leave us with five basic possibilities. 1.) Either his prophecies are false and people can view them as false. 2.) They can be false and people can view them as valid. 3.) They are valid and people can view them as false. 4.) They are valid and people can view them as valid. 5.) His predictions are neither false nor valid, but simply consist of psychic visions (premonitions received through means of alchemy and ancient knowledge) combined with astrological calculations, therefore, "sometimes right, sometimes wrong".

One prudent course of thought might be to be aware of the perceived contents of Nostradamus' prophecies consider the impact that the fulfillment of any particular prediction may have (in case it later proves to be correct), and then either construct a plan of prevention (if you think you are empowered with the ability to effect or alter the perceived outcome of a particular quatrain), or adopt a *wait and see* attitude regarding their fulfillment.

Let's examine Nostradamus' quatrains (and other writings) to see what information they contain. You, the reader, can then decide if you feel they are relevant to our past, present, and future.

HYPOTHETICAL CHRONOLOGY OF THE FUTURE

The challenge was to unveil the future as we enter the third millennium A.D. Nostradamus was a man who had a message, yet making sense of his message would be in vain unless a clearer view of potential future events could be obtained.

This abridged version of *The Centuries* attempts to focus on events which could possibly be fulfilled between 2000 and 2050. However, some of the quatrains included in this book may not be fulfilled until decades or centuries later.

If it appears that Nostradamus was accurate in his predictions pertaining to the last four centuries, then odds are his future predictions pertaining to natural disasters, Euro/Arabic conflicts, the war with the future third antichrist, and other events, are most likely accurate and relevant as well. We could build a case for the accuracy of the quatrains pertaining to the future based upon the perceived accuracy of Nostradamus' quatrains pertaining to the past.

With this in mind, we should consider that Nostradamus was a Frenchman of Jewish descent, he was a Christian and appeared to be interested in protecting his homeland of France, the followers of Christianity (as well as all of humanity) against future danger and the potential enemies of peace.

In an attempt to make sense of the future we can develop hypothetical scenarios of possible future events by linking certain quatrains together with other quatrains of similar subject matter, time frames, and geographical regions.

Due to Nostradamus' intentional confusion of linear time in the sequence of the quatrains it is possible to construct hypothetical scenarios of future events which might later be proven correct, or incorrect (considering the fact that we, in most cases, can only guess in which century any particular quatrain was intended to be fulfilled). Though this process could be analogous to solving the "ultimate" crossword puzzle (regarding time frames and events), this perplexing challenge remains fair-game. After all, we are in possession of the pieces of the puzzle, so our challenge is to recognize topical themes, and attempt to determine the time sequence of their potential future fulfillment.

With this in mind, the following are brief hypothetical scenarios of what may possibly lay ahead in the future, if some of the quatrains included in this book were intended to be fulfilled before the year 2050. These "worst-case" scenarios are followed by a wide range of potential years in which "some" of these events could possibly occur.

With the exception of quatrain #10-72 (which plainly states the year 1999) and quatrains #2-46 and #10-74 (which mention the change of a millennium -- suggesting the times around the years 2000 or 3000), all the other dates presented in this chapter were obtained by information contained in the astrological quatrains. Please refer to the chapter titled the Astrological Quatrains for a detailed explanation of how these potential dates were derived.

Rather than attempting to formulate a sequential year-to-year chronology, general themes concerning future wars and natural disasters are presented, followed by some of the hypothetical dates in which they have the potential to occur (between 2000 and the year 2050 A.D.).

Though present political and military alliances may endure into the future, readers should consider the possibility that these alliances, as they exist now, may differ slightly from the ones which might be formed (or restructured) during the progression of the 21st century. Therefore, the possibility for the emergence of new international alliances and confederations (some being favorable to the West, others adverse) certainly exists, especially in Africa, the Middle East, the former Soviet Union, and various parts of Asia.

Quatrain # 2-89 appears to suggest that the United States and Russia would one day be "friends" again, and their combined power would appear to grow. Since the collapse of the Iron Curtain, and up to the millennial era, this has indeed been the case. However, quatrain #4-95 and #5-78 seem to suggest that this friendship might be short lived (if these quatrains are in fact references to the United States and Russia). If by chance this later becomes true, the reversal of friendship between them could impact many global events to come.

In quatrain # 10-72, Nostradamus predicted an event for July (or September) of 1999 which involved some type of military combat, or other event, by means of the sky. It appears that it foreshadowed NATO's air-war in Serbia, the military tension between China and Taiwan, Russia's war in Chechyna, and the tragic death of John F. Kennedy Jr. Due to the timeliness of this prophecy, this particular quatrain aroused great curiosity among the public.

Beyond the events around the change of the millennium, it appears that conflicts between Christian and Islamic nations have the potential to occur. This could involve one or a combination of the following nations: Iran, Algeria, Morocco, Pakistan, Tunisia, Syria, Libya, Sudan, Iraq, various nations of the former Soviet Union, and others; against Turkey, Italy, France, Germany, Austria, Spain, Portugal, Greece, Macedonia, Hungary, the United States, Israel, the United Kingdom, and various allies of these nations.

By land, various Islamic armies (and their allies) might one day invade Turkey, Macedonia, Greece, Hungary, the former Yugoslavia, Austria, and eventually march towards Italy, attacking the Italians and other forces located there. From Italy, the invaders could then attack other nations in various parts of Europe. It appears that Greece might endure chemical or biological warfare in these conflicts (see quatrains #9-91, #5-47, and #6-21). Algeria, Tunisia, Morocco, and Libya may attempt to vex Egypt by land. By sea, these same North African nations appear to invade the southern coastline of France, Monaco, and Spain (then deeper into Europe).

Some of these conflicts could occur in one massive sweep. Or, they might take place over an extended period of years. In addition to land war, these conflicts seem to involve heavy naval warfare in the Mediterranean, Tyrrhenian and Aegean Seas. The nations of N.A.T.O. (or its future equivalent) and their various allies appear to eventually prevail in these conflicts.

The fate of Israel remains unclear. However, in paragraph #34 of the Epistle, Nostradamus states that Jerusalem might be assailed on all sides, and a Western naval force (from the United States and or other nations in the New World) will help Israel in fighting the forces of its future adversaries.

According to astrological information the years for the potential occurrence of these conflicts (between the period of 2000 to 2050) might be: 2000, 2002, 2013, 2015-16, 2017, 2019, 2021, 2030, 2037, 2038, and 2044.

One should consider the possibility that Euro/Arabic or "Muslim/Christian" conflicts might occur before, during, or after the war with the yet-to-arrive third antichrist. How Euro/Arabic conflicts inter-relate with the war with the third antichrist is unclear at this time. Some of them will be part of his war, and some of them might be precursory or unrelated independent events.

Nostradamus appears to suggest that the future third antichrist will come from a region east of the Black Sea. In paragraph #23 of the Epistle he states that "the grand Empire of the Antichrist shall begin in the region of the former empire of Attila" (Attila was the leader of the Asian Huns who invaded Europe during the fifth century). Nostradamus refers to the third antichrist as "the new Xerxes" (Xerxes was the Persian king who unsuccessfully invaded Greece in 480 B.C.).

Nostradamus intentionally used the names "Attila" and "Xerxes" as allusions to personality types and geographical areas. Thus, in a geographical sense, this suggests that he was referring to various regions of eastern Europe, Asia, and the Middle East.

The army of the third antichrist (an enemy of peace) will begin its trek towards Europe from a region between the Caspian and Black Seas. It appears that they will pass through Alania (southwestern Russia) and Armenia, then into Turkey (quatrain #5-54). From there they invade most all of Europe.

The naval forces of the third antichrist will be accompanied by the Libyan fleet into the Mediterranean and Adriatic Seas (quatrain #1-9). One of the climaxes of this future conflict appears to be a colossal naval engagement in the Adriatic Sea (quatrain #5-27). Island locations which sustain damage in this war include Malta, Euboea, Sicily, Sardinia, the Dodecanese Islands, and the Cyclades.

If the Russians are "not" allied with Europe and the West during the beginning of this war, Nostradamus states in the Epistle that a northern king from Aquilon (an allusion to Russia) will eventually help to set things right.

This suggests that if the Russians are allied against Europe and the New World at the start of this conflict, they will reverse their position at some future point during the hostilities, and militarily realign themselves with Europe and the West in an effort to quash the "Easterners". As used in Nostradamus' Epistle, "Easterners" would be a reference to the citizens of China, former Soviet nations in central and eastern Asia, the Muslim nations of the Middle East and Asia, and or other countries of the Orient.

Therefore, in consideration of all the prophetic information contained in the quatrains and Epistle, it appears likely that China, in an alliance with certain Muslim nations (and other countries) might be the source of future troubles for many nations around the world.

Apparently, various nations who embrace Christianity will be military targets of the third antichrist. Nostradamus clearly states in his Epistle that the followers of Christianity will face a horrific persecution in the future.

The war with the future third antichrist, according to Nostradamus, will last for the duration of 27.5 years (suggesting a protracted war). N.A.T.O., S.E.A.T.O. (or their future equivalent) and their allies appear to be victorious over the third antichrist's forces. However there appears to be great losses on both sides of this futuristic conflict.

Nostradamus appears to suggest that various regions will one day be struck by missiles (in Europe, the West and elsewhere). New York City might be the location of a direct hit (see quatrains #4-99 and #6-97).

In paragraph #33 of the Epistle, Nostradamus states that a pestilence will develop in the future which will remove two-thirds of the world's population. Could this be a reference to futuristic nuclear or biological war? If so, could this possibly be connected with the third antichrist's war?

When will the third antichrist make his appearance? Will he appear sometime during the first or second quarter of the twenty-first century? It seems possible, yet the answer remains unclear. Hopefully he will never manifest himself and the world will be spared from his wrath.

However, if he makes his appearance before the year 2050, hypothetical years for events which might involve him could be: 2000, 2002, 2006, 2009, 2011, 2013, 2015, 2016, 2019, 2024, 2026, 2028, 2030, 2038, 2041, 2043, 2044, and 2049.

In his Epistle, Nostradamus stated that at some point in the future, global flooding will occur. No specific date is mentioned regarding its occurrence, except that it will happen sometime "after" the fall of the future third antichrist.

Some scientists have suggested that the possibility of universal flooding is not as remote as it may seem. Global warming appears to be real and the average temperature of the Earth continues to rise year after year, possibly due to carbon emissions from the combustion of coal and oil, and other human related factors (and not necessarily due to the natural variations of the Earth's climate).

If atmospheric heating continues, sea levels could rise as much as three feet in the next century, and if that occurs, the universal flood Nostradamus predicted could one day become reality. A world-wide flood would have a devastating effect upon the Earth.

In addition to flooding, if global warming continues, it could affect rainfall patterns resulting in droughts and famine, affecting the spread of various infectious diseases. And considering the fact that Nostradamus penned many predictions pertaining to droughts, famines, floods, and pestilences, it should serve as a warning to us to consider the long term consequences of this perplexing phenomenon.

Some modern commentators feel that Nostradamus hints at the possibility of a future polar shift, as per the text in paragraph #24 of the Epistle. In example, the on-going heating of the Earth could melt the ice in the polar regions creating not only floods, but producing conditions that could allow for an "off balancing" of the Earth on its axis.

If a polar-shift were to occur, it would cause our planet to quickly shift upon its axis, making a correction to reestablish a new center of its gravity. In the opinion of many modern scientists, in geological terms the Earth is long over due for a polar shift. A polar shift would be quite devastating and could trigger earthquakes and tidal waves (as well as the long term failure of crops and eco-systems).

Some have hypothesized that the gravitational effect created by an alignment of various planets within our own solar system could also serve as a catalyst to produce a polar shift. Another event which could trigger a polar shift could be a collision between the Earth and an asteroid or comet (as occurred on Jupiter in 1994).

According to Velikovsky, a student of Einstein, polar shifts have occurred frequently throughout the geological history of the Earth as referenced in his books *Earth in Upheaval* and *Worlds in Collision*. And in the opinion of many modern scientists, in geological terms -- the Earth is long overdue for a polar shift.

It remains speculation as to whether or not Nostradamus was trying to suggest a polar shift by use of the phrase "the grand translation". But if we consider that Nostradamus frequently used synonyms in his writing, we should consider it as a future possibility.

If a universal flood, massive earthquakes, a polar shift, or a mighty tidal wave were to occur at some point in the future, it could act as an accelerant, initiating hostilities between nations who might otherwise be at peace with one another. A catastrophe of great magnitude might compel the militaries (and citizens) of the various nations affected by it to panic in the chaos and fight over the remaining food and resources, as they scramble for safe ground.

In regards to future earthquakes (between 2000-2050), possible dates for their occurrence, as per astronomical information contained in the quatrains are as follows: earthquakes in America and/or Italy -- 2015, 2016, 2044; earthquakes in Asia -- 2013 and 2026; world-wide earthquakes -- 2048. But readers should bare in mind that Nostradamus did not make predictions for "every" earthquake which will rock our Earth in the future. Earthquakes can occur (in various regions) at anytime and with no warning at all.

After the defeat of the third antichrist, and the passing of the great flood, Nostradamus states in his Epistle that a one thousand year period of peace will prevail upon the planet. Then, new wars appear to present themselves (perhaps around the year 3100).

Hopefully the future will be more positive than the gloomy hypothetical scenarios presented in this chapter. After all, considering that Nostradamus took "the good times" for granted, we must assume that many positive and wondrous events will transpire inbetween future periods of peril. With the exception of natural disasters, which mankind can affect, but cannot presently control, the future is somewhat in our hands to mold. Or is it?

Perhaps the challenge presented to humanity by Nostradamus' writings is to be observant, to heed the warning signs he left for our benefit. Hopefully, then, we will be better able to formulate intelligent alternatives to disaster.

If we heed Nostradamus' warnings and make a concerted effort to preserve the Earth's environment, and avoid disputes among nations, then his predictions will have served the purpose of steering mankind away from self-destruction.

If, on the other hand, we prove to be incapable of avoiding conflicts and disasters, then at least we have some idea of what the darker side of the future may hold.

GLOSSARY OF TERMS, ALLUSIONS, AND GEOGRAPHIC LOCATIONS (PREFACE & QUATRAINS)

AENOBARBE, an allusion to Charles De Gaulle.

ALANIA, a region of southwestern Russia located between the Volga River, the River Don, and the Caucasus mountains, formerly the land of the Alans.

ALCHEMY, a mystical system for man's salvation of his soul and ultimate reunion with his divine source. The system consisted of symbols, rituals, procedures, and doctrines which were guarded with great secrecy. The four elements (Earth, Air, Fire, and Water) played a major role in alchemy. In many ways, alchemy was the precursor of modern chemistry. The foremost duty of the alchemist was to improve upon divine creation and develop it further. The "oneness" of all things was one of their fundamental principles.

AMPHIBOLOGICAL, ambiguity arising from a grammatical construction that can be understood in more than one way.

ANTICHRIST, an individual who is an enemy of Christ and an antagonist of his teachings.

AQUILON, derived from the Latin word "Aquilonaris" (northern), an allusion to Russia and possibly other former Soviet states and various parts of northern Asia.

AQUITAINE, a historical region of southwestern France between the Pyrenees and the Garonne River.

ARETHUSA, an orchid native to the eastern region of North America, perhaps an allusion to the United States and/or North America. It is also an anagram for "Earth, USA".

BARBARIANS, in ancient Greece this would suggest uncivilized persons living to the east of Greece.

BYZANTIUM, a Greek city on the site which Constantine built the great city of Constantinople (presently Istanbul), an allusion to Turkey.

CELTS, the ancient people of western and central Europe including the Britons and the Gauls (the French and the British).

DALMATIA, a region of Croatia along the eastern coast of the Adriatic Sea.

DRIZZLE, an allusion to a substance which falls from the sky, perhaps a combination of rain and fall-out.

ETHNOGRAPHIES, geographical regions inhabited by ancient or primitive societies (i.e., parts of Africa, Australia, North and South America, and Asia).

FLEMISH, pertaining to Flanders, (the Dutch).

GALLIC, of or pertaining to ancient Gaul (or modern France).

GAUL, an ancient name for modern France, a Frenchman, represents France.

GREAT OCEAN, an allusion to the Atlantic Ocean.

GREAT ST. BERNARD PASS, a land pass through the Alps mountain range between France and Italy.

HESPERIA, in Greek mythology "the Lands of the West" (an allusion to America and the New World).

HISTER, an allusion to Adolf Hitler. "Hister" is just one letter off from the word "Hitler".

INSUBRIA, an old Roman name for Lombardy, an allusion to Italy.
ISLES, when this word is used with a capital "i" (I) in the text of a quatrain, it appears to be an allusion to the British Isles.
JUDICIAL ASTROLOGY, a type of astrology by which the acts and fates of men and nations might be foreknown.
KING, a reference to a king or monarch. Sometimes "king" is used as an allusion to a national leader, i.e., a president or prime minister.
LIGUARIA, a coastal region of northwest Italy, an allusion to Italy.
LOMBARDY, a region of northern Italy, an allusion to Italy.
LUISTANIA, an ancient name for modern Portugal.
MAHOMETAN, the followers of the prophet Mohammed, Muslims, people of the Islamic faith.
MANTUA, a city (and/or region) of northern Italy, an allusion to the Italians.
MARS, in Roman Mythology, the god of war. In astrology the planet Mars can suggest war and conflict. Thus Mars is an allusion to war. When "Mars" appears in an astrological quatrain, it pertains to the planet Mars.
MESOPOTAMIA, the land between the two rivers of the Tigris and Euphrates, ancient name for modern Iraq.
NEGREPONT, an old Italian name for the Greek island of Euboea in the eastern Mediterranean Sea.
NEPTUNE, the mythical Roman God of the Oceans who carries a trident (a three-pronged spear).
NORMAN, one of a Scandinavian people who conquered Normandy in the tenth century, suggesting modern France, or the French.
OCLADES, a region of Spain.
OGMIOS, an allusion to either a person or a movement (or dynasty) of some type. In Celtic folklore, Ogmios was a deity equated with Hercules (a man of great strength). If intended as an allusion to a person, Ogmios may suggest a future European political or military leader (probably French). If intended as an allusion to an organization, movement, or dynasty, then Ogmios might be an allusion to N.A.T.O., or a futuristic European military organization.
PERSIA, an ancient country in southwest Asia, an allusion to modern Iran.
PESTILENCE, a fatal epidemic disease.
PHALANX, a formation of infantry troops.
PHILIP, possibly an allusion to Great Britain or a future British leader.
PLAGUE, a highly infectious epidemic disease (this could include anything from AIDS to chemical or biological war).
PONTIFF, a pope.
PROPHECY, a prediction, the inspired utterance of a prophet, a foretelling of future events.
PROPHET, one who declares what will happen, a person who speaks by divine inspiration, a predictor or soothsayer.
REDS, an allusion to the British.
RHODES, a Greek island located off the coast of Greece.
SAXONS, members of the Germanic tribe who inhabited northern Germany, an allusion to the citizens of Germany.

SAVOY, a region of France in the southeast bordering on Switzerland and Italy.

SCEPTER, a staff held by a sovereign as an emblem of authority, usually inferring "royal" authority.

SELIN, an allusion to a future Islamic leader who will make war upon Europe and the West. In the personal opinion of the author, "Selin" is possibly an allusion to the future third Antichrist.

THE BARK OF SAINT PETER, an allusion to the Catholic Church, and possibly an allusion to a pope.

THE BOAR, an allusion to General Blücher, the Prussian "Boar" who fought with Wellington against Napoleon at the Battle of Waterloo in 1815.

THE COCK, an allusion to the nation of France.

THE EAGLE, a powerful bird of prey which symbolically represents a nation with a powerful military. The "eagle" is an allusion to Napoleon Bonaparte in the quatrains pertaining to the Napoleonic era. It appears to be used as an allusion to America in the quatrains intended for more modern times.

THE GREAT ONE, an allusion to a pope.

THE HOLY ONE, an allusion to a pope.

THE LEOPARD, an allusion to the Duke of Wellington. Napoleon referred to the English heraldic lion as the "leopard", thus the "Leopard of England" became Napoleon's nickname for the Duke of Wellington.

THE LION, an allusion to the British, as in the symbol of the English "lion".

THE NEW CITY, in a macro sense this appears to be an allusion to the New World. In a micro sense, perhaps it is an allusion to New York City, or in a broader sense the United States.

THE THREE BROTHERS, possibly an allusion to the Kennedy brothers (John, Robert, Edward) in some quatrains, and in others it is an allusion to their homeland (the United States of America).

THE UNITED BROTHERS, an allusion to Hitler and Mussolini during the era of World War II quatrains.

TOPOGRAPHIES, the features and accurate description of a place or geographical region.

TREMBLES, to shake involuntarily as from fear, to quake, shiver, or to express fear or anxiety.

TUSCANY, a region of northwest Italy, an allusion to the Italians.

TWO GREAT ROCKS, an allusion to two super powers; possibly Asia and North America, or the Euro/Asian land mass and the Americas.

VEX, to annoy, confuse, baffle, or puzzle. As Nostradamus used the term vex, it could also suggest "battle" in some quatrains.

WATER, in astrological terms it represents feelings and emotions. "Water" can also suggest flooding.

WHITES, an allusion to the French.

THE PREFACE OF MICHAEL NOSTRADAMUS
TO HIS BOOK, *THE PROPHECIES*

DEDICATED TO CAESAR NOSTRADAMUS
MY SON - LONG LIFE AND HAPPINESS

(1) Your late arrival,[1] Caesar Nostradamus my son, has caused me to bestow a great deal of time through nocturnal watchings[2], to leave you in writing, a memorial to refer to after the bodily death of your father, that might serve for the common benefit of mankind, which the Divine Spirit has allowed me to learn through the revolution of the stars.[3] Since it has pleased the immortal God that thou have appeared into the natural light of this world, and your years are not yet calculated astronomically, and your months are incapable to receive into thy weak brain, what I must record what will happen after my time. It is impossible to leave you in writing, that which might suffer by the injury of time, for the inherited gift of occult prediction shall remain confined in my own bowels and will go to the grave with me.

(2) Considering that events of human origin are uncertain, and all is regulated (and governed by) the incalculable power of God, inspiring us not through Bacchic[4] fury nor by Lymphatic[5] motion, but through astronomical assertion. *Only those inspired by the divine power, can predict particular events in a spirit of prophecy.*

(3) For years I have made many predictions a long time in advance of events which have now come to pass, and in particular regions attributing the entire accomplishment to divine power and inspiration.

(4) Other predicted events (both fortunate and unfortunate) have come to pass in the world with increasing promptness, for I was willing to remain silent and pass over matters that might prove to be injurious if published, both as related to the present tense, and for most of the future, if put into writing. Kingdoms, sects, and religions will make changes so complete and diametrically opposite, that if I were to reveal the events of the future, the leaders of the kingdoms, sects, and religions would find it so disagreeable with what they would like to hear, that they would condemn that, which future ages will know and perceive as the truth. Considering what the true

---

[1] Nostradamus' son, Caesar, was born in early 1555 and was but a tiny baby when the first four "centuries" were originally published in the year 1555. Though the Preface was dedicated to his blood son, it is commonly believed that the word "son" was actually used in a symbolic sense, and is a dedication to the people of the future (Nostradamus' spiritual sons), as well as to the interpreters and students of his writings.

[2] Personal observations of celestial bodies (the Sun, Moon, planets, stars, comets, etc...).

[3] Through judicial astrology and astronomical study.

[4] Drunkenness.

[5] In ancient times, those who were "mad for love".

savior Jesus Christ said, "*give not which is holy unto dogs, nor cast your pearls before swine, lest they trample them under their feet and turn and rend you (tear you apart).*[6] This is the reason for my withholding my tongue from the vulgar and my pen from paper.

(5) However, later on for the common good, I gave way and by dark and abstruse sentences, the most urgent of future causes, as per my perceptions, and in a way that would not upset their gentle sentiments they were put into writing. All my prophecies were written under a cloudy figure and above all things, are prophetic. However, *thou hast hidden these things from the wise and prudent and hast revealed them to the small and weak.*[7] To prophets, through the grace of God and the good angels, have had handed to them the spirit of prophecy through which they perceive things at a distance and forecast future events. Nothing can be accomplished without Him, whose great power and goodness are so great to all his creatures so long as they put their faith in Him, much as they may be subject to other influences, on account of their similarity to the nature of their good genius, this power and prophetic heat approach us like the rays of the Sun, which are casting their influence upon bodies, both elementary and non-elementary.

(6) For ourselves, who are but human, we can discover nothing by our own (unaided) knowledge, or by the angle of our intelligence, about the secrets of God our creator. *It is not for you to know the times or hours.*[8]

(7) However, now or in the future, there may be some individuals who arrive to whom God the Almighty, by means of fanciful impressions, may wish to reveal more secrets of the future to, integrated with judicial astrology in the same manner as in former times, when a certain power and voluntary faculty possessed them as a flame of fire.[9] By His inspiration, they were able to judge divine and human virtue. Divine works, which are universal, God will complete, things which are contingent the good angels direct, the third type, the evil angels.

(8) My son, perhaps I speak to thee here a bit too obscurely. But regarding hidden prophecies which come to one by the subtle spirit of fire, by which the understanding being disturbed by the contemplation of the remotest of stars, remains active. The pronouncements are recorded in writing, without bias, and without taint of excess verbiage. But why? Because everything proceeds from the divine power of the almighty God, from whom all goodness emanates.

(9) Further my son, though I inserted the name "prophet", it is not my wish to assume a title so sublime for the present. *For he who is now called a prophet, was*

---

[6] A verse from the Bible (Matthew vii.6).

[7] These things were hidden from kings, leaders, and influential people, and were revealed to common folk (the small and weak). This is a modification of a Biblical verse, see Matthew xi.25.

[8] A verse from the Bible (Acts 1.7).

[9] A flame of fire resembles a "tongue" and is representative of prophetic utterance. In the opinion of Grotius (1583-1645, a Dutch jurist, statesman, and commentator), a flame of fire, as observed atop a lit candle, represents the "duality of nature", possessing the purifying qualities of luminosity (as in the spiritual world), as well as the opposite nature of the material world. Also see the Bible (Acts ii.3).

once called a "seer". In strict terms my son, a prophet is one who sees things remote from the natural knowledge of all men. Or, to state the case, through the perfect light of the prophecy appearing before him, the prophet may see things both divine and human, which cannot come about since the effects of future prediction stretch to such remote periods.

(10) The secrets of God are incomprehensible and their virtue belongs to a sphere quite remote from natural knowledge, and derive their immediate origin from the free will, manifesting the appearance of things which otherwise would not be known either by human augury, or by hidden knowledge or secret virtue under Heaven, even from the present fact of all eternity, which comes to embrace all time. Only through the means of some indivisible eternal power, and through means of Herculean[10] agitation, the causes are made known by celestial movements.[11]

(11) Understand my son that I am not saying that the knowledge of this matter can not impress itself upon your tender brain, nor am I saying that futuristic events are not within the grasp of knowledge of reasoning men. If future events are, not withstanding, purely the creation of the "intellectual soul" of current events, then future events are by no means too greatly concealed.

(12) The perfect knowledge of events cannot be acquired, without divine inspiration, considering that all prophetic inspiration derives its prime motivating principle from God the creator, next from good fortune, and finally from nature. Because of this, independent causes being independently produced or not produced, the prophecy occurs in part, where it was predicted, proportionately to the degree of which similar events have manifested similarly, or failed to manifest themselves. Considering that human understanding is intellectually created, it cannot see or penetrate occult or hidden things, unless it is aided by the voice emanating from limbo, by means of the thin flame, revealing in which direction the knowledge of future events is inclined.

(13) Further my son, I insist that you never apply your understanding on such vanities and reveries, as dry up the body and bring perdition to the soul, disturbing your weak senses.[12] I especially caution you against the seduction of a more than abominable magic,[13] denounced by the Holy Scriptures and the Canons of the Church.[14]

(14) Exempt from this judgement, however, is judicial astrology.[15] By the aid of this judicial astrology combined with divine inspiration, revelation, and long nightly

---

[10]An allusion to a very powerful force (pertaining to Hercules).

[11]As revealed through the science of astronomy.

[12]Perhaps a health wise warning from Nostradamus, who was a noted physician, alerting people to the dangers of alcohol abuse, smoking, and substance abuse (which "dry-up" the senses).

[13]Perhaps a warning for people to avoid the lure of Black Magic, etc....

[14]The doctrines of the Roman Catholic Church (and/or the dogmas of Christianity).

[15]According to Nostradamus, participation in the study of astrological arts and sciences is very acceptable and should never be falsely grouped into the category of "unacceptable practices" by the Christian religion.

watches and calculations[16], we reduced our prophecies to writing. Not withstanding that occult philosophy was not condemned by the church, I could never persuade myself to meddle in it. However, I had many volumes concerning occult philosophy laid before me which had been concealed a long time. Yet dreading what might happen after I had read them, I presented them to Vulcan[17] and as he devoured them flames of fire licking the air shot forth in an unaccustomed brightness, clearer than the light of a natural flame. It resembled more the explosion of gun powder and suddenly illuminated the house as if the whole were wrapped in sudden conflagration. To assume, in the future, that you might not be led astray searching for the perfect transformation, solar or lunar, or of incorruptible metals hidden under the earth or sea, I reduced them to ashes.

(15) But I do want to make clear to you, the judgement which perfects, by means of the celestial judgement. By this method you may have cognizance of future things, while avoiding completely, all fantastic imaginations which may arise. Through divine and supernatural inspiration, integrated with astronomical computations, one can name places and periods of time accurately, which the occult property has relation to, by the virtue and faculty divine, in whose presence the three aspects of time (past, present, and future) become clasped into one by eternity, *for all things are naked and open.*

(16) All from which my son you can easily comprehend, notwithstanding your tender brain, the things that are to happen can be predicted by the nocturnal and celestial lights, which are natural, coupled with the spirit of prophecy. Not that I would assume the name or capacity of a "prophet". However, by revealed inspiration, as a mortal man my senses place me no farther from heaven than the feet are from the Earth. *I am able not to err, fail, or be deceived*, though I am the greatest sinner in this world and heir to all human afflictions.

(17) Yet being amazed sometimes in my ecstatic work, I am overtaken by an ecstasy, having rendered my nocturnal studies agreeable through lengthy calculations. I have composed books of prophecy, each of which contains one hundred astronomical quatrains of forecasts, which I have sought to polish through a bit obscurely, and which are perpetual prophecies from the 16th century to the year 3797, at which some persons my son, may perhaps frown upon considering such a vast extent of time and treatment of everything under the Moon, and the universal treatment of causes throughout the Earth. If you live to the natural age of a man, you shall see in your climate and beneath the heaven of your nativity, the events of the future that have been foretold.

---

[16] Astrological calculations.

[17] In Roman mythology Vulcan was the god of fire. Nostradamus is saying that he burnt his occult books.

(18) Though only God himself knows the eternity of the light proceeding from him, I say frankly to all persons to whom God has wished to reveal his limitless magnitude, as immeasurable and incomprehensible as it is, that it is something hidden and divinely manifested. It is manifested by two principle means, as contained in the knowledge of the inspired one who prophesies.

(19) One arrives by infusion, which clears the supernatural light for he who predicts by astral process, or predicts by inspired revelation, which is almost a participation in the eternal divineness. Through this means comes the prophet, to judge of that which his share of divine spirit has accorded him, via communication with God, and the natural "intuition" granted to him.

(20) Know that what is predicted is true and had its origin in heaven. The light, and the thin flame, are together effective, and descend from a heavenly origin, no less than does natural light. The latter renders philosophers quite sure of themselves, due to the principles of a first cause, they have penetrated the innermost abysses, attaining the loftiest of doctrines.

(21) I must not wander too far, my son, from the capacity of thy senses. I find that letters[18] shall suffer a great and incomparable loss, and I find the world before the "universal conflagration,"[19] suffering such deluges and deep submersion, that scarcely any land will remain not covered with water, and for so long a period that all will perish, except for Ethnographies and Topographies. Both before, and after these floods, many countries shall suffer from such a scarcity of rain, and so great an abundance of fire, that there will fall from heaven burning stones to such an extent, that hardly anything shall remain unconsumed. This will occur shortly before the "final conflagration."[20]

(22) Though the planet Mars will complete its cycle, during the end of its second period he will recommence his course. Some people will gather in Aquarius[21] for several years, and again in Cancer[22] for an even longer duration of time. Presently we are led by the Moon, through means of the power of the supreme and eternal God, and before she completes her entire circuit the Sun shall come, then later Saturn. According to the celestial signs, Saturn's reign will return, so all calculated, the world is drawing towards an anaragonic revolution.[23]

(23) From the moment I am writing this, before 177 years, 3 months, and eleven days, through pestilence, famine, war, and for the most part floods, the world between this day and that, both before and afterwards, shall be so greatly

---

[18] An allusion to the alphabet, books, knowledge, education.
[19] Perhaps the first world wide disaster by fire (due to war or nature?) which precedes a great flood.
[20] Unlike the "universal conflagration", which appears to occur first, the "final conflagration" appears to be a reference to a disaster which occurs before the final end of the Earth (perhaps near the year 3797).
[21] Perhaps an allusion to the astrological age of Aquarius, which we are presently entering.
[22] Perhaps an allusion to the future astrological age of Cancer.
[23] Suggesting destruction.

diminished, and its population so reduced, that there will hardly be enough people around to work the fields, and the lands will be left without agriculture for as long a duration of time as they had been when tilled.

(24) According to celestial judgement, we are currently in the seventh millinery, which concludes all and introduces us to the eighth, where the firmament of the eighth sphere is located, which in a latitudinary dimension, is the place where God completes the revolution, where the heavenly bodies will return to their courses, and the upper motion which renders the Earth stable and fixed for us, *"whence it shall not deviate from age to age,"*[24] unless "God's will" be accomplished, and not otherwise.

(25) Through uncertain opinions exceeding all natural reason by Mahometan dreams,[25] sometimes God the Creator, through the ministry of angels of fire, as through missive fire, presents to our external senses and eyes, the causes of predicted future events deemed significant to future happenings. These should manifest themselves to one who prophesies anything.

(26) The presage made by the exterior light arrives infallibly to judge, partly with and through means of, the exterior light, though the part which seems to come by the "eye of understanding", arrives only through the lesion of the imaginative sense.

(27) The reason for this is quite self evident, for the whole is predicted by means of divine inspiration, and through the angelic spirit possessed by the individual who is thus inspired to prophesy, rendering him anointed with vaticinations which visit and illuminate him, arousing his fantasy through various nocturnal apparitions. Through astronomic calculations combined with the holiest future prediction, he prophesies, taking nothing into consideration except the hardiness of his own free courage.

(28) At this hour my son, come to understand that I have determined through my astral revelations in accordance with revealed inspiration, that the "sword of death" is approaching us now in the forms of pestilence, war of which is more horrid than three generations of men have witnessed and famine, which will fall upon the Earth and return at frequent intervals. For the stars bring into harmony with such a revolution, in accordance to the phrase *I will visit their iniquities with a rod of iron and will strike them with blows.*[26]

(29) For God's mercy, my son, will not spread abroad for a long period of time, until the major part of my prophecies have been accomplished, and through this accomplishment, resolved. And several times during the course of these sinister storms, our Lord will say, *I will trample them, and break them, and not show pity.*[27]

---

[24]Though the language here is unclear, some scholars have speculated that this could be a subtle reference to a polar shift.

[25]The desires of persons of the Islamic faith.

[26]This phrase resembles a verse in the Bible (Psalms ii.7).

[27]This phrase resembles a verse in the Bible (Isai. Lxiii.3).

(30) Thousands of accidents and events will arrive due to floods and continual rains, as I have more fully referenced in writing in my other Prophecies, designating the geographic locations, times, and terms prefixed, in order for all men coming after me may see them and have knowledge of the events (and circumstances) that occur infallibly, as we have marked by other predictions and quatrains, where we speak more clearly. Although they (the quatrains) were composed and covered with a veil of cloud, their meanings should be clear enough to be understood by men of good intelligence, for *when the time arrives for the removal of ignorance*, the totality of these events shall stand out with even greater clarity.

(31) I am ending here my son. Please take this gift from your father, Michel Nostradamus, who wishes to explain to thee every prophecy contained in the quatrains included here. I beseech the immortal Father that he be willing to provide you with a long life of happy and prosperous felicity.

From Salon (France), this first of March, 1555.

Étant assis de nuit secret étude,
Seul reposé sur la selle d'airain:
Flamme exiguë sortant de solitude, Fait prospérer qui n'est à croire vain.

1 - 1

Sitting at night in secret study; alone resting on the brass tripod. A slight flame comes out of the solitude and makes successful that which should not be believed in vain.

NOSTRADAMUS' PROPHETIC METHODS REVEALED

These first two quatrains provide us with information regarding Nostradamus' prophetic methods. Nostradamus sits at night, alone in his secret study room above his home in France. He rests on his brass tripod (a contraption used in his prophetic rituals). "A slight flame (meaning unclear, perhaps suggesting a spirit) comes out of the solitude and makes successful that (Nostradamus' prophetic activities) which (according to Nostradamus) should not be believed in vain" (or dismissed or taken for granted).

La verge en main mise au milieu de BRANCHES,
De l'onde il moulle et le limbe et le pied:
Un peur et voix frémissant par les manches:
Splendeur divine. Le divin près s'assied.

1 - 2

The rod in the hand is placed in the midst of the Branches. With water he sprinkles both limb and his foot. A voice, fear; he trembles in his robes. Divine splendour; the divine one seats himself nearby.

NOSTRADAMUS' PROPHETIC METHODS REVEALED

Nostradamus explains the routine used in his prophetic activities. A rod in his hand is placed in the midst of the branches. He sprinkles both limb and foot with water. He hears a voice and trembles in his robes. "Divine splendor" overwhelms him and a "divine one" (some type of spiritual entity) is seated by him. Perhaps this suggests that an angel, or spirit guide of some sort, assisted Nostradamus in his prophetic activities.

Le corps sans âme plus n'être en sacrifice: Jour de la mort mis en nativité: L'esprit divin fera l'âme félice, Voyant le verbe en son éternité.	2 - 13	The body without a soul, no longer will be sacrificed. At the day of death it is brought to rebirth. The Divine Spirit makes the soul rejoice, upon its seeing the eternity of the word.

A SPIRITUAL COMMENTARY

"The body (suggesting the physical body of a human being) without a soul (suggesting that upon the death of our physical human body -- when our spiritual 'soul' departs from its temporary human body), no longer will be sacrificed (upon death, the suffering of our physical human body will terminate). At the day of death (upon the death of our physical body) it (our spiritual soul) is brought to rebirth (following bodily death, our soul, considered to be 'eternal' by most of the world's religions, will experience a spiritual rebirth of some type). The Divine Spirit (suggesting God) makes the soul rejoice, upon its seeing the eternity of the word" (when our soul arrives in heaven, it will experience spiritual bliss, when the truth of God is revealed to it). People who have survived near-death experiences describe their blissful glimpse into the spiritual realm in much the same way as Nostradamus does in this quatrain. Nostradamus reveals his spiritual nature in this and the following quatrain.

Le divin verbe donra à la sub-stance, Compris ciel, terre, or occulte aulait mystique: Corps, âme esprit ayant toute puissance, Tant sous ses pieds comme au siège Celique.	3 - 2	The divine word will give to the substance, all which contains heaven and Earth, gold hidden in the mystic deed. Body, soul and spirit having all power. Everything is beneath his feet, as at the seat of heaven.

A SPIRITUAL STATEMENT

"The divine word (suggesting the divine word of God) will give to the substance, all which contains (both) heaven and Earth (suggesting the spiritual realm, and Earth -- the material plane), gold hidden in the mystic deed (perhaps suggesting that Nostradamus viewed his mystical prophetic spiritual practices as something which yielded "gold", or beneficial results). Body, soul, and spirit having all power (suggests richness through self empowerment and spiritual awareness). Everything is beneath his feet, as at the seat of heaven." The last line of this quatrain seems to suggest that God is all powerful on Earth, as he is at the seat of heaven (in the spiritual realm).

De cinq cents ans plus compte l'on tiendra Celui qu'était l'ornement de son temps: Puis à un coup grande clarté donra Qui par ce siècle les rendra très contents.	3 - 94	For five hundred years more they will take notice of him who was the ornament of his time. Then suddenly a great revelation will he give, making the people of this same century well pleased.

MANKIND'S VIEW OF NOSTRADAMUS' PREDICTIONS

"For (a period of) five hundred years more they (mankind) will take notice of him (Nostradamus), who was the (self described) ornament of his time. Then suddenly a great revelation will he give (suggesting that one of Nostradamus' predictions will come true), making the people of this same century well pleased" (if we add 500 years to the date of Nostradamus' death in 1566, we arrive at the year 2066, a few years after the return of Halley's Comet). Apparently this unstated prophesied "revelation", which will be fulfilled sometime in the 21st century, will be an accurately predicted event and will somehow please the people of that time (how it serves to please the people is unstated). Nostradamus stated in the Preface to *The Prophecies*, that as time passed, his predictions would be seen to carry more weight by mankind.

Napoleon Bonaparte as First Consul of France.

Par l'univers sera fait un Monar-
que,
Qu'en paix et vie ne sera
longuement:
Lors se perdra la piscature
barque,
Sera régie en plus grand
détriment.

1 - 4

In the world there will be a
monarch who will have little
peace and a short life. Then
the fishing bark will be lost,
ruled to its greatest detriment.

NAPOLEON BONAPARTE

Here are the quatrains pertaining to the Napoleonic era. "In the world there will be a monarch (a sovereign such as a king or emperor -- suggesting Napoleon Bonaparte, who was crowned Emperor of France on December 2, 1804 while holding a replica of Charlemagne's scepter) who will have little peace (suggesting that this monarch will be engrossed in military matters) and a short life (Napoleon died at the relatively, young age of fifty-two, a 'short life'). Then the fishing bark (an allusion to the Papacy - the 'bark' of St. Peter) will be lost, ruled to its greatest detriment" (which seems to accurately suggest Napoleon's imprisonment of Pope Pius VI, who died in captivity in 1799, and Pope Pius VII, who was Napoleon's prisoner from 1809 to 1814).

Au mois troisième se levant le
Soleil,
Sanglier, Léopard au champ
Marspour combattre:
Léopard laissé au ciel étend son
oeil,
Un Aigle autour du Soleil voit
s'ébattre.

1 - 23

In the third month, at sunrise,
the Boar and the Leopard
engage on the battlefield. The
fatigued Leopard looks up to
the heavens and sees an eagle
playing around the Sun.

WATERLOO; NAPOLEON, WELLINGTON, BLÜCHER

"In the third month (during the third month following Napoleon's arrival in Paris from exile in Elba), at sunrise (at dawn), the Boar (an allusion to Prussian General Blücher) and the Leopard (Napoleon's nickname for the English Duke of Wellington) engage on the battlefield (resulting in the famous Battle of Waterloo in Belgium). The fatigued Leopard (an allusion to Wellington and his English troops, who according to Wellington himself 'were beginning to feel fatigued by evening-time that day') looks up to the heavens and sees an Eagle (an allusion to Napoleon) playing around the Sun" (An anti-climatic poetic gesture in reference to Napoleon, *the eagle* -- "in flight", retreating after his defeat at Waterloo) defeat that day). After his departure from exile on Elba, Napoleon arrived in Paris on March 20, 1815. The Battle of Waterloo took place on June 18, 1815. Thus, just as Nostradamus predicted, this event indeed occurred within "the third month" following Napoleon's return to his capital (the end of the third month being June 20th).

Le grand Empire sera tôt translaté, En lieu petit qui bien tôt viendracroître: Lieu bien infime d'exiguë comté Où au milieu viendra poser son sceptre.	1 - 32	The great Empire will soon be exchanged for a little place, which will very soon begin to grow. A lowly place in a petty country in the middle of which he will arrive to lay down his scepter.

NAPOLEON BONAPARTE, ST. HELENA, ELBA

"The great Empire (an allusion to Napoleon's French Empire) will soon be exchanged for a little place (the little Island of Elba, located off the western coast of Italy, where Napoleon lived following his first abdication and exile from France in 1814), which will very soon begin to grow" (perhaps a reference to Napoleon's thoughts of leaving Elba and growing the French Empire). After his escape from Elba on February 26, 1815, Napoleon began his famous 100 Day Campaign. After his defeat at Waterloo, followed by his second abdication and capture, Napoleon set sail as a prisoner to be exiled, on an English vessel bound for the British island of St. Helena (located to the west of South Africa, another "lowly place in a petty country"), where he arrived to "lay down his scepter" (a staff which denotes royalty and leadership), and died at the age of 52 in British custody. Napoleon's last words were "France, the great army", a reference to the great army of the Republic of France, which he had so successfully commanded.

Un Empereur naîtra près d'Italie, Qui à l'Empire sera vendu bien cher: Diront avec quels gens il se rallie Qu'on trouvera moins prince que boucher.	1 - 60	An Emperor will be born near Italy, who will cost his Empire greatly. They will say among his peers when they see his allies, that he is less a prince than a butcher.

NAPOLEON BONAPARTE

"An Emperor (suggesting Napoleon Bonaparte, crowned Emperor of France on December 2, 1804) will be born near Italy (Napoleon was born 'near Italy' on the island of Corsica, located west of the Italian mainland in the Mediterranean Sea), who will cost his Empire (an allusion to the French Empire) greatly (in terms of human lives, and other things as well). They will say among his peers when they see his allies (suggesting that it will be rumored among various Frenchmen), that he is less a prince than a butcher" (suggesting that Napoleon would be perceived to be more of a military man, and less of a royal figure, by some of his peers and enemies). Nostradamus may have used the word "butcher" as a symbolic reference to the 1,000,000 people who lost their lives fighting Napoleon's forces in Europe, Russia, Africa, and elsewhere.

Entre deux mers dressera promontoire Que puis mourra par le mors du cheval: Le sien Neptune pliera voile noire, Par Calpre et classe auprès de Rocheval.	1 - 77	A promontory will be erected between two seas. A man who will die later by the bit of a horse: Neptune unfurls a black sail for this man; the fleet through Gibraltar and near Rocheval.

THE BATTLE OF TRAFALGAR

"A promontory (a high ridge of land jutting out into the sea) will be erected between two seas" (suggesting Gibraltar, a seaport in southern Spain between the Atlantic Ocean and the Mediterranean Sea, where the French, Spanish, and English fleets fought a desperate battle in 1805 during Napoleon's reign). A man who will die later by the bit of a horse (appears to be a reference to French Admiral Villeneuve, who was strangled to death by a strip of leather -- a rein, part of a horse's bridle, by one of Napoleon's men upon returning to France in reprisal for allowing himself to be taken prisoner by the British). Neptune (an allusion to the mythological Roman God of the Oceans who) unfurls a black sail for this man (a reference to the death of British Admiral Nelson, who died due to his battle wounds on his return voyage to Great Britain); the fleet (the French fleet) through Gibraltar (the Straight of Gibralter, the vital waterway between Spain and northern Africa, which connects the Atlantic Ocean with the Mediterranean Sea) and near Rocheval" (perhaps suggesting Cape Roche in Spain).

Terre Italique près des monts tremblera, Lion et Coq non trop confédérés, En lieu de peur l'un l'autre s'aidera, Seul Castulon et Celtes, modérés.	1 - 93	The land of Italy near the mountains will tremble. The Lion and the Cock not strongly united. Because of fear they will help each other. Only Spain and the French moderate.

NAPOLEON'S INVASION OF ITALY

"The land of Italy near the mountains (suggesting the Alps, the major mountain range of south-central Europe) will tremble (as it did when Napoleon and his army first invaded Italy in 1795). The Lion (an allusion to England, in reference to its "Lion" symbol) and the Cock (an allusion to France) not strongly united (as they developed feelings of antagonism towards each other during these times). Because of fear (of war?) they will help each other (England and France later formed an alliance). Only Spain and the French moderate" (in some unclear manner). Though this quatrain seems to fit the general conditions of the Napoleonic era, it may have been intended for future times, and is thus included in a later chapter.

Le chef qu'aura conduit peuple infini Loin de son ciel, de moeurs et langue étrange: Cinq mil en Crete et Thessalie fini, Le chef fuyant sauvé en marine grange.	**1 - 98**	The chief who will conduct great numbers of people far from their own skies, to foreign customs and languages. Five thousand will die in Crete and Thessaly, the chief saved in a sea going supply ship.

NAPOLEON AND KLËBER'S EGYPTIAN CAMPAIGN

"The chief (suggesting Napoleon) will conduct great numbers of people (suggesting legions of French troops) far from their own skies, to several foreign customs and languages. Five thousand will die in Crete (presently a Greek island in the Mediterranean Sea, southeast of Greece) and Thessaly" (presently a division of central Greece along the Aegean Sea). The French sailed to foreign lands and engaged the Turkish army who controlled Crete and Thessaly, Napoleon reduced their troop strength to 5,000 men after several battles. In Egypt, General Klëber won a brilliant victory over British Admiral Lord Keith at the Battle of Heliopolis on March 20, 1800. "The chief saved in a sea going supply ship" (when he left Egypt, Napoleon sailed away in a wooden supply vessel back to France).

Par grands dangers le captif échappé: Peu de temps grand la fortune changée. Dans le palais le peuple est attrapé, Par bon augure la cité assiégée.	**2 - 66**	The captive escapes through great dangers. The great one has a change of fortune. In the palace people are trapped, by good omen, the besieged city.

ESCAPE FROM ELBA, NAPOLEON'S 100 DAYS

"The captive (suggesting Napoleon, a "captive" on the island of Elba) escapes through great dangers (Napoleon "escaped" from Elba, successfully eluding a British naval vessel, on February 26, 1815). The great one (possibly suggesting Napoleon) has a change of fortune (if Napoleon is intended here, this could suggest "a good change of fortune" - his escape from Elba, or it could suggest good fortune turning to bad - a foreshadowing of things to come). In the palace people are trapped, by good omen, the besieged city" (though unclear, these last two lines might suggest to the joyous crowds of Parisians' who carried Napoleon into his palace upon arriving in Paris after his escape from Elba). The phrase, "the besieged city", seems to infer Paris. It is possible that the phrase "the great one" could have a double meaning, and could possibly be an allusion to a pope.

GRAND Pau, grand mal pour Gaulois recevra, Vaine terreur du maritime Lion: Peuple infini par la mer passera, Sans échapper un quart d'un million.	2 - 94	Great Po will receive great evil from Gaul, vain terror to the maritime Lion. An infinite number of people will pass by the sea and a quarter of a million will not escape.

NAPOLEON, SEA TRAVEL, THE POPE

The "Great Po (a river located near Mount Viso in northwestern Italy, a geographical allusion to Italy) will receive great evil (suggesting death and destruction) from Gaul (the ancient name for France, and a reference to Napoleon's military invasions of Italy), vain terror to the maritime Lion (an allusion to British naval forces, the 'Lion' being their famous symbol, and a reference to the naval battles fought between the British and French fleets). An infinite number of people will pass by the sea" (a reference to French forces who passed through the seas and fought for France in various countries, where the resulting military engagements left at least a quarter of a million men dead, in other words "not escaping").

Terroir Romain qu'interpretait augure, Par gent Gauloise par trop sera vexée: Mais nation Celtique craindra l'heure, Boreas, classe trop loin l'avoir poussée.	2 - 99	Roman land that as the omen interpreted, will be greatly vexed by the Gallic citizens. But the French nation will come to dread the time of the North wind having pushed their fleet too far.

NAPOLEON'S ITALIAN & RUSSIAN CAMPAIGNS

"Roman land (suggesting the nation of Italy, of which Rome is the capital) as the omen interpreted (perhaps suggesting this very quatrain as an omen), will be greatly vexed (by war) by the Gallic citizens" (Gallic pertains to Gaul, the ancient name for France, thus the French invasion of Italy and Russia is suggested here). "But the French nation will come to dread the time of the north wind having pushed their fleet too far." The last two lines are a reference to the peril encountered by Napoleon's army during their costly invasion of Russia, pushing their land "fleet" of caravans, wagons, and troops too far inside Russia, before they retreated back to France (as Hitler would later discover, the northern winds of the Russian winter can take a heavy toll upon any army which is unprepared for it). The French began their Russian campaign with 500,000 troops. By the time it was over, fewer than 20,000 French troops returned to France (a disastrous loss of men, equipment, and strategic positioning).

Avant l'assaut l'oraison pro- noncée, Milan pris d'Aigle par embûches deçus: Muraille antique par canons enfoncée, Par feu et sang à merci peu reçus.	3 - 37	Before the assault a speech is delivered; Milan, deceived by an ambush will be captured by the Eagle. The ancient walls are driven in by cannon; through fire and blood few receive quarter.

NAPOLEON IN ITALY

"Before the assault (preceding a military assault by French forces) a speech is delivered (an accurate reference to the fact that Napoleon, who was regarded as a gifted orator, instilled a sense of honor and motivation in his troops by giving them lengthy pre-battle speeches); Milan (an Italian city in Lombardy), deceived by an ambush (this Italian stronghold was taken twice by Napoleon's forces) will be captured by the Eagle (an allusion to Napoleon and his victorious sieges of Milan). The ancient walls are driven in by cannon (Napoleon, who began his military career as an artillery man, certainly pounded the city of Milan with French artillery); through fire and blood (war) few (Italian soldiers) receive quarter" (thus dying in combat). Yet another reference to Napoleon's campaigns in Italy.

Gaulois par sauts, monts viendra pénétrer: Occupera le grand lieu de l'Insubre: Au plus profond son ost fera entrer, Gennes, Monech pousseront classe rubre.	4 - 37	The Gaul will penetrate the mountains in leaps and will occupy the great land of Insubria. He will make his army penetrate deep, Genoa and Monaco will repulse the red fleet.

NAPOLEON, ITALY, AND MONACO

"The Gaul (a Frenchman, an allusion to Napoleon and his French army) will penetrate the mountains (suggesting the Alps, through the Great St. Bernard Pass) in leaps and will occupy the great land of Insubria (an old Roman name for Lombardy, a region of northern Italy). He (Napoleon) will make his army penetrate deep (into the land of Italy, which indeed occurred), Genoa (a city in Italy) and Monaco (a small coastal European principality) will repulse the red fleet" (in 1800, Genoa was attacked by Austria, and Monaco by the British, the "red fleet" might suggest the British and their famous red uniforms, known as red-coats).

Prêt à combattre fera defection, Chef adversaire obtiendra la victoire: L'arrière-garde fera defension, Les défaillants morts au blanc territoire.	4 - 75	One who was ready to fight will desert, the chief adversary will obtain victory. The rear guard will make a defense, those faltering, dead in a white territory.

THE BATTLE OF WATERLOO, 1815

"One who was ready to fight will desert (is a reference to French General Grouchy and his 30,000 troops who were separated from Napoleon's men, when Grouchy finally received Napoleon's orders, he refused them), the chief adversary will obtain victory, (the Duke of Wellington, an Englishman, was Napoleon's 'chief adversary', who with his ally Prussian General Blücher, obtained victory over the French). The rear guard will make a defense" (is a reference to the actions of the French Imperial Guard during the Battle of Waterloo). Napoleon lost half a day of maneuvering at Waterloo, resulting in 60,000 exhausted French troops (lacking infantry support) battling 125,000 enemy troops, in the mud. "Those faltering, dead in a white territory" (appears to be a reference to the French retreat in the Russian campaign, some years earlier).

The labouring dragon's roar: 'Unless ye slay me, ye cannot be called sages.'

La sacrée pompe viendra baisser les ailes,
Par la venue du grand législateur:
Humble haussera, vexera les rebelles,
Naîtra sur terre aucun émulateur.

5 - 79

The sacred pomp will come to lower its wings at the coming of the great legislator. He will raise the humble and vex the rebellious; his like will not again appear on the Earth.

NAPOLEON AND THE POPES

This quatrain is a reference to the ill treatment Napoleon gave Popes Pius VI and VII, as referenced by phrase "the sacred pomp (suggesting a pope) will come to lower its wings (suggesting a surrender) at the coming of the great legislator (Napoleon, 'the great legislator', was a noted jurist and the architect of the Code Napoleon, a system of civil law). He (suggesting Napoleon) will raise the humble (the French Revolution and Napoleon's campaign's raised the patriotic spirits of the common men of France) and vex the rebellious" (condemning various rebellious Frenchmen during the French revolution). According to Nostradamus, "his likes (Napoleon's) will not again appear on the Earth".

Milan, Ferrare, Turin, et Aquilleye, Capue, Brundis vexés par gent Celtique: Par le Lion et phalange aquilée, Quand Rome aura le chef vieux Britannique.	5 - 99	Milan, Ferrare, Turin & Aquileia, Capua and Brindisi vexed by the Celtic nation: by the Lion and his imperial phalanx, when the old British chief will have Rome.

NAPOLEON'S ITALIAN CAMPAIGNS

"Milan, Ferrare, Turin, Aquileia, Capua and Brindisi (cities throughout Italy, an allusion to the region of Italy) vexed by the Celtic nation" (Italy was 'vexed' by France -- the Celtic nation, during Napoleon's military campaigns). The last two lines of this quatrain seem to be a reference to Cardinal York, the last of the Stuarts (a family name of rulers who governed Scotland, England, and Great Britain). Cardinal York ('the old British chief') died in Rome in 1807.

De la cité marine et tributaire La tête rase prendra la satrapie: Chasser sordide qui puis sera contraire, Par quatorze ans tiendra la tyrannie.	7 - 13	From the marine tributary city, the shaven head will take up the satrapy; to chase the sordid man who will then be against him, for he will hold the tyranny for fourteen years.

NAPOLEON AND HIS REIGN

"From the marine tributary city (suggesting the coastal city of Toulon, in France), the shaven head (suggesting Napoleon and his famous hair cut) will take up the satrapy (a territory under the rule of a governor, in this case the Englishman, Sir Arthur Wellesly, who made Toulon a tributary city of the British), to chase the sordid man who will then be against him (perhaps suggesting certain members of the French Directory who ruled the democratic republic), for he (Napoleon) will hold the tyranny for fourteen years" (from 1800 to 1814).

PAV, NAY, LORON plus feu qu'à sang sera,
Laude nager, fuir grand aux surrez:
Les agassas entrée refusera,
Pampon, Durance les tiendra enserrés.

8 - 1

Pau, Nay, Loron will be more of fire than blood, swimming in praise, the great one will flee to the confluence of rivers. The Pius he will refuse entry. The All-Depraved ones and the Durance will keep them confined.

NAPOLEON

"Pau, Nay, and Loron" are three small villages located in the ancient region of Béarn in southwestern France. These villages are approximately ten or fifteen miles apart from one another. This indicates the birth of something from French soil. Previous commentators see the choice of these words and letters to be intended as an anagram for "Napaulon", which is most likely the correct inference intended here ("Napaulon Roy"). In Corsica, (Napoleon's birthplace) the spelling "Napaulon" was not uncommon. Thus, "Napoleon will be more of fire than blood" (suggests Napoleon will be more "war-like" than "royal" in his nature). Napoleon certainly "swam in great praise" (and respect). The line "the great one will flee to the confluence of rivers" (the Rhône and Isère Rivers in France, is a reference to Pope Pius VI who was held captive by Napoleon in Valence, where he died as his prisoner in 1799). The exact meaning intended by this last line is unclear.

De soldat simple parviendra en empire,
De robe courte parviendra à la longue:
Vaillant aux armes en Église où plus pire,
Vexer les prêtres comme l'eau fait l'éponge.

8 - 57

From simple soldier he will attain to Empire, from the short robe he will attain to the long robe. Valiant in arms, much worse towards the Church, vexing the priest as water does a sponge.

NAPOLEON VEXES THE VATICAN

Napoleon evolved from the lowly position of artillery lieutenant ("a short robe") to the position of Emperor of the French Empire (which suggests "a long imperial robe", like the type worn by kings and emperors). Napoleon was indeed "valiant in arms, and much worse towards the Church, vexing the priest as water does a sponge" (a reference to the imprisonment of Popes Pius VI and VII).

Vent Aquilon fera partir le siège, Par murs jeter cendres, chaux et poussière: Par pluie après, qui leur fera bienpiege, Dernier secours encontre leur frontière.	9 - 99	The Aquilon wind causes the siege to be raised, to throw over the walls, cinders, lime and dust, through rain afterwards which does them more harm, the last aid is met at their frontier.

NAPOLEON'S RETREAT FROM RUSSIA

"The Aquilon wind (the Russian, or northern wind) causes the siege to be raised (Napoleon's siege of 'the North', suggesting the French siege of Russia and Moscow), to throw over the walls, cinders, lime and dust (Moscow was set on fire during this siege, thus the reference to 'cinders, lime and dust'), through rain afterwards which does them more harm (the French retreated from Moscow under horrendous weather conditions, thus the reference to 'rain, wind, and snow'), the last aid is met at their frontier" (the French met friendly forces at the borders of the French frontier). This quatrain could be a reference to the Nazi siege of Moscow, during World War II, but seems to fit well with Napoleon's siege (and retreat) in Russia.

Le captif prince aux Itales vaincu Passera Gennes par mer jusqu'à Marseille: Par grand effort des forens survaincu, Sauf coup de feu, baril liqueur d'abeille.	10 - 24	The captive prince conquered in Italy travels from Genoa to Marseilles by sea; through a great effort the foreigners will be overcome, safe from gunshot, a barrel of bees' honey.

NAPOLEON'S 100 DAYS

"The captive prince (suggesting Napoleon), conquered in Italy travels from Genoa to Marseilles by sea (Napoleon escaped from the island of Elba located off the coast of Italy, and crossed the Gulf of Genoa landing at the French port city of Marseilles), through a great effort the foreigners (suggesting the French) will be overcome (is a reference to the Battle of Waterloo, fought on soil foreign to France - in Belgium) safe from gunshot, a barrel of bee's honey (suggesting the famous emblem of bee hives, which Napoleon adopted as his symbol). According to commentator Le Pelletier, the "honey" of the French Republic was spilled at Waterloo.

Gaulois qu'empire par guerre occupera, Par son beau-frère mineur sera trahi: Pour cheval rude voltigeant traînera, Du fait le frère longtemps sera haï.	10 - 34	The Gaul who holds his empire through war will be betrayed by his younger brother-in-law. He will be drawn by an untrained nervous horse, for the deed, the brother to be hated for a long time.

THE KING OF NAPLES AND NAPOLEON

"The Gaul (a Frenchman, suggesting Napoleon) who holds his empire (the French Empire) through war will be betrayed by his younger brother-in-law" (this line and the ones which follow, are a reference to Joachim Murat, the King of Naples in 1814). Murat promised Talleyrand a large sum of money in return for the ministers' princedom of Benevento, causing Talleyrand to drop a plot against him, enabling Talleyrand to concoct a scheme to kidnap the Emperor from Elba, where Napoleon was exiled. Napoleon, in the back of his mind, probably never forgave Murat for this deed, "hating him for a long time".

La barque neuve recevra les voyages, Là et auprès transféreront l'Empire: Beaucaire, Arles retiendront les otages, Près deux colonnes trouvées de Porphyre.	10 - 93	The new bark will travel there and nearby they will transfer the empire. Beaucaire and Arles will hold on to the hostages near where two columns of porphyry are found.

NAPOLEON AND THE POPES

"The new bark (suggesting 'the bark of St. Peter', the Papacy) will travel there (suggesting Popes Pius VI and VII, who traveled to France, where they were imprisoned by Napoleon), and nearby they will transfer the empire (suggesting the French annexation of the Papal States in 1810), Beaucaire and Arles (two French cities located near the Rhone River) will hold on to the hostages (the city of Valence, where Napoleon imprisoned Popes Pius VI and VII, 'the hostages') near where two columns of porphyry are found" (near two columns of crystal stones -- the exact meaning of this line is unclear).

Adolf Hitler, leader of Germany during World War II.

La tour de Boucq craindra fuste Barbare, Un temps, long temps après barque hesperique: Bétail, gens, meubles, tous deux feront grand tare, Taurus et Libra, quelle mortelle pique!	**1 - 28**	Tobruk will fear the barbarian fleet, then much later the Western fleet. Cattle, people, possessions, all will be wasted. What a deadly combat in Taurus and Libra.

NAVAL WARFARE, COMBAT, TOBRUK

And now the quatrains which pertain to World War II. "La tour de Boucq" suggests Tobruk (a coastal city in Libya). "Tobruk will fear the barbarian fleet (suggesting the Italians, who controlled Tobruk in the early days of World War II), then much later the Western fleet" (suggesting America and the Allies). A deadly combat occurred in April (during the astrological Sun sign of Taurus) when German General Rommel, the sly and chivalrous Desert Fox (who commanded the famed Africa Korps) attacked the brave Australian defenders of Tobruk, ending his siege around November (a few weeks after the end of the Sun sign of Libra, which is October 23rd). The British then launched Operation Crusader. "Cattle, people, possessions, all will be wasted" (is a reference to the heavy fighting which occurred during the battles).

L'oiseau de proie volant à la sénestre Avant conflit fait aux François parure: L'un bon prendra, l'un ambiguë sinistre, La partie faible tiendra par bon augure.	**1 - 34**	The bird of prey flying to the window, before battle preparations made by the French. One will regard it as good, others ambiguous or uncertain. The weak party will view it as a good omen.

A FRENCH VIEW OF HITLER

"The bird of prey (suggesting German prop-driven dive bombers) flying to the window (literally 'flying' beyond the borders of Germany), before battle preparations made by the French (suggesting the construction of the defensive Maginot Line, and other pre-war preparations). One (suggesting either the Spanish, Italians, or Japanese?) will regard it (the rise of Hitler and the Third Reich) as a good omen, others uncertain (of Hitler's intent). The weak party (possibly suggesting Franco, Mussolini, the Japanese, or other unidentified parties) will view it (the rise of the Third Reich) as a good omen (perhaps viewing it as something "good" in the beginning)."

Du tout Marseille des habitants changée,
Course et poursuite jusqu'auprès de Lyon.
Nabonne, Tholouse par Bourdeaux outragée:
Tués captifs presque d'un million.

1 - 72

The inhabitants of Marseilles completely changed, fleeing and pursued up to near Lyons. Narbonne, Toulouse upset by Bordeaux; the dead and captives are nearly one million.

FRANCE AND WORLD WAR II

A general reference to the war time plight of French citizens (suggested by the phrase the inhabitants of Marseilles, a costal city in France) which seems to fit the awful circumstances of the German invasion and occupation of France, during World War II. Lyons, Narbonne, Bordeaux and Taulouse are all French cities. A reference is made to the one million people who are "dead and captive" (a reference to European military and civilian casualties).

D'un chef vieillard naîtra sens hébété,
Dégénérant par savoir et par armes:
Le chef de France par sa soeur redouté,
Champs divisés, concédés aux gendarmes.

1 - 78

It will be born of an old leader with dulled senses, degenerating in both knowledge and in arms. The leader of France feared by his sister. Fields of battle divided, granted to the troops.

MARSHAL PÉTAIN AND THE NAZIS

"It will be born of an old leader with dulled senses, degenerating in both knowledge and in arms" (appears to be a reference to the alleged collaboration with the Nazi's by French General Marshal Pétain, and possibly others). Pétain was a hero of World War I. But by the time of World War II, Pétain was too aged to be effective as a military commander, and some accused him of conspiring with the Germans. "The leader of France (Charles De Gaulle or someone else?) feared by his sister (if by chance Nostradamus is suggesting that Germany is France's sister, since they border one another, perhaps he meant that the German's initially viewed the military power of France with respect). "Fields of battle divided, granted to the troops" (suggests French and German forces, who were scattered about in various areas of France during the beginning of World War II).

Auprès des portes et dedans deuxcités Seront deux fléaux, et onc n'aperçuun tel, Faim dedans peste, de fer hors gensboutés, Crier secours au grand Dieu immortel.	2 - 6	Near the ports and within two cities will be two scourges, the like of which was never seen. Hunger, plague within, people thrown out by steel, crying for help from the great immortal God.

THE NUCLEAR ATTACK ON JAPAN

"Near the ports and within two cities (suggesting Hiroshima and Nagasaki in Japan) will be two scourges (suggesting two massive fires), the like of which was never seen (up to that point in history). Hunger, plague within, people thrown out by steel (human bodies hurled about due to atomic bomb blasts), crying for help from the great immortal God." Great misery was endured by the Japanese survivors of the first atomic blasts, who surely cried out to their God (or Gods) after being victimized by atomic blasts, radiation burns, and sickness. An American B-29 bomber (nicknamed the 'Enola Gay' by its crew) dropped the first atom bomb on Hiroshima on August 6, 1945. Three days later, Nagasaki was bombed. These unfortunate bombings compelled Japan to surrender to the Allies, ending World War II.

Naples, Palerme, Sicile, Syracuses, Nouveaux tyrans, fulgures feux célestes: Force de Londres, Gand, Bruxelleset Suses, Grand hécatombe, triomphe faire festes.	2 - 16	Naples, Palermo, Sicily and Syracuse new tyrants, celestial fires in the skies. A force from London, Ghent, Brussels and Susa: a great murderous slaughter, then triumph and festivities.

EUROPEAN NATIONS ALLY AGAINST AXIS POWERS

"Naples, Palermo, Sicily and Syracuse (cities in Italy) new tyrants (suggesting Mussolini and his followers), celestial fires in the skies (suggesting battle and aerial warfare). A force from London (the capital of Great Britain), Ghent, Brussels (cities in Belgium) and Susa" (southwestern Iran; will confront the Axis enemy). Britain, Belgium, and Iran were all on the side of the Allies during World War II. "A great murderous slaughter (an accurate description of World War II, from 1939 to 1945), then triumph and festivities" (which certainly occurred in Europe, and around the world, on Victory Europe Day - May 7, 1945, and Victory Japan Day - Sept. 2, 1945, celebrating the end of World War II).

Bêtes farouches de faim fleuves tranner: Plus part du champ encontre Histersera, En cage de fer le grand fera traîner, Quand rien enfant de Germain observera.	2 - 24	Beasts ferocious with hunger will swim across the rivers, the greater part of the army will be against Hister. The great one will cause him to be dragged in a cage of iron, when the German infant observes no law.

ADOLF HITLER AND THE NAZIS

"Beasts ferocious with hunger (suggesting Adolf Hitler and the German army) will swim across rivers (and borders), the greater part of the army (suggesting the French and Allied armies) will be against Hister" (a clever allusion to Adolf Hitler). Nostradamus misspelled Hitler's name by one letter. This is one of his remarkable name choices which most people agree is far beyond just coincidence. Perhaps Nostradamus is teasing us here. "The great one (suggesting the Allies) will cause him (Hitler) to be dragged in a cage of iron when the German infant (Hitler and Nazism) observes no law."

	2 - 40	
Un peu après non point longue intervalle, Par mer et terre sera fait grand tumulte: Beaucoup plus grande sera pugne navale, Feux, animaux, qui plus feront d'insulte.		Shortly afterwards, without a long interval, a great uproar will be raised by land and sea. Naval battles will be much greater. Fires, animals which will create greater insults.

THE TRANSITION FROM WORLD WAR I TO WORLD WAR II

This quatrain appears to pertain to the end of World War I, and the beginning of World War II. "Fires, animals which will create greater insults" (appears to be a reference to improved technology in weaponry). In Nostradamus terminology, the phrase "shortly afterwards" could easily suggest a period of approximately twenty years or so (World War I ending in 1918, and World War II beginning in 1939).

	3 - 32	
Le grand sépulcre du peuple Aquitanique S'approchera auprès de la Toscane, Quand Mars sera près du coin Germanique Et au terroir de la gent Mantuane.		The huge grave for the people of Aquitaine will approach from the direction of Tuscany. When Mars is in the corner of Germany and in the lands of the Mantuan people.

A WARNING FOR FRANCE

"The huge grave (suggesting mass death and destruction) for the people of Aquatine (a historical region of southwestern France, suggesting the people of France) will approach from the direction of Tuscany (a region of northwest Italy, an allusion to the nation of Italy). When Mars (suggesting war since in astrology the planet Mars often symbolizes war) is in the corner of Germany and in the lands of the Mantuan people" (suggesting Italy, since Mantua is a region, and city, in northern Italy). This quatrain is an accurate description of World War II. Nostradamus intended this quatrain to serve as a warning to the citizens of France, alerting them to dangers which would evolve in Germany and Italy during the 20th century.

Du plus profond de l'Occident d'Europe, De pauvres gens un jeune enfant naîtra, Qui par sa langue séduira grandetroupe: Son bruit au regne d'Orient plus croîtra.	3 - 35	In the deepest part of the west of Europe, a child will be born of a poor family, who by his speech will seduce a great troop. His reputation will increase in the Kingdom of the East.

ADOLF HITLER

"In the deepest part of the west of Europe (which could include Germany), a child will be born of a poor family (which Adolf Hitler was), who by his speech will seduce a great troop (Hitler, who was well known as a ranting orator, indeed seduced the great army of Germany through the power of his speeches). His reputation will increase in the Kingdom of the East" (this last line seems to suggest the war time bond between Hitler's Germany, and their Japanese allies, a "Kingdom of the East").

L'enfant naîtra à deux dents en la gorge, Pierres en Tuscie par pluie tomberont: Peu d'ans après ne sera blé ni orge, Pour saouler ceux qui de faim failliront.	3 - 42	The child will be born with two teeth in his mouth; stones to fall during the rain in Tuscany. A few years after there will be neither wheat nor barley to satisfy those who will faint from hunger.

THE BIRTH OF TOTALITARIANISM

The child born with two teeth in his mouth (perhaps a symbolic description of the birth of totalitarianism, which was born into the world, but died during its childhood, never reaching maturity). The "two teeth" of this child is perhaps a symbolic reference to Nazism and Fascism, which "bit" into Europe during the 1930's and 40's. "Stones to fall during the rain in Tuscany" (a region of northwest Italy), describes the destruction in Italy during World War II. The last lines are a general description of the hardships endured by the general population of European citizens during the horrible years of World War II (1939-1945).

Auprès du Rhin des montagnes Noriques Naîtra un grand de gens trop tardvenu, Qui défendra Saurome et Pannoniques, Qu'on ne saura qu'il sera devenu.	3 - 58	Near the Rhine from the Norican mountains will be born a powerful man of the people, arriving too late. He will defend Poland and Pannonians and one will never know what became of him.

THE COMING OF ADOLF HITLER

"Near the Rhine (a major European river rising in Switzerland, and flowing north through Germany and the Netherlands) from the Norican mountains (a mountain range in Austria) will be born a powerful man of the people (suggesting Adolf Hitler) arriving too late (arriving "too late" to successfully fulfil his agenda). He will defend Poland (the first nation Hitler invaded under a false pretense) and Pannonians" (which suggests the nation of Hungary, another European country Hitler later controlled). It was during these invasions that the Germans developed their famous *Blitzkrieg* technique of attack. "And one will never know what became of him" (is a reference to Hitler's body, which was never officially located after his alleged suicide in his bunker in Berlin, during the Allied invasion of Germany at the end of World War II).

Le camp plus grand de route misen fuite, Guère plus outre ne sera pourchassé: Ost recampé et légion réduite, Puis hors des Gaules du tout serachassé.	4 - 12	The greatest army put to flight in a disorderly manner scarcely pursued further. The army reassembled and the legion reduced, it will be driven out of Gaul completely.

THE GERMANS TO BE DRIVEN OUT OF FRANCE

"The greatest army (apparently a reference to the French military, which later proved to be 'greater' than the German army) put to flight in a disorderly manner (by the Germans during the early days of World War II) scarcely pursued further. The army reassembled and the legion reduced (a reference to De Gaulle's 'reassembly' of the French military upon his return from London), it (the German army) will be driven out of Gaul (the ancient name for France) completely". Near the end of World War II, the Parisians turned their guns on the Germans, giving them hell as they retreated from Paris (driving them, or 'it', out of France 'completely').

D'où pensera faire venir famine,
De là viendra le rassasiement:
L'oeil de la mer par avare canine
Pour de l'un l'autre dorna huile, froment.

4 - 15

From the location where they will think to bring famine, from there will come the relief. The eye of the sea, like a greedy dog; for the one will give oil and wheat to the other.

GREAT BRITAIN AND THE LEND-LEASE ACT

"From the location where they (the Germans) will think to bring famine (Great Britain), from there (from Great Britain) will come the relief (a reference to the Allied invasion of Normandy on D-Day, June 6, 1944, which was launched from Great Britain). The eye of the sea, like a greedy dog (might refer to periscopes and German submarine warfare in the North Atlantic -- the phrase "greedy dog" might suggest "wolf pack", which is what German submarine groups referred to themselves as during the war); for the one will give oil and wheat to the other" (is an amazing line). "The one" is an allusion to the United States, "the other" is an allusion to Great Britain. This act of "one giving oil and wheat to the other" is an extraordinarily accurate description of what was officially known as The Lend-Lease Act of World War II (the American policy of sharing food, oil, resources and military equipment with their war-time allies). During World War II many Allied merchant seamen died on Liberty Ships on their voyages from the United States to Great Britain (and Russia) due to German submarine and torpedo-bomber attacks.

Le changement sera fort difficile:
Cité, province au change gain fera:
Coeur haut, prudent mis, chassé lui habile,
Mer, terre, peuple son état changera.

4 - 21

The change will be very difficult. Both city and province will gain by the change. A high hearted prudent man highly placed, will be chased out by the cunning one. By land and sea people will change their estate.

CONDITIONS IN FRANCE DURING THE NAZI OCCUPATION, CHARLES DE GAULLE AND HITLER

"The change (suggesting the German occupation of France) will be very difficult (for the people of France to get used to). A high hearted prudent man highly placed (suggesting French General De Gaulle) will be chased out by the cunning one" (due to German actions, directed by the 'cunning' Hitler, De Gaulle left France and traveled to Great Britain). "By land and sea the people will change their estate" (suggests that by battle over the land, and by Allied invasion from the sea, the French people change the hardship in their country, "their estate", finally to be liberated from Nazi control).

Les fortresses des assiégés serrés, Par poudre à feu profondés en abîme: Les proditeurs seront tous vifs serrés, Onc aux sacristes n'avint si piteux schisme.	4 - 40	The fortress of the besieged, shut up by gunpowder, submerged into a pit; the traitors will be packed away alive, never has such a pitiful schism happened to the sextons.

THE DEATH OF ADOLPH HITLER

"The fortress of the besieged (a reference to Hitler's underground bunker in Berlin), shut up by gunpower ('besieged' by American, British, and Russian infantry and armored units), submerged into a pit; the traitors (the Nazis, traitors of peace and of peace treaties) will be packed away alive (perhaps suggesting Hitler's last days in his Berlin bunker before his suicide), never has such a pitiful schism (a disaster) happened to the sextons" (grave diggers, a reference to mass death resulting from war).

Après victoire de rabieuse langue, L'esprit tempré en tranquil et repos: Victeur sanguin par conflit fait harangue, Rôtir la langue et la chair et les os.	4 - 56	After the victory of the raving tongue, the spirit tempered in tranquil repose. During the battle, the bloody victor makes speeches, roasting the tongue, the flesh and the bones.

HITLER, THE NAZIS, AND THE HOLOCAUST

"After the victory of the raving tounge (a reference to the temporary military victories of Hitler, well known for his 'raving tounge' and lengthy oratories), the spirit tempered in tranquil repose. During the battle (through-out the course of various battles during World War II -- especially the early ones), the bloody victor (Hitler, a bloody, yet temporary victor) makes speeches (another reference to Hitler and his ranting oratories), roasting the tongue, the flesh and bones" (an amazing reference to the incineration, and death, of approximately 6 million Jews during World War II, 1939-45). Several million other people were also heinously killed and incinerated by the Nazis during the war which included gypsies, political prisoners, the physically handicapped, the mentally retarded, and others. This horrible act became known as the *Holocaust*.

Le vieux moqué et privé de sa place, Par l'etranger qui le subornera: Mains de son fils mangées devantsa face, Le frère à Chartres, Orl Roüan trahira.	4 - 61	The old man, mocked and deprived of his place by the foreigner who will suborn him. The hands of his sons are eaten before his face, betraying his brother at Chartres, Orléans and Rouen.

MARSHAL PÉTAIN

"The old man (suggesting Marshal Pétain, a French military commander and hero of World War I), mocked and deprived of his place by the foreigner (suggesting Adolf Hitler) who will suborn him (allegedly inducing Pétain to commit wrong and unlawful acts). The hands of his sons (the young men of the French army) are eaten before his face (a reference to the inability of the French to stop the invading Germans), betraying his brother (his fellow Frenchmen and the other allies - his 'brothers' in arms) at Chartres, Orleans and Rouen" (three cities in France where the Allies eventually advanced towards).

En lieu bien proche non éloigné deVenus, Les deux plus grands de l'Asie et d'Affrique, Du Ryn et Hister qu'on dira sontvenus, Cris, pleurs à Malte et côté Ligustique.	4 - 68	In a place not far from Venus, the two greatest ones of Asia and Africa, from the Rhine and Hister they will come; cries and tears at Malta and the Ligurian coast.

ITALY, JAPAN, GERMANY AND HITLER

"In a place not far from Venus (perhaps an allusion to Venice, Italy), the two greatest ones of Asia (suggesting Japan) and Africa (suggesting the Italians, who successfully invaded northern Africa during the beginning of World War II), from the Rhine (a river in Germany, an allusion to the nation of Germany), and Hister (an allusion to 'Hitler' -- Nostradamus misspelling his name by one letter) they (suggesting the Axis triumvirate of Germany, Italy, and Japan) will come (to attack their neighbors); cries and tears at Malta (a British island in the Mediterranean Sea south of Sicily, blockaded by the Italian military during the war) and the Ligurian coast" (Liguaria is a coastal region of northwest Italy which was targeted by Allied bombers during World War II).

Pres du grand fleuve, grand fosse, terre egeste, En quinze parts sera l'eau divisée: La cité prise, feu, sang cris conflit mettre, Et la plupart concerne au collisee.	4 - 80	Near the great river, a great ditch, earth dug up, the water divided into fifteen parts. The city taken, fire, blood, cries and conflict given, the greatest part concerned with the collision.

PARIS, THE MAGINOT LINE

"Near the great river (suggesting the Rhine, a major European river) a great ditch, earth dug up, the water divided into fifteen parts (suggesting the Maginot Line - a defensive military line created by the French, which quickly fell into German hands), the city taken, fire, blood, cries and conflict given, the greatest part concerned with the collision" (suggesting the series of famous battles fought throughout this region of France during the early and late stages of World War II). During the beginning of World War II, the French misread German intentions, hypothesizing that the Germans would attempt to invade France through Switzerland, which resulted in the creation of the Maginot Line. Nostradamus was accurate here.

Mer par solaires sûre ne passera, Ceux de Venus tiendront toute l'Affrique: Leur regne plus Saturne n'occupera, Et changera la part Asiatique.	5 - 11	Those of the Sun will not cross the sea in safety, the people of Venus will hold all of Africa. Then Saturn occupies their realm no longer and that part of Asia will change.

ITALY, AFRICA, JAPAN

"Those of the Sun (an apparent allusion to the Japanese, whose national flag resembles a rising Sun), will not cross the sea in safety (Japan, unable to sail in the Pacific without being attacked, never 'crossed' the Pacific Ocean past Hawaii), the people of Venus (suggesting Venice, Italy, an allusion to the Italians) will hold all of Africa (a reference to the fact that the Italians conquered parts of northern Africa during the early years of World War II). Then Saturn (known in astrology as the planet of obstacles and punishment) occupies their realm (the sphere, domain, or kingdom of Japan) no longer, and that part of Asia will change". The last two lines of this quatrain appears to suggest that "following" a period occupied by "obstacles and punishment" (the years of Japan's unsuccessful involvement in World War II), the nation of Japan (a "part of Asia") will "change", suggesting post-war success.

À son haut prix plus la larme sabee, D'humaine chair par mort en cendre mettre, À l'île Pharos par Croissars perturbée, Alors qu'à Rhodes paraîtra dur espectre.	5 - 16	The frankincense having lost its value, human flesh through death is burnt to ashes; the island of Pharos disturbed by Crusaders, when at Rhodes will appear ghosts.

GREECE, AFRICA, DEATH CAMPS

"The frankincense having lost its value, human flesh through death is burnt to ashes (suggesting the death of Jews and others who the Germans killed in death camps and cremated, a reference to the *Holocaust*), the island of Pharos (near Alexandria, Egypt, close to Tobruk, the location of several invasion attempts by the armies of Hitler), disturbed by Crusaders (perhaps an allusion to the Allied armed forces from traditionally Christian nations, i.e., the United States, Great Britain and Australia; but could possibly be an alllusion to the Nazis, 'men of the cross', possibly suggesting the *swastika cross*), when at Rhodes (a Greek island northeast of Crete, symbolically suggesting the nation of Greece) will appear ghosts" (a reference to the death of Italian and German soldiers who invaded Greece in 1940-41).

La liberté ne sera recouvrée, L'occupera noir, fier, vilain, inique, Quand la matière du pont sera ouvrée, D'Hister, Venise fâchée la république.	5 - 29	The liberty will not be regained; a proud, villainous and unjust black man will occupy it. When the matter of the Pontiff is opened by Hister, the republic of Venice will be vexed from the Danube.

HITLER, THE VATICAN, ITALY

"The liberty (after World War I) will not be regained, a proud, villainous and unjust black (black hearted) man (suggesting Hitler) will occupy it. When the matter of the Pontiff (the pope) is opened by Hister (Hitler), the Republic of Venice (an allusion to the nation of Italy) will be vexed from the Danube" (the "Danube" is a major river in Germany, thus the use of this word is an allusion to the nation of Germany). This quatrain is a general description of the military alliance between Germany and Italy (where the Vatican is located) during World War II. It is fair to say that Italy was "vexed" by Hitler. Again, Nostradamus used the word "Hister" to represent Hitler, misspelling Adolf's last name by one letter!

Charles De Gaulle

Le grand Empire sera tôt désolé Et translaté près d'arduenne silue: Les deux bâtards par l'aîné décollé, Et regnera Aenobarbe, nez de milve.	5 - 45	The great Empire soon to be desolated, and transfers to near the forest of Ardennes. The two bastards decapitated by the oldest one. Aenobarbe, the hawk-nosed one will rule.

FRANCE AND CHARLES DE GAULLE

"The great Empire (an allusion to Napoleon's French Empire, or in more modern terms - The Republic of France) soon to be desolated (will be in a state of ruin, gloom, and misery) and transfered to near the forest of Ardennes (a forested plateau in northern France, southeastern Belgium and Luxemburg, possibly suggesting that the valid leadership of France will be transferred from Paris to a region near the forest of Ardennes, perhaps an allusion to Charles De Gaulle and his stay in Great Britain-- located 'near' the Ardennes, just across the English Channel), the two bastards (an allusion to the incompetent French Generals Giraud and Corap, who failed to hold back the Germans after the Battle of Sedan) decapitated (poetically symbolizing 'ruin') by the oldest one (Marshall Pétain?). Aenobarbe, the hawk-nosed one (apparently an allusion to Charles De Gaulle, easily recognized by his large nose -- the hawk-nosed one) will rule" (leading the patriotic French people in their victory over the Germans). De Gaulle was later elected President of the Republic of France in January of 1959, and again in 1965. The "Ardennes" was the location of the Battle of the Bulge (in December of 1944).

La gent de Dace, d'Angleterre, Polonne Et de Boësme feront nouvelle ligue: Pour passer outre d'Hercules la colonne, Barcins, Tyrrens dresser cruelle brigue.	5 - 51	The people of Dacia, England and Poland and Bohemia will form a new alliance. In order to pass beyond the pillars of Hercules, the Spanish and the Italians will plan a cruel plot.

EUROPEAN POLITICAL ALLIANCES

"The people of Dacia (Romania), England, Poland and Bohemia (Czechoslovakia) will form a new alliance (which they indeed formed in 1939). In order (perhaps for the naval forces of the Germans) to pass beyond the pillars of Hercules (the Straits of Gibraltar, the strategic water way eight to 27 miles wide which extends for 36 miles between the Atlantic Ocean and the Mediterranean Sea), the Spanish and the Italians will plan a cruel plot" (which suggests the Spanish revolution of the 1930's, which Hitler supported, and Mussolini's rise to power in Italy). Perhaps these events affected the flow of naval traffic in Mediterranean sea lanes during World War II.

Translatera en la grande Germanie, Brabant et Flandres, Gand, Bruges, et Bolongne: La trêve feinte, le grand Duc d'Armenie Assaillira Vienne et la Cologne.	5 - 94	He will change into the greater Germany, Brabant and Flanders, Ghent, Bruges and Boulogne. The truce feigned, the grand Duke of Armenia will assault Vienna and Cologne.

HITLER, EUROPE, WORLD WAR II

"He (suggesting Adolf Hitler) will change into the greater Germany, Brabant (a province in central Belgium) and Flanders (a region of northern France and western Belgium), Ghent (a region of northwest central Belgium), Bruges (a region of northwestern Belgium) and Boulogne" (a seaport in northern France). All these regions were allied against the Axis powers and were affected by Hitler during World War II. The mention of "the truce feigned" is a possible reference to the non-aggression pact which was signed between Germany and Russia at the beginning of the war, but was later broken by Hitler when he began Operation Barbarossa against the Russians. "The truce feigned" might also be a reference to the phoney peace treaty Hitler signed with Chamberlin before the War. The "grand Duke of Armenia" is a possible reference to the Russian leader Stalin, who was born in Armenia. The Russians, however, never assaulted Vienna during World War II.

Hitler intentionally began Operation Barbarossa on the day of June 22 (which was the same day of June that Napoleon began his invasion of Russia approximately 140 years earlier).

Norneigre et Dace, et l'îsle Britannique,
Par les unis frères seront vexés:
Le chef Romain issu de sang Gallique
Et les copies aux forêts repoussées.

6 - 7

Norway and Dacia and the British Isles, will be troubled by the united brothers. The Roman leader, derived from French blood; his forces thrust back into the forests.

EUROPE VEXED BY HITLER & MUSSOLINI

"Norway, Dacia (Romania) and the British Isles (countries who were allied against Germany and Italy during World War II) will be troubled by the united brothers (suggesting Hitler and Mussolini - Hitler's ally and 'brother in spirit'). The Roman leader (a reference to Mussolini?), derived from Gallic (French) blood (this line eludes me), his forces thrust back into the forests" (is perhaps a reference to troops, or to European resistance movements which were popular in France, Yugoslavia, and other Axis occupied countries during World War II).

Roi trouvera de qu'il désirait tant,
Quand le Prélat sera repris à tort:
Réponse au Duc le rendra malcontent,
Qui dans Milan mettra plusieurs àmort.

6 - 31

The King will find that which he desired so greatly; when the Prelate will be unjustly taken. The reply to the Duke will make him unsatisfied; in Milan several will be put to death.

ITALY, MUSSOLINI

This quatrain appears to be a general reference to events in Italy during the 1930's, between Mussolini, Victor Emanual, and the King of Italy. "The Prelate (in liturgical churches, one of a higher order of clergy) will be unjustly taken" (appears to be a reference to conditions in the Vatican, and the difficulties of Church matters, during World War II). The Italian dictator Mussolini executed several of his political rivals in "Milan" (a city in Italy). Allied forces later invaded Italy, liberating it from Fascist and Nazi control.

De la partie de Mammer grand Pontife,
Subjuguera les confins du Danube:
Chasser les croix, par fer raffe ni riffe,
Captifs, or, bagues plus de cent mille rubes.

6 - 49

The great Pontiff of the party of Mars, will subjugate the borders of the Danube. The cross to pursue through sword, hook or crook, captives, gold, jewels, over one hundred thousand rubies.

HITLER, THE NAZIS AND THE SWASTIKA

"The great Pontiff of the party of Mars (suggesting Adolf Hitler, high priest of the Nazi war party) will subjugate (conquer or subdue) the borders of the Danube" (the Danube River flows from Germany east to Rumania). Nostradamus was both accurate and clever in his choice of words here. "The cross (swastika cross) pursues through sword (death), hook or crook" (through death, lies and the hooked or "crooked" cross). "Captives" refers to prisoners of war, and occupants of death camps. This might also suggest citizens who lived as prisoners within their own nations, due to the occupation. Hitler was somewhat temporarily successful at capturing various treasures in parts of Europe, referred to in this quatrain as "gold, jewels and one hundred thousand rubies."

En grand regret sera la gent Gauloise,
Coeur vain, léger croira témérité:
Pain, sel, ni vin, eau, venin ni cervoise,
Plus grand captif, faim, froid, nécessité.

7 - 34

In great grief will be the Gallic people, vain and light-hearted, they will believe in rashness. No bread, salt, wine, water, liquor nor ale, great captivity, famine, cold and need.

CONDITIONS IN FRANCE DURING WORLD WAR II

A clearly stated quatrain describing the grief stricken emotions, and difficult living conditions, the people of France endured under the Nazi occupation of their homeland during World War II.

Le grand naîtra de Veronne et Vicence, Qui portera un surnom bien indigne. Qui à Venise vouldra faire vengeance. Lui-même pris homme du guet et signe.	8 - 33	The great one will be born of Verona and Vincenza who will carry a very unworthy surname; he who at Venice will wish to take vengeance, himself taken in by a man of the watch and sign.

MUSSOLINI (THE ITALIAN DICTATOR)

"The great one (suggesting Benito Mussolini - Fascist ruler of Italy during the 1930's and up until the end of World War II) will be born of Verona and Vincenza (two cities in northern Italy near where Mussolini was born) who will carry a very unworthy surname (suggesting that the Italians would eventually scorn his name); he (suggesting Mussolini) who at Venice (a city in Italy where Mussolini later lost his glory) will wish to take vengeance (upon the enemies of his rebellion), himself taken in by a man of the watch and sign," (perhaps a reference to Hitler's seduction of Mussolini).

Dedans les Îles les enfants transportés, Les deux de sept seront en désepoir: Ceux du terrouer en seront supportés, Nom pelle pris des ligues fui l'espoir.	8 - 64	Into the Isles, the children transported, two out of seven in despair. Those of the soil will be supported by it, the name shovel taken, the hope of "the league" fails.

BRITAIN, THE FAILURE OF THE LEAGUE OF NATIONS

"Into the Isles (suggesting the British Isles) the children (troops, young men) will be transported (mostly by sea), two out of seven in despair (suggesting that 28% of the population of the British Isles would be vexed by their enemy, Hitler). Those of the soil (an unnamed party) will be supported by it" (unclear to me). The next part of the quatrain is confusing, yet "shovel" may be a reference to the digging of trenches or graves during wartime. "The hope of the league fails", is a remarkable reference to the failure of the League of Nations, the precursor of the modern United Nations, to keep peace in Europe after World War I. The document called the Covenant of the League of Nations, formed Part I of the Treaty of Versailles, which ended World War I. The League of Nations was a visionary dream of American President Woodrow Wilson.

Le vieux frustré du principal espoir, Il parviendra au chef de son empire: Vingt mois tiendra le regne à grandpouvoir, Tyran, cruel en délaissant un pire.	8 - 65	The old man disappointed in his principal hope, he will attain to the leadership of his Empire. Twenty months he will hold the realm with great force, tyrannical, cruel, giving way to one worse.

MARSHAL PÉTAIN, FRANCE

"The old man (suggesting the aging French General Marshal Pétain) disappointed in his principal hope (of defending France against a German invasion), he (Marshal Pétain) the leadership of his Empire (Pétain became the leader of France in July of 1940). Twenty months he will old the realm with great force, tyrannical, cruel, giving way to one worse" (after holding power for twenty months, Pétain transfered his leadership to Laval, the reference to "one worse", preceding De Gaulle's return to France). During World War I, Pétain coined the phrase "they shall not pass", which was a patriotic reference to holding the line against the Germans, who wished to invade Paris. However, during World War II, many accused Pétain of collaborating with the Nazis.

De Castel Franco sortira l'assemblée,	9 - 16	Out of Castile, Franco will come to the assembly, the ambassadors will not be agreeable and cause a schism. The citizens of Riviera will be in the squabble, and they deny him entry to the great Gulf.
L'ambassadeur non plaisant fera schisme:		
Ceux de Ribiere seront en mêlée,		
Et au grand gouffre dénieront l'entrée.		

FRANCO AND THE SPANISH CIVIL WAR

"Out of Castile (a region of Spain), Franco (suggesting Francisco Franco) will come to the assembly (the leadership of Spain), the ambassadors will not be agreeable and cause a schism (a reference to Spanish political turmoil, and the resulting revolution by Franco and his men, from 1936-39). The citizens of Riviera (the supporters of Franco's rival, Primo de Riviera) will be in the squabble" (is a reference to the bloody civil war which resulted). The last line is a reference to Franco's exile to Morocco. Nostradamus names both Franco and Riviera by their surnames, which makes this a remarkable quatrain!

General Francisco Franco of Spain

Hercules Roi de Rome et d'Annemarc, De Gaule trois Guion surnommé, Trembler l'Italie et l'un de sainct Marc, Premier sur tous monarque renommé.	9 - 33	Hercules, King of Rome and of Hungary, three times the leader of France to be surnamed De Gaule. Italy and the one of St. Mark to tremble, the first monarch renowned over all the kings.

CHARLES DE GAULLE, MUSSOLINI

"Hercules (the mythological Roman hero of extraordinary strength and son of Zeus, suggests a strong man who is subordinate to one more powerful, as Mussolini was to Hitler), King of Rome and Hungary (is perhaps a reference to Hitler or Benito Mussolini). Three times the leader of France to be surnamed De Gaulle" is an amazing reference to Charles De Gaulle, naming him by his actual "surname". The reference to "three times" is a reference to the three periods De Gaulle led the French people (as a general during World War II, and as president in 1958 and 1965). Line three seems to be a general reference to Mussolini and the trembling of Italy (warfare). "The first monarch renowned over all the kings" might be a spiritual reference to Jesus Christ (the first monarch of all kings).

Un capitaine de la Grand Germanie Se viendra rendre par simulé secours Au Roi des Rois aide de Pannonie, Que sa révolte fera de sang grandcours.	9 - 90	A captain of the greater Germany will come to deliver false support; to the king of kings; to help Hungary; so that his war will cause a great shedding of blood.

ADOLF HITLER, WAR IN EUROPE

"A captain of the greater Germany (a reference to a German military man - Adolf Hitler), who will come to deliver false support (Hitler invaded several European nations during World War II, including Hungary, under the false pretense of offering support); to the king of kings (perhaps suggesting that Hitler will offer false support to the followers of Christianity?); to help Hungary; so that his war (World War II) will cause a great shedding of blood" (as history has recorded, millions of people died during World War II).

CENTURY I

Le mouvement de sens, coeur, pieds et mains
Seront d'accord, Naples, Leon, Sicile:
Glaives, feux, eaux: puis aux nobles Romains,
Plongés, tués, morts par cerveau débile.

1 - 11

The movement of senses, heart, feet and hands in agreement, Naples, Lyon and Sicily. Swords, fire, floods, then the noble Romans will sink, killed or dead because of a weak brain.

TROUBLE IN ROME

Now we arrive at the quatrains which appear to pertain to the future (as well as some which pertain to the recent past). "The movement of senses, heart, feet and hands in agreement (perhaps suggesting that the thoughts, emotional attitudes, and actions of the people in), Naples (a seaport city in southwestern Italy), Lyon (an industrial city in east-central France) and Sicily (an Italian island in the Mediterranean Sea, south of the Italian mainland) are parallel and in accord with one another (unified and or allied with one another). Swords (war and weapons), fire (destruction by war), floods, then the noble Romans (an allusion to the citizens of Italy) will sink, killed or dead (either submerged by flood or killed by war) because of a weak brain" (suggesting weak mindedness or negligence on the behalf of the Italians). This quatrain predicts trouble for the Italians during a future era, when they are allied with the French.

Par la discorde négligence Gauloise
Sera passage à Mahomet ouvert:
De sang trempé la terre et mer Senoise,
Le port Phocen de voiles et nefs couvert.

1 - 18

Because of French discord and negligence an entry shall be opened to the Mohammedans. The land and sea of Siena soaked in blood, and the port of Marseilles covered with ships and sails.

FRENCH DISCORD WILL CREATE OPENINGS FOR ARABIC FORCES DURING A EURO/ARABIC CONFLICT

"Because of French discord and negligence (suggesting French military or political discord?) an entry shall be opened to the Mohammedans (suggesting unnamed Islamic forces). The land and sea of Siena (a city in Italy) soaked in blood (suggesting war), and the port of Marseilles (a coastal city in France) covered with ships and sails" (suggesting naval vessels, perhaps belonging to France and/or other nations). This quatrain could be attributed to Napoleon. However, it might be a warning regarding a future conlfict involving the Italians (and the French) with an unnamed Islamic force.

La trompe fausse dissimulant folie Fera Bisance un changement de lois: Ira d'Egypte qui veut que l'on délie, Édit changeant monnaies et alois.	**1 - 40**	The false trumpet concealing madness causes Byzantium (Turkey) to change its laws. From Egypt will go forth a man who wants the withdrawal of edicts, devaluating the quality of coins.

CHANGES FOR TURKEY, AN EGYPTIAN WILL RISE TO POWER IN THE MIDDLE EAST

"The false trumpet concealing madness" perhaps suggests the public pronouncement of a false proclamation of some type (since trumpets used to sound in the courts of kings before proclamations were read to the public). Whatever its meaning, this action conceals some type of event, which "causes Byzantium (an allusion to Turkey) to change its laws" (perhaps some type of social or spiritual rebellion against the government). "From Egypt will go forth a man (an Islamic holy man, a military man, or civil leader?) who wishes the withdrawal of edicts" (the withdrawal of a decree or proclamation issued by an authority, perhaps meaning a change of laws or social values). The actions of this unnamed Egyptian appear to "devalue" the currency, or destabilize the economy of Turkey, Egypt, or another country.

Les fléaux passés diminue le monde, Longtemps la paix terres inhabitées: Sûr marchera par ciel, terre, mer et onde, Puis de nouveau les guerres suscitées.	**1 - 63**	The scourges passed, the world becomes smaller, Peace for a long time and populated lands: One will safely travel by air, land, sea and wave, then wars stirred up anew.

A PERIOD OF PEACE BETWEEN GREAT WARS

"The scourges passed (the word 'scourge' as used in quatrain #2-6, suggests the nuclear blasts in Japan and the end of World War II), the world becomes smaller (which suggests that the post-war world shrinks due to jet travel, automobiles, and electronic communications). Peace for a long time (40, 50, 60 years?) and populated lands (as has occurred since the end of World War II). One will safely travel by air (which is most often the case in modern times), land, sea and wave (suggesting electronic waves - radio, television, etc.), then wars stirred up anew" (near the change of the millennium, during the first quarter of the 21st century, or when?). This appears to be a quatrain relevant to our present times.

De nuit Soleil penseront avoir vu Quand le pourceau demi-homme on verra: Bruit, chant, bataille, au ciel battre aperçu, Et bêtes brutes à parler l'on orra.	1 - 64	At night they will think they have seen the Sun, when they see the half pig man. Noise, song, combat, battles in the skies. Brute beasts will be heard to talk.

NUCLEAR ATTACK AT NIGHT BY JET PLANES?

"At night they (an unnamed party in an unnamed location) will think they have seen the Sun (the unnamed party will witness an event which emits a great deal of light), when they see the half pig man (possibly suggesting a greedy leader of some unnamed country, or perhaps Nostradamus had a vision of a chubby combat pilot pulling "g"'s in his aircraft while dropping his bombs -- making his face appear pig-like). Noise (loud sounds, an outcry), song (suggesting music), combat (war), battles in the skies (modern aerial combat). Brute beasts (inanimate creatures; perhaps a 16th century description of modern electrical machines) will be heard to talk" (such as televisions, radios, computers, video games, telephones, audio systems, robots, etc...). This is obviously a quatrain relevant to modern times and the not-too-distant future.

An Allied pilot departs on a defensive mission against an invading enemy.

Pluie, faim, guerre en Perse non cessée, La foi trop grande trahira le monarque, Par la finie en Gaule commencée: Secret augure pour à un être parque.	1 - 70	Rain, famine, war in Persia not over, too great a faith will betray the monarch. Events begun in France will finish there, a secret sign for one to be moderate.

THE SHAH OF IRAN

"Rain (a reference to flooding, or to a lack of rain?), famine, war in Persia (an ancient name for modern Iran) not over (perhaps suggesting that Iran will be constantly involved in various conflicts over an extended period of years, i.e., its war with Iraq during the 1980's and its support of terrorism during the 1990's), too great a faith (suggesting a powerful belief in religion, in this case suggesting the religion of Islam) will betray (to give over into the hands of an enemy by treachery) the monarch (a supreme ruler or hereditary head of sovereign control -- a precise description of Shah Reza Pahlevi). Events begun in France (a reference to the actions of Ayatollah Khomeini, the Islamic holy man who was exiled from Iran to France, where he instigated an Islamic fundamentalist revolutionary movement against the Shah) will finish there (Khomeini's revolution will be completed in Iran), a secret sign for one (suggesting the Shah, President Carter, or someone else) to be moderate" (in their views and or actions towards Iran). The Islamic revolution in Iran forced the Shah of Iran into exile in 1979, allowing Khomeini to return to Iran and rule its government. These events resulted in an international hostage crisis between Iran and the United States causing great political anxiety for President Jimmy Carter.

La tour marine trois fois prise et reprise Par Espagnols, Barbares, Ligurins: Marseille et Aix, Arles par ceux de Pise, Vast, feu, fer, pillé Avignon des Thurins.	1 - 71	The marine tower captured and retaken three times by Spaniards, barbarians and Ligurians. Marseilles and Aix, Arles by those of Pisa, devastation, fire, sword, Avignon pillaged by the Turinese.

WARFARE IN EUROPE

"The marine tower (thought to represent the French city of Bauc, or possibly some other European coastal city) captured and retaken three times by Spaniards (the citizens of Spain), barbarians (an unnamed invading enemy), and Ligurians (Italians). Marseilles (a city in France) and Aix (a city in France), Arles (also a city in France, are all affected in some way) by those of Pisa" (by Italians from Pisa, or by foreign troops occupying Italy). "Devastation, fire, sword (war occurs), Avignon (a city in France) pillaged by the Turinese" (by Italians from the city of Turin, or by forces occupying Turin). Another mention of warfare in Europe.

France à cinq parts par neglect assaillie, Tunis, Argiels emus par Perseins: Leon, Seville, Barcelone faillie, N'aura la classe par les Venitiens.	1 - 73	France due to negligence shall be assailed on five sides. Tunis, Algiers stirred up by the Iranians. Leon, Seville and Barcelona having failed, for the Venetians, there will be no fleet.

FRANCE TO BRACE FOR ATTACK BY ISLAMIC FORCES

"France, due to negligence (due to military negligence and or political negligence) shall be assailed (military attacked) on five sides (from five directions). Tunis (the capital city of Tunisia) and Algiers (the capital city of Algeria, both Islamic nations located in North Africa) stirred up by the Persians (suggesting the nation of Iran, also an Islamic nation, who will provoke the actions taken by Tunisia and Algeria). Leon (a city in Spain), Seville (a city in Spain) and Barcelona (a seaport city in Spain) having failed (failing militarily) for the Venetians (the Italians) there will be no fleet" (to protect themselves against an enemy, and or to provide assistance to their Spanish allies). This interesting quatrain suggests that France, Spain, and Italy might one day be attacked by Islamic nations. A future Islamic naval invasion of Spain could originate from nations in North Africa (i.e., Tunisia, Algeria, and Morocco). If the invaders captured Spain, they could travel north to France, and east to Italy. Doom for Spain will affect the military security of both France and Italy.

La gent étrange divisera butins, Saturne en Mars son regard furieux: Horrible strage aux Toscans et Latins, Grecs, qui seront à frapper curieux.	1 - 83	The strange nation will divide the spoils. Saturn in Mars, in dreadful aspect. Great slaughter to the Tuscans and Latins, Greeks who will wish to strike.

GREECE AND ITALY ATTACKED

"The strange nation (an unnamed invading enemy) will divide the spoils (of war). Saturn in Mars, in dreadful aspect (perhaps suggesting, in astrological terminology, that traditional factions of domination, represented by the planet Saturn, will be devastated by war, as alluded to by the planet Mars). Great slaughter (war and blood shed) to the Tuscans (the people of western central Italy) and Latins (an allusion to the Italians), Greeks who will wish to strike" (this action will compel the Greeks to counter-attack or "strike-out" at the unnamed enemy). Some commentators attribute this quatrain to World War II, however, it may have been intended for future times.

	1 - 89	
Tous ceux de Ilerde seront dedans Moselle, Mettant à mort tous ceux de Loire et Seine: Secours marin viendra près d'haute velle Quand Espagnols ouvrira toute veine.		Those from Lerida located in the Moselle, killing all those from the Loire and Seine. The amphibious support will come near the high wall, when the Spanish open every path.

FRANCE TO BE INVADED BY FORCES OCCUPYING SPAIN

"Those from Lerida (a city in northeastern Spain, suggesting the Spanish, or unnamed forces stationed there) located in the Moselle (a river in northeastern France) killing all those from the Loire and Seine (rivers located in the northwest of France, suggesting the French or unnamed forces located on French soil). The amphibious support (friend or foe of the French?) will come near the high wall, when the Spanish open every path" (apparently through means of combat).

	1 - 91	
Les Dieux feront aux humains apparence, Ce qu'ils seront auteurs de grand conflict: Avant ciel vu serein épée et lance, Que vers main gauche sera plus grand afflict.		The gods will make it appear to the mortals that they are the authors of a great war: Sword and lance prior to the sky being seen unclouded, the greatest damage will be inflicted towards the left hand.

THE "GODS", THROUGH MAN, DESIGN A GREAT WAR

Nostradamus states that mortal men will think that they are the authors of a great war, but in reality, it will be an act of God or "the Gods" (*force majeure*, or the will of God). "Sword and lance prior to the sky being seen unclouded (perhaps suggesting a land war followed by aerial warfare). The greatest damage (according to Nostradamus) will be inflicted towards the left hand". As one holds a map of Europe, with the North to the top of the map, "the left" could suggest the New World. If looking at a map of the New World, "the left" could mean Asia. The meaning of "the left" is unclear, yet most commentators think "the left" refers to Europe and/or the New World. Considering the fact that aerial warfare was first introduced in World War I (1914-1918), this quatrain appears relevant to the 20th century (and or the future).

Terre Italique près des monts tremblera,
Lion et Coq non trop confédérés,
En lieu de peur l'un l'autre s'aidera,
Seul Castulon et Celtes, modérés.

1 - 93

The Italian lands near the mountains will tremble. The Cock and the Lion not strongly confederated. Because of fear they will help each other. Only Spain and France are moderate.

FRANCE AND THE U.K. WILL UNITE
IN ITALY TO FIGHT INVADING FORCES

This quatrain has been attributed to the Napoleonic era, yet it could possibly apply to future Euro/Arabic conflicts, or the future war with the third Antichrist. "The Italian lands (Italy) near the mountains (suggesting the Alps range) will tremble (due to war, due to earthquakes, due to what?). The Cock (an allusion to France) and the Lion (an allusion to Great Britain) not strongly confederated (due to battle field difficulties or political concerns?). Because of fear (of defeat?) they (France and Great Britain) will help each other. Only Spain and France are moderate". Apparently a situation in Italy compels France and Great Britain (the U.K.) to become close allies. How (or why) Spain and France are moderate is unclear.

Au port Selin le tyran mis à mort
La liberté non pourtant recouvrée:
Le nouveau Mars par vindicte et remort,
Dame par force de frayeur honorée.

1 - 94

At port, Selin the tyrant put to death, Liberty however is not recovered, the new Mars of vengeance and remorse. A lady is honored through force of terror.

A MIDDLE EASTERN LEADER
WILL BE DEFEATED AT A PORT

Apparently, a future Middle Eastern tyrant ("Selin", a fictitious or actual name of a person) will be "put to death" near a port (the geographical location of which is unknown). "Liberty however is not recovered (the death of 'Selin' does not end the hostilities), the new Mars (Mars is an allusion to war, thus a 'new' war will begin) of vengeance and remorse (probably against the victors of the conflict with Selin). A lady is honored (suggesting an individual woman, an allusion to France, the nations of liberty, or what?) through force of terror" (due to brave military actions during the time of a conflict)? "Selin" is mentioned in the quatrains (and Epistle) and appears to be a future adversary of Europe and the West (and is possibly the third Antichrist).

CENTURY II

Pour la chaleur solaire sus la mer De Negrepont les poissons demi cuits: Les habitants les viendront entamer Quand Rhod. et Gennes leur faudra le biscuit.	2 - 3	Because of the heat of the Sun upon the sea, the fish around Euboea will become half cooked. Local inhabitants will eat them when there is no food in Rhodes and Genoa.

DROUGHT AND FAMINE TO DEVELOP IN THE EASTERN MEDITERRANEAN

"Because of the heat of the Sun upon the sea (due to a heat wave, global warming or a nuclear blast?) the fish around Negrepont (an old Italian name for the Greek island of Euboea in the eastern Mediterranean Sea) will become half cooked. The local inhabitants will eat them when there is no food in Rhodes (the largest of the Greek Dodecanese Islands in the Aegean Sea southwest of Turkey) and Genoa" (a port city in northwest Italy on the Ligurian Sea). It seems that the lack of food during a future period of drought or wartime will force people to eat these "half cooked" fish or starve. This suggests that hard times might hit this region during a future crisis.

Depuis Monech jusqu'auprès de Sicille Toute la plage demeurera désolée: Il n'y aura faubourg, cité ni ville, Que par Barbares pillée soit et volée.	2 - 4	From Monaco as far as Sicily the entire coast will remain desolated. There will be no suburbs, cities nor towns which have not been robbed and pillaged by Barbarians.

THE EUROPEAN COASTLINE WILL BE DESECRATED DURING WAR

The entire European coast line between the region of Monaco (a small European principality located on the southern coast of France on the Mediterranean Sea, fifteen miles east of Nice) and Sicily (an Italian island south of the Italian mainland) will remain desolated" (devastated due to combat, or chemical or atomic war?). All the cities along this southern European coast line will be "robbed and pillaged by Barbarian invaders" (suggesting Middle Eastern invaders, North African invaders, or some other unnamed force). We have no clues here regarding the intended time frame for this futuristic European calamity.

Qu'en dans poisson, fer et lettre enfermée, Hors sortira qui puis fera la guerre, Aura par mer sa classe bien ramée, Apparaissant près de Latine terre.	2 - 5	When iron and letter are enclosed in a fish, out of it will come a man who will then make war. His fleet will have traveled far across the sea to appear near the Latin shore.

A FLEET TRAVELS TO ITALY

"When iron (weapons?) and letters (documents?) are enclosed in a fish (a 16th century description of a submarine?), out of it (out of the submarine) will come a man who will then make war (a reference to an aggressor or a liberator?). His fleet (identity unknown) will have traveled far across the sea (from Asia, from the Middle East, from Russia, or from America?) to appear near the Latin (Italian) shore." Could there be a link between this event, and quatrain #1-9 regarding a forecasted naval war in the Adriatic Sea?

Un peu devant monarque trucidé, Castor Pollux en nef, astre crinite: L'erain publique par terre et mer vidé, Pise, Ast, Ferrare, Turin terre interdite.	2 - 15	A short while before the monarch assassinated, Castor and Pollux in the ship, a bearded star. Public treasure emptied by land and sea, Pisa, Asti, Ferrara and Turin are lands under interdict.

MILITARY BATTLES IN ITALY IN 2061?

"A short while (a brief period of time) before the monarch (an unnamed monarch) is assassinated (by whom?), Castor and Pollux (the *Twin Stars* of the Gemini constellation, also the name of the ship which carried the Apostle Paul from the isle of Malta to Rome, see Acts 28:11, possibly an allusion to a pair of unnamed Christian leaders) in the ship (suggesting that 'Castor and Pollux', whoever they may be, might be located inside of a nautical vessel, possibly headed for Rome), a bearded star. Public treasure (Italian treasures?) emptied by land and sea (by an unnamed party), Pisa, Asti, Ferrara and Turin (Italian cities) are lands under interdict." The word "interdict" has two basic definitions. It can suggest the military halt of an enemy's advance. Or, in Catholicism, it is an ecclesiastical censure restricting the offending district or person from participation in most sacraments, including Christian burial. If "bearded star" suggests a comet, it may be a reference to Halley's Comet, which returns next in 2061. See footnote on page 178 in the Astrological tables.

L'ambassadeur envoyé par birèmes,
A mi-chemin d'inconnus repoussé:
De sel renfort viendront quatre trirèmes,
Cordes et chaînes en Negrepont troussé.

2 - 21

The ambassador sent by the biremes is repelled halfway by unknown men. Four triremes reinforced with salt will arrive, bound with ropes and chains in Negrepont.

NAVAL COMBAT AROUND EUBOEA

"The ambassador (identity unknown) sent by the biremes (an ancient two bridged oared galley or sailing vessel, perhaps suggesting naval forces) is repelled halfway (to some destination) by unknown men. Four Triremes (ancient sailing vessels larger than biremes) reinforced with salt (supplies?) will arrive, bound with ropes and chains in Negrepont "(an old Italian name for the Greek island of Euboea in the eastern Mediterranean Sea, mentioned in quatrain # 2 - 3 as a place that will be devastated during a time of drought, or war). This unclear event involves the Greeks and an unnamed naval power.

Le camp Ascop d'Europe partira,
S'adjoignant proche de l'îsle submergée:
D'Araon classe phalange pliera,
Nombril du monde plus grande voix subrogee.

2 - 22

The invincible army will depart from Europe collecting itself near the submerged island. The accursed fleet will bend the phalanx, the navel of the world a greater voice is substituted.

A EUROPEAN NAVAL FLEET REGROUPS

"The invincible army of will depart from Europe (from what geographic location in Europe?) collecting itself near the submerged island (an unnamed island which appears to have been submerged by flood). The accursed fleet (doomed, abominable) the identity of which we know not -- perhaps the foes of the European fleet) will bend (will strain) the phalanx (the infantry troops of an unnamed nation), the navel of the world (an unnamed place, perhaps suggesting Rome), a more powerful voice is substituted" (in place of what?). This quatrain seems to suggest that a European naval fleet will regroup near an unnamed island, and perhaps assist Italy in some way.

Lait, sang grenouilles escoudre en Dalmatie. Conflit donné, peste près de Balenne: Cri sera grand par toute Esclavonie, Lors naîtra monstre près et dedans Ravenne.	2 - 32	Milk, frog's blood will be prepared in Dalmatia. Battle engaged, a plague near Balliensis. A great cry will sound throughout Slavonia, then will a monster be born near and inside Ravenna.

WARFARE IN YUGOSLAVIA

"Milk" remains a mystery to me, except that Nostradamus mentions a "milky rain" in another quatrain that pertains to war. "Frog's blood" might be a 16th century description of future combat involving an amphibious military force. Whatever its meaning, it "will be prepared in Dalmatia" (a region of Croatia along the eastern coast of the Adriatic Sea). "Battle engaged (battle involving Croatian forces, or forces occupying Croatia, with an unnamed force seems to result in, or near, Dalmatia), a plague near Balliensis" (perhaps disease, chemical warfare, or something similar occurs near Balliensis, a city northeast of modern Capua, in Italy). "A great cry (of pain?) will sound throughout Slavonia" (a region of Croatia located between the Drava and Sava Rivers). This military action results in what Nostradamus calls "a monster being born near and inside Ravenna" (a city in northern Italy six miles inland from the Adriatic Sea). This yet-to-occur battle seems to involve war parties on both sides of the Adriatic Sea. Another quatrain which references a future Euro/Arabic conflict (see quatrain #9-60).

Un peu après non point longue intervalle, Par mer et terre sera fait grand tumulte: Beaucoup plus grande sera pugne navale, Feux, animaux, qui plus feront d'insulte.	2 - 40	Shortly afterwards, without a very long interval, a great uproar will be raised by land and sea. Naval battles will be much greater. Fires, animals which will create greater insults.

END OF WORLD WAR II, THE COMING OF FUTURE WARS

Shortly after (a great war?) a "great uproar" (a new war?) occurs by land and sea. The naval battles (in the new war) will be more intense than the ones in the previous war. "Animals" (weaponry?) will be created which will result in "greater insults" (greater killing power). Though this quatrain seems to fit the end of World War I, foreshadowing the beginning of World War II, could this quatrain be intended for the future?

	2 - 41	
La grande étoile par sept jours brûlera, Nuée fera deux soleils apparoir: Le gros mâtin toute nuit hurlera Quand grand pontife changera de terroir.		The great star will burn for seven days and the cloud will make the Sun appear double. The big mastiff will howl all night when the great pontiff changes his countries.

A POPE WILL FLEE THE VATICAN DURING WAR

"The great star will burn for seven days and the cloud will make the Sun appear double (possibly suggesting that a nuclear explosion will burn in an unnamed geographical area for seven days after exploding, or this might be a reference to a future astrological event). The big mastiff (an allusion to "the dogs of war") will howl all night (suggesting that a battle is opened during the night-time hours) when the great pontiff (a future unnamed pope) changes his countries" (suggesting that the unnamed pope will flee from Italy in order to avoid unnecessary exposure to some type of unstated danger). Perhaps this is a reference to future trouble during a Euro/Arabic conflict or the war with the third Antichrist.

	2 - 46	
Après grand trouble humain, plus grand s'apprête Le grand moteur les siècles renouvèle: Pluie, sang, lait, famine, fer et peste, Au ciel vu feu, courant longue étincelle.		After great trouble for humanity, greater troubles approach when the Grand Mover renews the cycle of the ages: Rain, blood, milk, famine, iron, and disease. In the heavens will be seen fire, a lengthy spark moves rapidly.

WAR NEAR THE CHANGE OF THE MILLENNIUM?

"After great trouble for humanity (wars, earthquakes, floods, famine), greater troubles (more complex problems) approach when the Grand Mover (an allusion to God) renews the cycle of the ages (since *The Prophecies* expire in 3797, this suggests either 2000 or 3000 A.D.). Rain (fall-out or flooding?), blood, milk (another reference to milk, which eludes me), famine, iron (machines of war), and disease. In the heavens (our atmosphere or beyond?) will be seen fire (a reference to war, or something astronomical?), a lengthy spark moves rapidly" (perhaps suggesting the visible glow from a missile, jet, or space ship as it passes through the sky). Or, perhaps Nostradamus might be referring to the Hale-Bopp Comet of 1997! The end of the Age of Pisces, and the beginning of the Age of Aquarius, may remotely be suggested in this quatrain (the cycle of astrological ages) rather than the change of the millennium. According to astrologers, the Age of Aquarius is approaching us, but there is no clear date for the change of astrological ages. See #10-72 and #10-74.

Classe Gauloise par appui de grande garde Du grand Neptune, et ses tridents soldat, Rougée Prouence pour soutenir grande bande: Plus Mars Narbon, par javelots et dards.	2 - 59	The Gallic fleet with the support of the main guard of great Neptune and his trident soldiers. Provence reddened to sustain this great band, fighting at Narbonne because of javelins and darts.

WARFARE IN FRANCE

"The Gallic (French) fleet with the support of the main guard (suggesting a N.A.T.O. fleet?), of great Neptune (Neptune is the Roman mythological God of the Oceans) and his trident warriors (marine or naval troops seem to be suggested here, which are apparently involved in some type of battle). Provence (a region of southeastern France on the Mediterranean Sea between the Rhône River and Italy), reddened to sustain this great band (meaning battle resulting from the presence of troops in this area), fighting (warfare) at Narbonne (a city in France) because of javelins and darts" (suggesting missiles?). This quatrain seems to be a general reference to future warfare in France.

La foi Punicque en Orient rompue, Gang. Iud, et Rosne Loire, et Tag changeront: Quand du mulet la faim sera repue, Classe espargie, sang et corps nageront.	2 - 60	The Punic faith broken in the East, Ganges, Jordan, Rhône, Loire & Tagus will change. When the hunger of the mule is gratified, the fleet in sprinkles and bodies swim in blood.

NAVAL WARFARE

"The Punic faith (pertaining to Phoenia, North Africa, or possibly the Islamic faith) broken in the East (possibly suggesting that an Islamic/Oriental, or North African/Oriental alliance is broken), Ganges (a river in India and Pakistan, sacred to Hindus, flowing 1560 miles from the Himalayas to the Bay of Bengal), Jordan (the principal river of Israel and Jordan, flowing south from Israel through the sea of Galilee to the Dead Sea), Rhône (a European river rising in Switzerland flowing generally west, then south to the Mediterranean), Loire (the longest river in France, flowing to the Bay of Biscay) and Tagus (a river rising in Spain, flowing to the Atlantic in Lisbon, Portugal) will change". How the geographic areas listed in this quatrain "change" is not specifically addressed. Perhaps they change politically or economically, or maybe they change due to war or flooding.

"When the hunger of the mule is gratified, the fleet in sprinkles and bodies swim in blood" is an interesting line. Its meaning is unclear, yet it could suggest several things. The donkey, not the mule, is the symbol for the American Democratic party, but could a U.S. Democratic president be alluded to here, or does "mule" suggest a stubborn world leader? Could "mule" symbolically represent a faction, or group, of individuals or nations? Again, its meaning is unclear.

The reference to "a fleet in sprinkles and bodies swim in blood" parallels language found in other quatrains and in the Epistle, which suggests the doom of an Arabic naval fleet in the Adriatic Sea. However, this quatrain could possibly be a reference to the doom of a Western fleet (as referenced in quatrain #2-86).

	2 - 61	
Euge, Tamins, Gironde et la Rochelle: O sang Troien! Mars au port de la flèche Derrière le fleuve au fort mise à l'échelle, Pointes à feu grand meurtre sus la brèche.		Bravo, ye men of the Thames, Gironde and La Rochelle; O Trojan blood, Mars at the port of the arrow. Beyond the river the ladder up to the fort, flashes of fire, great slaughter on the breach.

FUTURE WARFARE IN EUROPE

"Bravo, ye men of the Thames (a river in England, the British), Gironde (a region of southwestern France, the French) and La Rochelle (an area of France on the Bay of Biscay, suggesting the French). O Trojan blood (a reference to Troy, an ancient land in northwest Asia Minor, now Turkey), Mars (suggesting war) at the port of the arrow (an unnamed port or harbor, suggesting that the citizens or army of Turkey, or foreign troops located there, will be killed in battle near a sea harbor). Beyond the river (identity unknown) the ladder up to the fort, flashes of fire, great slaughter on the breach" (suggesting a military assault).

	2 - 62	
Mabus puis tôt alors mourra, viendra De gens et bêtes une horrible défaite: Puis tout à coup la vengeance on verra, Cent, main, soif, faim quand courra la comète.		Mabus will then soon die, there will come a dreadful destruction of people and beasts. Suddenly one will see vengeance, a hundred hands, thirst and hunger, when the comet will pass.

WARFARE AND DESTRUCTION IN 2061?

"Mabus (an unidentified person) will then soon die (after some type of action and shortly after his death) there will occur a dreadful destruction of people and beasts (by flood, war, plague, or famine?). Suddenly (unexpectedly) one will see vengeance revealed, a hundred hands (suggesting that 50 persons are involved in some type of vengeful act -- either as actors or victims), thirst and hunger (suggesting a period of drought and famine) when the comet will pass". Comet Hale-Bopp passed the Earth in spring of 1997. No specific event, as described in this quatrain occurred in the year 1997, or before. Halley's Comet passes near the Earth again (if Halley's is intended here) in 2061/62. So perhaps this event is intended for the distant future.

Several modern commentators have attached great significance to this quatrain, suggesting that Mabus might be the future third Antichrist. But in the opinion of this author, Mabus is an insignificant character who appears in only one quatrain. "Selin" appears in ten quatrains, and is ten times more likely than "Mabus" to be the so-called future third Antichrist. One author pointed out that "Mabus" spelled backwards, spells Sadam.

Armée Celtique en Italie vexée
De toutes parts conflit et grande perte:
Romains fuis, ô Gaule repoussée!
Près du Thesin, Rubicon pugne incerte.

2 - 72

The Celtic army will be vexed in Italy, on all sides will be conflict and great loss. The Italians fled, O France repelled; near the Ticino the battle at the Rubicon is uncertain.

THE FRENCH ARMY TO BE TROUBLED IN ITALY

"The Celtic (French) army will be vexed in Italy, on all sides will be conflict and great loss (suggesting a massive war). The Italians fled (flee Italy or where?), O France (the French) repelled (the French army appears to be repelled in combat in Italy); near the Ticino (a river rising in southern Switzerland flowing south into the Po River in northern Italy), the battle at the Rubicon (a small river in northern Italy near San Marino, flowing into the Adriatic Sea) is uncertain" (the outcome of the military engagement near the Ticino River is unclear). This quatrain appears to suggest that the French assist the Italians against an unnamed invading force.

Par feu du ciel lat cité presque aduste:
L'Urne menace encore Deucalion:
Vexée Sardaigne par la Punique fuste,
Après que Libra lairra son Phaeton.

2 - 81

By means of fire from the sky the city is almost burned down, The urn threatens Deucalion again. Sardinia vexed by the Punic ships. After Libra leaves her Phälton.

A FLEET WILL ATTACK SARDINIA

Apparently an unnamed city is almost burned down by "fire from the sky" (aerial combat or atomic fire?). "The urn (water or floods?) threatens Deucalion again (the Noah of Greek mythology, suggesting the Greeks?). Sardinia (an Italian island southwest of the Italian mainland located in the Mediterranean Sea) vexed by the Punic ships (possibly suggesting a North African fleet). After Libra leaves her Phälton" (an epithet of the Sun in Latin poetry). This could mean after Venus (ruling planet of the astrological sign of Libra) has left the Sun. The exact meaning of this last line is unclear.

Entre Campaignie, Sienne,
   Flora, Tuscie,
Six mois neuf jours ne pleuvra
   une goutte:
L'étrange langue en terre
   Dalmatie
Courira sus, vastant la terre
   toute.
	2 - 84	Between Campania, Siena,
		Florence and Tuscany, for six
		months and nine days it will not
		rain a drop. A foreign tongue
		will be spoken in Dalmatia, it
		will overrun the country,
		devastating the entire land.

INVADERS TO OVERRUN CROATIA AND YUGOSLAVIA

In the regions "between Campania (a region of southern Italy on the Tyrrhenian Sea), Siena (an area in Tuscany, Italy, 40 miles south of Florence), Florence (a city on the Arno River in Tuscany, Italy) and Tuscany (a region of northwest Italy), it will not rain a drop for six months and nine days (a drought develops due to problems with atmospheric conditions). A foreign tongue (a language foreign to Dalmatia, but which language?) will be spoken in Dalmatia (a region of Croatia along the eastern coast of the Adriatic Sea), it (suggesting foreigners) will overrun the country, devastating the entire land" (the unnamed foreign invaders will devaste Croatia). This is an interesting quatrain considering the recent tragic civil war in Yugoslavia.

Naufrage à classe près
   d'onde Hadriatique:
La terre tremble émue sus
   l'air en terre mis:
Egypte tremble augment
   Mahometique,
L'Héraut soi rendre à crier
   est commis.
	2 - 86	The fleet will wreck near the
		Adriatic Sea. The land trembles,
		stirred up into the air, then
		placed on land. Egypt trembles;
		Mohammedan increase. The
		Herald himself surrendering
		then appointed to cry out.

NAVAL WARFARE IN THE ADRIATIC SEA, EARTH CHANGES, EGYPT TREMBLES

"The fleet (whose fleet?) will wreck near the Adriatic Sea (an unidentified naval fleet will perish near the Adriatic Sea). "The land trembles, stirred up into the air, then placed on land" could suggest several things. It could suggest a nuclear blast, or an earthquake, or is perhaps just a poetic thought. It could remotely suggest a polar shift, as mentioned in the chapter Hypothetical Chronology of the Future. "Egypt trembles (due to natural disasters or war?); Mohammedan increase (an increase of troop strength in an Islamic force which effects Egypt in some way), the Herald (a state envoy from an unidentified nation) himself surrendering then appointed to cry out." Following a disaster for an Islamic naval fleet near the Adriatic Sea, earthquakes occur, an increase in the troop strength of an Islamic force appears somewhere (perhaps in Egypt). One of the warring parties sends their envoy out to seek surrender terms. Yet another quatrain pertaining to a future Euro/Arabic conflict.

Un jour seront demis les deux grands maîtres, Leur grand pouvoir se verra augmenté: La terre neuve sera en ses hauts êtres, Au sanguinaire le nombre raconté.	2 - 89	One day the two great masters will be friends; their great power will be seen to grow. The new land will be at the peak of its power, to the bloody one, the number is reported.

THE END OF THE COLD WAR

"One day the two great masters (suggesting two great nations?) will be friends (which suggests a prior period of unfriendliness); their great power (their collective power) will be seen to grow (their collective power makes them even stronger). The new land (suggesting the New World?) will be at the peak of its power" (which might prove to be a fair historical evaluation of conditions in America, Canada, and the rest of the New World as we approach the year 2000). Though the two great masters (or nations) are unnamed, this might suggest Russia and America (though speculation) who became "friends" after the collapse of the Iron Curtain (in November of 1989). "To the bloody one (or 'man of blood'), the number (what number?) is reported". This last line is unclear to me. However, former Russian President Gorbachev, and the famous birthmark on his forehead, comes to mind here.

Soleil levant un grand feu l'on verra, Bruit et clarté vers Aquilon tendants: Dedans le rond mort et cris l'on ouïra, Par glaive, feu, faim, mort les attendants.	2 - 91	At sunrise a great fire will be seen, noise and light extending towards Aquilon. Within the circle death, one will hear cries, death awaiting them through weapons, fire and famine.

MASS DESTRUCTION IN RUSSIA AND ASIA

"At sunrise a great fire (suggesting warfare and nuclear explosions?) will be seen, noise and light (thunderous bomb blasts?) extending towards Aquilon (the North, suggesting Russia and possibly other former Soviet states, and parts of Asia). Within the circle (a perimeter, or the Arctic circle?) death, one will hear cries, death awaiting them (the Aquiloners, and or others?) through weapons, fire and famine" (massive warfare and destruction). This quatrain might apply to the war with the third Antichrist or it could be an unrelated independent event. Though "Aquilon" appears to be an allusion to Russia (the target area suggested here), we have no clues regarding the identity of Aquilon's advesary in this quatrain.

	2 - 95	
Les lieux peuplés seront inhabitables: Pour champs avoir grande division Regnes livrés à prudents incapables: Lors les grands frères mort et dissension.		The populated places will become uninhabitable, great disagreement in order to obtain fields. Realms given to prudent incapable men. Then for the great brothers, death and dissension.

POPULATED AREAS WILL BECOME UNINHABITABLE

"The populated places (of various unnamed regions--perhaps in Europe and elsewhere) will become uninhabitable (due to war, overpopulation, disease or natural disasters?), great disagreement (war) to obtain fields (battle fields or agricultural fields?). Realms given to prudent incapable men (incapable leaders). Then for the great brothers (the 'three brothers' is an allusion to the Kennedy brothers and America, thus the phrase 'the great brothers' might also suggest the Kennedy's and America, or it might suggest 'three' allied nations or other things), death and dissension" (results). An interesting yet general quatrain.

	2 - 96	
Flambeau ardent au ciel soir sera vu, Près de la fin et principe du Rosne: Famine, glaive: tard le secours pourvu, La Perse tourne envahir Macedoine.		A burning torch will be seen in the sky at night near the end and source of the Rhône. Famine and weapon; relief provided too late, Persia turns to invade Macedonia.

IRAN WILL INVADE MACEDONIA

"A burning torch (a nuclear explosion, a missile, a fire, or something else?) will be seen in the sky at night near the source of the Rhône (a river which rises in central Switzerland flowing for 505 miles, ending near Arles, France). Famine and weapon (famine and war), relief provided too late (for which nation?), Persia (ancient name for modern Iran) turns to invade Macedonia" (the nation of Macedonia, and/or the regions of Greece, Bulgaria and the various new republics of Yugoslavia). This quatrain is a direct reference to a Euro/Arabic conflict, or possibly to the times of the third Antichrist. We have no clues as to the intended time frame of this quatrain, and it is probably connected to other quatrains suggesting future trouble involving Iran.

CENTURY III

Après combat et bataille navale,
Le grand Neptune à son plus haut beffroi:
Rouge adversaire de peur viendra pâle,
Mettant le grand Océan en effroi.

3 - 1

After the combat and naval battle, great Neptune in his highest belfry; Red adversary will become pale with fear, putting the great Ocean into a state of dread.

AFTER A NAVAL BATTLE, AN ADVERSARY TERRORIZES THE OCEANS

"After the combat (after a period of land or aerial combat) and naval battle (this future period of 'combat' also includes naval warfare), great Neptune (the mythological Roman god of the oceans) in his (Neptune's) highest belfry (the section of a tower in which bells are rung -- suggesting an urgent state); red adversary (in this particular quatrain 'red' possibly suggesting Russian?) will become pale with fear (suggesting a very defensive stance) putting the great Ocean (perhaps an allusion to the Atlantic Ocean) into a state of dread" (probably through means of additional naval combat). An interesting quatrain referencing future naval combat, but one that offers few specific clues.

Bordeaux, Roüan et la Rochelle joints
Tiendront autour la grande mer Océan,
Anglois, Bretons, et les Flamans conjoints
Les chasseront jusqu'auprès de Roane.

3 - 9

Bordeaux, Rouen & La Rochelle joined, will hold around the great ocean, the English, Bretons and Flemish allied will drive them as far as Roanne.

EUROPEANS WILL HOLD THEIR GROUND DURING WAR

"Bordeaux, Rouen and La Rochelle (three cities in France, suggesting the French) joined (with one another) will hold (their positions during war) around the great Ocean (perhaps an allusion to the Atlantic Ocean), the English and Bretons (the United Kingdom) and the Flemish (a region of France and Belgium, the French and Belgians) allied, will drive them (an unnamed invading enemy force) as far as Roanne" (a city in France located on the upper Loire River). Yet another quatrain dealing with future war in Europe.

De sang et faim plus grande calamité, Sept fois s'apprête à la marine plage: Monech de faim, lieu pris, captivité, Le grand mené croc ferrée cage.	3 - 10	Great calamity of blood and famine, seven times it approaches the sea shore. Monaco, from hunger, captured, in captivity. The great golden one caught in a metal cage.

MONACO TO BE CAPTURED BY SEA IN TIME OF WAR

"Great calamity of blood and famine (suggesting a time of war and few resources), seven times it (an enemy marine force or unnamed evil) approaches the sea shore (apparently a European shore line). Monaco (a small European principality on the Mediterranean Sea), from hunger, captured, in captivity (apparently Monaco, and perhaps southern France, will be plundered by war and captured by an unnamed invading enemy force). The great golden one (possibly a pope or European leader) caught in a metal cage" (will be held captive perhaps). A general description of a future invasion of Europe.

En Luques sang et lait viendra pleuvoir, Un peu devant changement de préteur: Grande peste et guerre, faim et soif fera voir Loin où mourra leur prince et recteur.	3 - 19	In Lucca it will rain blood and milk, shortly before a change of a governor. Great plague and war, famine and drought will be visible, far from where their prince and leader dies.

WARFARE IN LUCCA, ITALY

"In Lucca (a city from Roman times located north of Pisa, in Italy) it will rain blood (suggesting war) and milk" (the meaning of 'milk' is unclear, maybe a reference to some type of fallout, or other substance), shortly before a change of governor (before the change of a leader). Great plague and war, famine and drought will be visible (a state of war creates turmoil, famine, and drought), far from where their prince and leader (an Italian prince and leader, or someone else?) dies". Yet another reference to future war in Italy.

	3 - 23	
Si France passes outre mer lygustique, Tu te verras en îles et mers enclos: Mahommet contraire, plus mer Hadriatique: Chevaux et d'ânes tu rongeras les os.		If, France, you pass beyond the Ligurian Sea, you will find yourself shut up among islands and seas. Mahomet against you, more so the Adriatic Sea, you will gnaw the bones of asses and horses.

A WARNING TO FRANCE

Nostradamus clearly warns France to avoid the temptation of passing beyond the Ligurian Sea (the part of the Mediterranean Sea between Liguria, in Italy, and Corsica), possibly during a time of war. If France passes beyond the Ligurian Sea, they will be trapped on various islands and restricted to the seas. "Mahomet (suggesting Islamic nations and their military forces) against you (against France), more so the Adriatic Sea" (suggesting rough seas, or danger posed by unfriendly unnamed military forces located on, or near, the Adriatic). If France succumbs to this temptation, Nostradamus sees them "gnawing the bones of asses and horses". We have no clues regarding the intended time frame here. Was this quatrain intended for the Napoleonic era, or the future?

	3 - 27	
Prince Libyque puissant en Occident Français d'Arabe viendra tant enflammer. Savant aux lettres fera condescendant, La langue Arabe en Français translater.		The Libyan prince, powerful in the West, will come to inflame the French with Arabian; learned in letters, condescending the Prince will translate the Arab Language into French.

THE COMING OF A POWERFUL LIBYAN PRINCE

"The Libyan prince (a prince or ruler of the North African nation of Libya), powerful in the West (suggesting that the Libyan Prince, or leader, will be viewed as "powerful" by the nations of the West), will come to inflame (to arouse, or to intensify intolerably) the French with Arabian (the Libyan Prince will in some way upset the French); learned in letters (educated or linguistically talented), condescending (lowering one's self to the level with whom one is dealing) the Prince will translate the Arab language into French". "Translate" means expressing in another language, or conveying from one form or style into another. In theology, "translate" means to convey to heaven without natural death. Though unclear, it appears that the Libyan Prince will somehow give the French a hard time. Could this quatrain pertain to Col. Khadaffi, or to someone who will one day replace him in Libya?

Par toute Asie grande proscription, Même en Mysie, Lysie, et Pamphilie, Sang versera par absolution D'un jeune noir rempli de félonie.	3 - 60	Throughout Asia minor there will be great proscription, including Mysia, Lycia and Pamphilia. Blood will flow because of the absolution of a young dark king, filled with evil.

FUTURE WAR IN ASIA MINOR

"Throughout Asia minor there will be great proscription (to denounce or condemn), including Mysia (an ancient county in Asia minor, modern Turkey), Lycia (an ancient country on the southwest coast of Asia minor, modern Turkey) and Pamphilia (an ancient country on the southeast coast of Asia minor, modern Turkey). Blood will flow (warfare) because of the absolution (a Roman Catholic term for the formal remission of sin imparted by a priest as part of the sacrament of penance) of a young dark man filled with evil" (an unnamed enemy). "Proscription" may suggest the drafting of soldiers into the military. This probably refers to a Euro/Arabic conflict or to the times of the third Antichrist.

La grande bande et secte crucigère Se dressera en Mesopotamie: Du proche fleuve compagnie légère, Que telle loi tiendra pour ennemie.	3 - 61	The great band and sect of the crusaders will array in Mesopotamia. The light company of the nearby river, that such laws will hold for enemies.

OPERATION DESERT STORM

"The great band and sect of the crusaders (suggesting a powerful group of warriors or knights from the nations of Christianity, i.e. Great Britain, France, and America-- traditional nations of Christianity, and their allies) will array (draw up troops in battle order) in Mesopotamia (ancient name for modern Iraq). The light company (suggesting Iraq - energy producers) of the nearby river (suggesting the Tigris or Euphrates River), that such laws (the laws of the crusaders, or possibly U.N. sanctions) will hold for enemies" (the Iraqis). Though unclear, this description fits the situation of Operation Desert Storm quite well. The U.S., French and British (nations of Christianity, possibly viewed as "crusaders" by Iraq) sent a mighty force of troops to Iraq during the recent Gulf War. The Iraqis' regarded the "no fly zone" law, and other U.N. conditions of peace, as adverse to their national interests. See quatrains #6-33 and #8-70.

Proche del duero par mer Tyrrene close, Viendra percer les grands monts Pyrénées. La main plus courte et sa perce glose, À Carcassonne conduira ses menées.	3 - 62	Near the Douro closed by the Cyrrene sea he will come to pierce the great mountains of the Pyrenees. The shortest hand and his opening noted he will conduct his plots in Carcassonne.

INVADERS WILL CROSS SPAIN INTO FRANCE

"Near the Douro (a river in the mountains near Burgo and the Bay of Biscay in Spain) closed by the Cyrrene (the 'Cyrenian' Sea is another name for the Mediterranean) he (possibly an Asian or Arabic military man) will come to pierce the great mountains of the Pyrenees (the mountain range between Spain and France). The shortest hand (traveling the shortest route) and his opening noted (his movement observed), he (the unnamed foreign invader) will conduct his plots in Carcassonne" (a city in southern France on the Aude River, where this invader will make war).

Le chef de Perse remplira grande Olchades, Classe trirème contre gens Mahometiques De Parthe, et Mede: et piller les Cyclades: Repos longtemps au grand port Ionique.	3 - 64	The Persian leader will occupy great Olcades. A fleet of triremes against the Mohammedan people. From Parthia and Media, the Cyclades pillaged: then a long rest in the great Ionian harbour.

SPAIN TO BE INVADED BY IRANIAN FORCES

"The Persian leader (or in modern times -- an Iranian leader) will occupy great Olcades (suggesting modern Spain). A fleet of triremes (ancient sailing vessels, suggesting naval forces) against the Mohammedan people (apparently unnamed naval ships, perhaps a European or NATO fleet, send naval forces against the Iranian and other Muslim forces). From Parthia (a city in northeastern Iran) and Media (an ancient region of northwestern Iran) the Cyclades (a group of Greek islands in the southern Agen Sea) pillaged (suggesting that possibly the Iranians and their allies are responsible for this action), then a long rest (for some unnamed party) in the great Ionian harbor" (the Ionian Sea is a section of the Mediterranean Sea between southern Italy and western Greece). This could suggest that the Iranian/Islamic force, or possibly an opposing naval force, will anchor in an unnamed harbor on the coast line of the Ionian Sea following an intense period of naval warfare.

Peuple sans chef d'Espagne d'Italie Morts, profligés dedans le Chersonèse: Leur dict trahi par légère folie, Le sang nager partout à la traverse.	3 - 68	The leaderless people from Spain and Italy dead, overcome within the Peninsula. Their dictator betrayed by negligent folly, bodies swim in blood throughout the latitude.

SPAIN AND ITALY WILL BE OVERCOME BY ENEMIES

"The leaderless people of Spain and Italy dead (suggesting the nations of Spain and Italy lose many citizens due to war), overcome within the peninsula (an unnamed peninsula). Their dictator (a Spanish or Italian dictator, or perhaps their enemy's dictator?) betrayed by negligent folly (through some type of negligence), bodies swim in blood (due to war) throughout the latitude" (laterally across Spain and Italy and an unnamed peninsula in Europe).

Pau, Verone, Vicence, Sarragousse, De glaives lion terroirs de sang humides: Peste si grande viendra à la grande gousse, Proche secours, et bien loin les remèdes.	3 - 75	Pau, Verona, Vicenza, Saragossa, from distant weapons, the lands wet with blood. A very great plague will come with the great pod, relief near but the remedies far away.

WARFARE AND PLAGUE IN EUROPE

"Pau (a city in southern France), Verona (a city in northeastern Italy), Vicenza (a city in northeastern Italy) and Saragossa (a city in northeastern Spain), from distant weapons (missiles?) the lands (these European lands will be) wet with blood. A very great plague (war and disease?) will come (arrives) with the great pod (the identity of the pod is a mystery, could this perhaps linked with RAYPOZ from quatrain # 9 - 44?). Relief near, but the remedies (for this situation are) far away". We have no clues as to the intended time frame for this quatrain.

Freins, Antibol, villes autour de Nice, Seront vastées fort par mer et par terre: Les sauterelles terres et mer vent propice, Pris, morts, troussés, pillés, sans loi de guerre.	3 - 82	Frejus, Antibes, the towns around Nice will be thoroughly devastated by sea and land; the locusts by land and sea, the wind being favorable, captured, dead, bound, plundered without law of war.

THE COAST OF FRANCE WILL BE INVADED BY SEA

"Frejus, Antibes and Nice (cities in France) will be thoroughly devastated by sea and land (it appears they will be devastated by a coastal invasion from the sea), locusts by land and sea (may suggest helicopters or planes). The wind seems favorable for their assault. Citizens or soldiers (perhaps French) "captured, dead, bound, plundered without law of war" (suggesting French citizens will be killed and held captive, plunged into chaos by lack of civil law and order during a time of war). We have no clues regarding the time frame for this calamity.

Le grand Satyre et Tigre de Hyrcanie, Don presenté à ceux de l'Océan: Un chef de classe ira de Carmanie, Qui prendra terre au Tyrren Phocean.	3 - 90	The great Satyr and Tiger of Hyrcania; gift presented to the people of the Ocean: the leader of a fleet will set forth from Carmania and take land at the Tyrren - Phoenean.

AN ARAB FLEET WILL SAIL TO EUROPE

"The great Satyr (a mythological demon with pointed ears, or a lecher, perhaps an allusion to the third Antichrist) and Tiger of Hyrcania (suggesting a leader from an Iranian coastal area on the Caspian Sea, perhaps an ally of the 'great Satyr'), a gift (of some type) presented to the people of the Ocean (the identity of the Ocean people is unclear, maybe a naval force). The leader of a fleet (an unnamed fleet) leaves from Carmania (a port in Iran at the mouth of the Persian gulf) and takes the land at the Tyrren Phoenean" (location unclear, possibly suggesting an Italian port on the Tyrrhenian Sea). Yet another reference to a Euro/Arabic conflict.

Dans Auignon tout le chef de l'empire Fera arrêt pour Paris désolé: Tricast tiendra l'Annibalique ire: Lyon par change sera mal consolé.	3 - 93	In Avignon, the leader of the whole empire will make a stop on the journey to desolated Paris: Tricast will hold the anger of Hannibal: Lyons will be poorly consoled for the change.

TROUBLES IN FRANCE

"In Avignon (a city on the Rhone River in southeastern France), the leader of the whole empire (a French leader, or enemy leader?) will make a stop (where and for what purpose?) on the journey to desolated Paris (suggesting that Paris will one day be desolated due to war or other reasons?). Tricast (meaning unclear, perhaps suggesting a group of three nations or entities) will hold (ward off or possess?) the anger of Hannibal (the Carthaginian warlord of North Africa who conquered the Romans in the second century (B.C. -- suggesting in modern terms an Islamic leader of a North African nation). Lyons (a city in France) will be poorly consoled for the change." Could this refer to a future Euro/Arabic conflict or the future war with the third Antichrist?

Nouvelle loi terre neuve occuper Vers la Syrie, Iudée et Palestine: Le grand empire barbare corruer, Avant que Phebés son siècle determine.	3 - 97	A new law to occupy the new land around Syria, Judea and Palestine. The great barbarian Empire will deteriorate before the Moon completes her cycle.

THE BIRTH OF ISRAEL

"A new law to occupy the new land around Syria, Judea and Palestine." This could possibly suggest the birth of the nation of Israel, which officially occurred a few years after World War II in 1948 (remember that Nostradamus was of Jewish descent). "The great barbarian Empire (an unnamed empire, perhaps suggesting Middle Eastern and/or North African nations) will deteriorate before the Moon completes her cycle" (which is completed again in the year 2080).

Aux champs herbeux d'Alein et du Varneigne,
Du mont Lebron proche de la Durance,
Camps de deux parts conflit sera si aigre,
Mesopotamie défaillira en la France.

3 - 99

In the green fields of Alleins and Vernegues of the Luberon mountains near Durance, the conflict on both sides will be so intense for both armies that Mesopotamia shall fail in France.

AN INVASION OF FRANCE DURING A EURO/ARABIC CONFLICT

"In the green fields of Alleins and Vernegues (French cities near Salon) of the Luberon mountains (a mountain range in France) near Durance (a river in France), the conflict on both sides (of some battle or war) will be so intense for both armies that Mesopotamia (if taken literally, 'Mesopotamia' suggests Iraq) shall fail in France" (suggesting doom for the forces invading France).

CENTURY IV

Devant Roüan d'Insubres mis le siège,
Par terre et mer enfermés les passages:
D'Haynault, et Flandres, de Gand et ceux de Liege
Par dons laenees raviront les rivages.

4 - 19

Before Rouen the attack laid by the Insubrians, the passages shut by land and sea. By Hainaut & Flanders, by Ghent and those of Liége, through cloaked gifts they will ravage the shorelines.

ITALIANS TO LAY SIEGE IN FRANCE; IN THE NETHERLANDS AND BELGIUM THE SHORE LINE IS ATTACKED BY SEA

"Before Rouen (in front of Rouen, a city in northern France where Joan of Arc died in 1431) the attack laid by the Insubrians (the Italians), the passages shut by land and sea (roads and sea lanes closed by war?). By Hainaut (an area of southwest Belgium) and Flanders (a part of northern France and western Belgium), by Ghent (a city in northwest Belgium) and those of Liege (a city in eastern Belgium), through cloaked gifts they (a friend or foe?) will ravage the shorelines".

Ès lieux et temps chair au poisson donnera lieu,
La loi commune sera faite au contraire:
Vieux tiendra fort puis ôtée du milieu,
Le Panta Choina Philon mis fort arrière.

4 - 32

In those places and times that meat gives way to fish, the communal law will be made in opposition. It will hold strongly, then removed from the scene, then "lovers of all things common & social" put far behind.

THE CREATION AND FALL OF SOCIALISM

"In those places and times when meat gives way to fish (suggesting upper-class life styles being reduced to more common levels, as in socialism), the communal law (socialism or communism) will be made in opposition (to another type of law, capitalism, the Czar). It will hold strongly (resisting the change), then removed from the scene, then lovers of all things common and social (communism and socialism) put far behind" (capitalism replacing socialism). This quatrain was generally fulfilled in 1989 with the collapse of the Soviet Union. The Soviets moved quickly to replace socialism with democracy and a free-market system of economics.

	4 - 38	
Pendant que Duc, Roi, Reine occupera,		While he engrosses the Duke, King and Queen, the Byzantine
Chef Bizant du captif en Samothrace:		leader is held captive in Samothrace. Before the assault
Avant l'assult l'un l'autre mangera:		one will devour the other. Reverse side metaled will follow
Rebours ferré suivra du sang la trace.		the resulting trail of blood.

A TURKISH LEADER TO BE HELD CAPTIVE IN GREECE

"While he (an unnamed leader or individual) engrosses (occupies the attention of) the Duke, King and Queen (suggesting leaders of an unnamed nation), the Byzantine leader (suggesting a Turkish leader) is held captive (is kidnapped, or incarcerated by unnamed persons, possibly Greeks) in Samothrace (a small Greek island in the northeastern Aegean Sea). Before the assault (a military attack) one will devour the other" (suggesting Turkey and Greece will devour one another, or two other unnamed nations?). The phrase "reverse side metaled" remains a mystery. I have not a clue to its meaning. However, this "reverse side metaled will follow the resulting trail of blood" (apparently due to the resulting combat). Tension between Turkey and Greece has existed for years.

	4 - 39	
Les Rhodiens demanderont secours,		The Rhodians will strongly request help, abandoned by the
Par le neglect de ses hoirs délaissée.		neglect of their heirs. The Arab Empire will lower its course, its
L'empire Arabe révélera son cours,		cause set right again by "the Lands of the West".
Par Hesperies la cause redressée.		

GREECE WILL BE ATTACKED DURING AN ARABIC CONFLICT

"The Rhodians (suggesting the Greek occupants of the island of Rhodes, the largest of the Dodecanese Islands in the Aegean Sea located southwest of Turkey, which was ceded by Italy to Greece in 1947) will strongly request help (suggesting that the Greeks in Rhodes will cry for aid and assistance, probably during a time of military conflict), abandoned by the neglect of their heirs (suggesting that the Rhodians will be abandoned by the neglect of the people who might later occupy Rhodes, possibly their enemies?) The Arab Empire (suggesting a powerful futuristic confederation of Arabic or Islamic nations?) will lower its course (will reveal their plans or initiate a course of action), its cause (the cause of the Arab Empire) set right again (clearly defined, or put on course or advanced) by the Lands of the West" (suggesting America and/or the nations of the New World).

	4 - 43	
Seront ouïs au ciel les armes battre: Celui an même les divins ennemis: Voudront loix saintes injustement débattre: Par foudre et guerre bien croyant à mort mis.		Arms will be heard clashing in the skies: in the same year the divine ones are enemies: they will want unjustly to question the holy laws, through lightning and combat the complacent ones will be killed.

AERIAL COMBAT, CHRISTIAN VALUES THREATENED

In the year that great aerial combat will appear to be prevalent in the skies, "the divine ones (suggesting a pope and the occupants of the Vatican, or who?) will be enemies (of an unnamed party). They (the unstated enemies of the divine ones) will want unjustly to question the Holy Laws (suggesting Christian doctrines). Through lightning and combat (warfare), the complacent ones (individuals or parties) will be killed" (will die due to war or inaction). An interesting, yet general quatrain. It is remarkable that Nostradamus mentions aerial combat in the first line of this quatrain. The intended time frame of this event is either the 20th century, or beyond, since aerial combat became popular during World War I (1914-1918).

	4 - 50	
Libra verra regner les Hesperies, De ciel et terre tenir la monarchie: D'Asie forces nul ne verra péries, Que sept ne tiennent par rang la hiérarchie.		The Balance will see "the Lands of the West" govern, holding the rule over the skies and Earth. No one will see the forces of Asia destroyed, only seven hold the hierarchy in succession.

AMERICA HOLDS BALANCE OVER THE WORLD

"The Balance (Libra in astrology, represents law, balance and justice) will see Hesperies (the Lands of the West -- America and the New World) govern, holding the rule over the skies and Earth (holding a strong military rule over the land, seas, and skies). No one will see the forces of Asia (Asian military forces) destroyed (suggesting a state of perpetual conflict in Asia), only seven (suggesting seven unstated someones or somethings) hold a hierarchy in succession" (exact meaning unclear). Could popes be intended here? Quatrain # 9 - 92 mentions "seven" somethings (or someones) who will hold a position for the period of seventeen years. Could this quatrain be connected to quatrain #9-92?

Soleil ardent dans le gosier coller, De sang humain arroser terre Etrusqu: Chef seille d'eau, mener son fils filer, Captive dame conduicte en terre Turque.	4 - 58	To swallow the burning Sun in the throat, the Tuscan land washed with human blood, the leader will lead his son away, the captive lady led into the Turkish lands.

DEVASTATION IN ITALY

"To swallow the burning Sun in the throat (trying to digest the devastation of a nuclear bomb, conventional attack or a drought?), the Tuscan lands (Italy) will be washed with human blood." The leaders and their families apparently leave this region in a mass exodus. "The captive lady" (an individual woman, Lady Liberty, the Catholic Church or something else?) appears under siege and will be led into Turkish territory.

Selin monarque l'Italie pacifique, Regnes unis par Roi Chrétien du monde: Mourant voudra coucher en terre blesique, Après pirates avoir chassé de l'onde.	4 - 77	Selin is king, Italy is at peace, By the Christian King of the World kingdoms are united, his death approaching, dying he will desire to rest upon the soil of Blois, after chasing the pirates from the seas.

A CHRISTIAN LEADER WILL UNITE NATIONS

"Selin is king (suggesting a future Middle Eastern leader of an unnamed country), Italy is at peace, by the Christian King of the World (suggesting a powerful world leader of a Christian country, or perhaps an allusion to a future pope) kingdoms are united (this unnamed Christian leader will unite and harmonize many nations), dying he will desire to rest upon the soil of Blois (whoever is dying here -- a pope, a Christian leader, or perhaps a leader of France, will wish to return to French soil, 'Blois' being a city in France), after chasing the pirates from the seas (after he helps to vanquish the naval forces of Selin from the seas, perhaps from the Adriatic and/or Mediterranean Seas). See quatrains #1-94, #4-77, #6-42, #6-58 and #6-78.

La regne à deux laissé bien peu tiendront, Trois ans sept mois passés feront la guerre: Les deux Vestales contre rebelleront, Victor puîné en Armonique terre.	4 - 95	The realm left to two, they will hold it a very short time, after three years and seven months having passed they will make war, two Vestals to rebel in opposition, the Victor, the younger in the land of Armonique.

AMERICA AND HER ADVERSARY?

"The realm (the domain or sphere) left to two (controlled by two unnamed powers), they (the two powers) will hold it a very short time (the union of the two unnamed powers will soon dissolve), after three years and seven months having passed (three years and seven months after the beginning or end of some event involving or affecting the two unnamed powers), they (the two unnamed powers or other parties?) will make war (upon each other, or united with one another against a third party?), two vestals (pertaining to Vesta, a mythological Roman goddess, perhaps suggesting two other nations) to rebel in opposition (against the two united powers, against the two united powers making war on a third party, or do the 'two vestals' fight one another?), the Victor (of this future conflict), the younger in the land of Armonique ('Armonique' suggests Brittany, thus 'the younger in the land of Armonique' might suggest America). If America and Russia happen to be the "two" powers intended here, could this suggest that they might one day face one another in a conflict? Hopefully, for reasons of peace, America and Russia are not intended here. Edgar Cayce, *the sleeping prophet*, saw great hope for the future of Russia.

Les Albanois passeront dedans Rome, Moyennant Langres demipler affublés, Marquis et Duc ne pardonnent à homme, Feu, sang, morbiles point d'eau faillir les blés.	4 - 98	The people of Alba will pass into Rome, by means of Langres the large mob suppressed. The Marquis and the Duke will pardon no man, fire, blood and smallpox, no water, the crops to fail.

ALBANIA WILL INVADE ITALY

"The people of Alba (suggesting Albania?) will pass into (or invade) Rome (the capital of Italy and seat of the Vatican), by means of Langres (a city in France, the French) the large mob (the invaders from Alba -- an allusion to Albania?) suppressed (through battle or other means?). The Marquis and Duke (of which country we know not) will pardon no man, fire, bloodshed and smallpox (unmerciful warfare and disease result), no water, the crops fail" (the Italian eco-system temporarily fails due to war and drought).

CENTURY V

Avant qu'à Rome grand aie rendu l'âme, Effrayeur grande à l'armée étrangère: Par escadrons, l'embûche près de Parme, Puis les deux rouges ensemble feront chère.	5 - 22	Before the great man gives up his soul at Rome, there is great terror among the foreign army. An ambush by the squadrons takes place near Parma, then the two red ones will make festivities together.

AN AMBUSH NEAR PARMA BEFORE THE DEATH OF A POPE?

During a period "before the great man (suggesting an unnamed pope, a national leader, or another great man) gives up his soul (suggesting death) at Rome (the capital of Italy and seat of the Vatican), there is great terror among the foreign army (an unnamed foreign army -- friend or foe?). An ambush by the squadrons takes place (we are not told if it is by enemy forces or friendly forces) near Parma (a city in northwest Italy), then the two red ones will make festivities together." The "red ones" as used in this context, might suggest enemies, or bloody ones, but its exact meaning is unclear.

Par feu et armes non loin de la marnegro, Viendra de Perse occuper Trebisonde: Trembler Pharos, Methelin, Sol alegro, De sang Arabe d'Adrie couvert onde.	5 - 27	Through fire and weapons, not far from the Black Sea, he will come from Persia to occupy Trebizond. Pharos and Mytilene tremble, the Sun lively, the Adriatic Sea covered with Arab blood.

AN ARMY COMES FROM IRAN TO OCCUPY TURKEY

"Through fire and weapons (warfare) not far from the Black Sea, he (an unnamed person, perhaps the third Antichrist or another enemy) will travel from Persia (Iran) to occupy Trebizond (a province in northeastern Turkey on the coast). Pharos (an island located in the Bay or Harbor of Alexandria, part of the Cyclade Islands) and Mytilene (the Greek island of Lesbos) will tremble (due to the actions of this man from Iran), the Sun lively (perhaps an allusion to the nations of Europe), the Adriatic Sea (an arm of the Mediterranean Sea between Italy and the Balkan Peninsula) covered with Arab blood" (apparently the Arabic fleet will face a horrible defeat by unnamed adversaries in the Adriatic Sea). No time frame is mentioned in this quatrain. Could "Selin" be the Iranian leader referred to as "he" in quatrains #5-54 and #9-73?).

Par chapeaux rouges querelles et nouveaux schismes Quand on aura élu le Sabinois: On produira contre lui grands sophismes, Et sera Rome lésée par Albanois.	5 - 46	Quarrels and new schisms by the red hats when the Sabine is elected. They produce great sophisms against him. Rome will be injured by those of Alba.

ITALY TO BE INVADED BY ALBANIA (OR ITS OCCUPIERS)

"Quarrels and new schisms by the red hats (suggesting Catholic Cardinals?) when a Sabine (an Italian) is elected (elected as pope?). They (unnamed parties or the cardinals) produce great sophisms (a plausible, but unsound argument, intended to deceive) against him (the new pope?). Rome (the capital of Italy and home of the Vatican) will be injured by those of Alba" (an allusion to the nation of Albania?). Could this be linked to quatrain # 5-91 (in the Astrological chapter) or to quatrain #4-98?

Le grand Arabe marchera bien avant, Trahi sera par les Bisantinois: L'antique Rodes lui viendra au-devant, Et plus grand mal par austre Pannonois.	5 - 47	The great Arab will march far to the fore, he will be betrayed by the Turks. Ancient Rhodes will come forward to meet him and more harm through the Austrian Hungarians.

A POWERFUL ARAB WILL BE BETRAYED BY TURKEY; HE WILL CONFRONT GREECE, HUNGARY, AND YUGOSLAVIA

"The great Arab (identity unknown) will march far to the fore, he will be betrayed by the Byzantians (the Turks). Ancient Rhodes (the largest of the Greek Dodecanese Islands in the Aegean Sea, southwest of Turkey, which was seceded by Italy to Greece in 1947) will come forward to meet him (the great Arab?) and more harm through the Austrian Hungarians." Rhodes might be the military base for a battle against the great Arab and his forces which results in greater harm to the Pannanois (modern Hungary and the new nations of the former Yugoslavia). This suggests that the Hungarians, Austrains and the former Yugoslavians will also fight the Arab army as they march into eastern Europe. This is a very straightforward quatrain referencing a future Euro/Arabic conflict (a clear warning in light of on-going difficulties in this region).

Après la grande affliction du sceptre, Deux ennemis par eux seront défaits: Classe d'Afrique aux Pannons viendra naître, Par mer et terre seront horribles faits.	5 - 48	After the great affliction of the scepter two enemies will be defeated by each other. A fleet from Africa will appear before the Hungarians; terrible deeds will take place on land and sea.

A FLEET TRAVELS FROM AFRICA TO HUNGARY

"After the great affliction of the scepter (following a painful power struggle of some type) two enemies (identities unstated) will be defeated by each other (will cause one another great harm in some way, perhaps through war). A fleet (an unidentified fleet which departs) from Africa (friend or foe?) will appear before the Hungarians, (the African fleet travels northward to the Adriatic Sea, perhaps to Albania, Italy or Yugoslavia), terrible deeds (war and chaos) will take place on land and sea" (apparently the fleet from Africa invades the European shoreline enroute to Hungary, resulting in war).

La loi du Sol, et Venus contendus, Appropriant l'esprit de prophétie: Ni l'un ni l'autre ne seront entendus, Par Sol tiendra la loi du grand Messie.	5 - 53	The law of the Sun in strife with Venus, appropriating the spirit of prophecy. Neither the one nor the other will be understood; the great Messiah's law retained through the Sun.

CHRISTIANITY AND ISLAM IN STRIFE

"The law of the Sun (in astrological terminology perhaps suggesting 'the laws of Christianity') in strife with Venus (in astrological terminology perhaps suggesting Islam), appropriating the spirit of prophecy. Neither the one nor the other (religions) will be understood (Christians will fail to understand the ways of Islam, and Islamic people will fail to understand the ways of the Christians), the great Messiah's law (the teachings of Jesus Christ) retained through the Sun" (retained through God, nature, and the nations of Christianity). Hopefully, at some point in the future, the followers of these two powerful religions will someday transcend their cultural and spiritual differences, and establish a more peaceful relationship with one another.

De la Felice Arabie contrade,
Naîtra puissant de loi Mahome-
   tique:
Vexer l'Espagne conquester la
   Grenade,
Et plus par mer à la gent Ligust
   -ique.
	5 - 55	In the country of Arabia Felix, will be born one powerful in the laws of Mahomet. Vexing Spain and conquering Grenada, and more from the oceans against the Ligurians.

AN ARAB, WELL EDUCATED IN THE
ISLAMIC FAITH, ATTACKS SPAIN, THEN ITALY BY SEA

"In the country of Arabia Felix (which consists of parts of Saudi Arabia, Yemen, and the Aden Protectorate), will be born one (a holy man?) powerful in the laws of Mahomet (Islam). Vexing Spain and conquering Grenada (the last Moorish outpost in Spain, which fell in 1492), and more from the oceans against the Ligurians" (the Italians). Yet another reference to a future Euro/Arabic conflict in Europe.

Sur les rochers sang on verra
   pleuvoir,
Sol Orient, Saturne, Occidental:
Près d'Orgon guerre, à Rome
   grand mal voir,
Nefs parfondrées et pris le Tri-
   dental.
	5 - 62	Blood seen to rain on the rocks, Sun in the East, Saturn in the West. War near Orgon, at Rome great evils seen. Sunken ships on the bottom and the Trident taken.

TROUBLE IN ROME AND
FRANCE DURING TIMES OF NAVAL WAR

"Blood seen to rain on the rocks (suggesting a period of war), Sun in the East (in astrological terminology perhaps this suggests a period of prosperity in Asia - the East), Saturn in the West (in astrology Saturn is the planet of obstacles and punishment, thus this suggests that someone, or some adverse conditions, drag down the West in some manner). War near Orgon (a small city in France), at Rome great evils seen. Sunken ships (of what nation?) on the bottom (of which ocean or sea?) and the Trident taken" (a 'trident' is a three pronged spear carried by the classical gods of the oceans - Neptune and Poseidon, it is associated with naval power). This appears to suggest a period of intense naval warfare. Could "Trident" be a reference to a "Trident" submarine? Perhaps this is related to the third Antichrist's war.

	5 - 68	
Dans le Danube et du Rhin viendra boire Le grand Chameau ne s'en repen tira: Trembler du Rosne et plus fort ceux de Loire, Et près des Alpes Coq le ruinera.		The great Camel will come to drink in the Danube and of the Rhine, and will not repent of it. Those of the Rhône to tremble and even more, those of the Loire; near the Alps the Cock will waste him.

EUROPE INVADED

"The great Camel (suggesting persons from the Middle East or North Africa) will come to drink in (will depart from their homeland and arrive in the regions of) the Danube (a river rising in Germany flowing east to Rumania) and of the Rhine (a river rising in Switzerland flowing north through Germany and the Netherlands), and will not repent of it (suggesting that these European areas will be invaded). Those of the Rhône (a river rising in Switzerland, flowing through France to the Mediterranean - suggesting the Swiss and the French) to tremble, and even more, those of the Loire (the longest river in France - again suggesting the French), near the Alps (a European mountain range arcing from France to Albania) the Cock (an allusion to France) will waste him" (suggesting the French military will defeat the Arabic invaders). Here we have yet another prediction concerning a future military conflict between European and Middle-Eastern (and/or North African) nations.

A N.A.T.O. F-16 Falcon on patrol over Germany.

	5 - 78	
Les deux unis ne tiendront longuement, Et dans treize ans au Barbare Satrape: Aux deux côtés feront tel perdement, Qu'un bénira la Barque et sa cappe.		The two do not remain allied for long, and in thirteen years to the Barbarian Satrap, causing such great loss on both sides, that one will bless the bark of St. Peter and its cloak.

AN AMERICAN AND RUSSIAN ALLIANCE BROKEN?

"The two (suggesting two nations, or possibly two opposing confederations of nations) do not remain allied (in harmony with one another) for long, and in 13 years to the Barbarian Satrap (the key word here is 'Satrap', defined as a governor of a province in ancient Persia, from Middle English -- *Satrape*, from Old Persian, *khshathrapavan* -- protector of the country), causing such great loss (suggesting war) on both sides, that one (one of the nations or groups of nations involved in this future conflict) will bless the bark of St. Peter and its cloak (suggesting the papacy and the Catholic faith)".

If the two allied or united things represent nations (speculation on behalf of your author), then the recent friendship between Russia and the USA comes to mind. If one adds thirteen years to the date of their friendship (November 1989, the collapse of the Iron Curtain), we arrive at the year 2002. However, in June of 1994, Russia signed an agreement with N.A.T.O. called the "Partnership for Peace" plan (if we add thirteen years to this date we arrive at the year 2007).

Though it is tempting to cling to the possibility that this quatrain pertains to Russia and America (considering the possibility that quatrain #2-89 is a reference to their recent friendship), this quatrain is actually quite vague. This might be one of those quatrains which is tempting for a commentator to apply to his own times, but in reality, it might have been intended for a future period of time. Bearing this realistic possibility in mind, this quatrain could be interpreted as if it pertains to Russia and America. However, this remains speculation.

Hopefully, Russia and the United States aren't "the two" nations suggested in this quatrain. Continued cooperation between Russia and the United States will certainly help to ensure global peace and security.

If Nostradamus intentionally used the word "*Satrape*" as a direct reference to Iran, then Iran might be one of the nations responsible for the potential future fall out of the two unnamed nations in this quatrain.

Logmion grande Bisance approchera, Chassée sera la Barbarique Ligue: Des deux lois l'une l'estinique lâchera, Barbare et franche en perpétuelle brigue.	5 - 80	Ogmios will approach great Byzantium, the Barbarian league will be driven out. Of the two laws the heathen one will fail, Barbarian and freeman in perpetual struggle.

OGMIOS WILL REMOVE ANTICHRIST III FROM TURKEY

"Ogmios (an allusion to a Celtic Hercules - a future European military or political leader) will approach great Byzantium (an allusion to Turkey), the Barbarian league (perhaps a reference to the forces of the third Antichrist) will be driven out (from Turkey, and or possibly other regions). Of the two laws (religions) the heathen one (a heathen is anyone who is not of the Christian, Jewish, or Islamic faith, so perhaps an Asian or African religion is suggested here) will fail (will eventually collapse or be conquered), Barbarian and freemen in perpetual struggle (suggesting an on-going power struggle). Ogmios is mentioned in quatrain #6-42 and in paragraph #47 of the Epistle.

Ceux qui auront entreprise subvertir, Nompareil regne, puissant et invincible: Feront par fraude, nuits trois advertir, Quand le plus grand à table lira Bible.	5 - 83	Those who will have an undertaking to subvert an unparalleled realm, both powerful and invincible. They will deceive, warning for three nights, when the greatest one is reading his Bible at the table.

A GREAT LEADER, WHILE READING HIS BIBLE,
WILL BE DECEIVED BY AN ENEMY (BEFORE WAR)

"Those (an unnamed party, a single nation or confederation of nations?) who will have an undertaking (a task or mission) to subvert (to destroy completely, to ruin) an unparalleled realm, both powerful and invincible (which appears to be a powerful Christian nation or group of nations - perhaps in the New World or Europe). They (the unnamed subverters?) will deceive (the powerful and invincible realm?), warning for three nights (some type of warning will be made during a three day period prior to some event or battle), when the greatest one (the more powerful person or leader -- apparently a Christian) is reading his Bible at the table". This is an interesting, yet general quatrain.

Par les Sueues et lieux circonvoisins, Seront en guerre pour cause des nuées: Camp marins locustes et cousins, Du Leman fautes seront bien dénuées.	5 - 85	Through the Swiss and surrounding places they will war due to the clouds. A swarm of marine locusts and gnats, the faults of Geneva will be laid quite bare.

THE SWISS WILL GO TO WAR

"Through the Swiss and surrounding places (suggesting the nation of Switzerland and the surrounding European nations) they (the Swiss and other European nations) will war due to the clouds (due to enemy planes in the clouds or suggesting chemical clouds or drifting atomic fallout?). A swarm of marine locusts and gnats (perhaps a 16th century description of military planes or helicopters launched from atop a ship), the faults of Geneva (a major city in Switzerland on the Rhone River) will be laid quite bare" (exposed). This is perhaps a reference to negligence which will result (or has already resulted) due to a poorly drafted peace treaty or other situation, constructed in Geneva, Switzerland. Geneva was the location of the League of Nations, which failed to avert World War II (which might explain the phrase 'the faults of Geneva will be laid quite bare'). If this quatrain is intended for the future, perhaps some of the parties who sign a future peace treaty (or political agreement) in Geneva will do so in bad faith. Though no time-frame is mentioned here, this quatrain might refer to World War II. However, it could possibly apply to the future.

Par les deux têtes, et trois bras séparés, La cité grande sera par eaux vexée: Des grands d'entr'eux par exil égarés, Par tête Perse Bisance fort pressée.	5 - 86	Divided by the two heads and three arms, the great city will be troubled by water. Some of the great men among them astray in exile. Turkey is hard pressed by the Iranian leader.

TURKEY WILL BE "HARD PRESSED" BY IRAN

The symbolism in the first line eludes me. "The great city (identity unknown) will be troubled by water (by flood or by a naval force?). Some of the great men among them (Cardinals, European citizens or others?) astray in exile (in an unknown location). Turkey (which borders Iran to the west) is hard pressed by the Iranian leader." Another quatrain, perhaps linked to others, which predicts that Iran will one day vex its neighbor Turkey (a member of N.A.T.O.).

Dedans Hongrie par Boheme, Nauarre, Et par bannière saintes séditions: Par fleurs-de-lis pays portant la barre, Contre Orleans fera émotions.	5 - 89	Into Hungary from Bohemia, Navarre and under that banner holy insurrections. The country of the Fleur-de-lys carrying the bar, they will cause disturbances against Orléans.

FUTURE WARFARE IN HUNGARY & BOHEMIA

Apparently an army will pass "into Hungary (the European nation east of Austria, a new member of N.A.T.O.) from Bohemia (a region of western Czechoslovakia, a new member of N.A.T.O.), Navarre (a former kingdom extending from Spain into France) and under that banner (the banner of Navarre - suggesting Spain and France, presently members of N.A.T.O.) holy insurrections (a revolt against civil authority or a constituted government, seems to occur). The country of Fleur-de-lys (possibly representative of the Bourbon family, a French royal family -- suggesting France) carries the bar (leading the insurrection into Hungary?), they (an unnamed party) will cause disturbances against Orleans" (a city in north central France south of Paris). This suggests that the French enter Hungary in order to protect her during a time of future crisis.

Dans les cyclades, en perinthe et larisse, Dedans Sparte tout le Peloponnesse: Si grande famine, peste par faux connisse, Neuf mois tiendra et tout le chersonèse.	5 - 90	In the Cyclades, in Perinthus and Larissa, in Sparta and all of the Peloponnesus; a very great famine, plague through false ashes: it will last nine months throughout the entire peninsula.

CHEMICAL (OR ATOMIC) WARFARE IN GREECE

"In the Cyclades (a group of Greek islands in the southern Aegean Sea), in Perinthus and Larissa (Greek cities in eastern Thessaly), in Sparta (a city in southeastern Peloponnesus) and all of the Peloponnesus (the medieval name of a peninsula lying south of the Gulf of Corinth in Greece), a very great famine, plague through false ashes (suggesting chemical agents or nuclear fall out?), it will last nine months throughout the entire peninsula" (this suggests that most of Greece will be affected by these 'false ashes'). The exact meaning of "false ashes" is unclear. Apparently this quatrain predicts hard times for the Greeks during a period of future war.

Nautique rame invitera les ombres,
Du grand Empire lors viendra conciter:
La mer Aegée des lignes les encombres,
Empêchant l'onde Tirrenne defflottez.

5 - 95

The nautical fog will invite the shadows and then it will come to provoke the great Empire. In the Aegean Sea the remains of wood, obstructing the diverted Tyrrhenian Sea.

NAVAL WARFARE IN THE AEGEAN AND TYRRHENIAN SEAS

This quatrain is not very clear. It seems to suggest that a "nautical fog (meaning unclear) invites the shadows" (death?) which provokes the great Empire (French, American, British, or another great power?). In the Aegean Sea (between Greece and Asia Minor) the remains of bits of wood (perhaps suggesting the destruction of naval vessels), obstructing the diverted Tyrrhenian Sea" (this action seems to effect a situation, possibly a battle, in the Tyrrhenian Sea, which is located between the Italian island of Sicily and Tuscany, a northwestern region of Italy, near France). Though attributed to Napoleon by some commentators, could this quatrain be intended for future times?

À quarante-huit degré climatérique,
A fin de Cancer si grande sécheresse:
Poisson en mer, fleuve, lac cuit hectique,
Bearn, Bigorre par feu ciel en détresse.

5 - 98

At the forty-eighth degree of the climacteric, at the end of Cancer, there is a very great dryness. Fish in the sea, river and the lake boiled hectic, Bearn and Bigorre in distress from aerial fire.

WAR IN EUROPE

"At the 48th degree of the climacteric (suggesting the forty-eighth day of a series of events, or perhaps the forty-eighth degree of latitude north. If latitude is meant here the European cities of Paris, Munich, Vienna, and Budapest might be the locations suggested), at the end of Cancer (the Sun sign of Cancer ends on July 22nd), there is a very great dryness (due to war or environmental conditions?). Fish in the seas, rivers and lakes are boiled hectic (from drought or atomic war?), Bearn and Bigorre (counties in Navarre, in Spain and France) in distress from aerial fire" (aerial warfare or nuclear fire?).

Le boute-feu par son feu attrapé, De feu du ciel à Calcas et Cominge: Foix, Aux, Mazere, haut vieillard échappé, Par ceux de Hasse, des Saxons et Turinge.	5 - 100	The incendiary trapped in his own fire; of fire from the sky at Carcassonne and Comminges: Foix, Auch & Mazeres, the high ranking old man escaped, by people of Hesse, Thuringia and some Saxons.

FRANCE UNDER AERIAL ATTACK, THE GERMANS WILL HELP TO SAVE A LEADER

The phrase "the incendiary trapped in his own fire" places this in the 20th century or in future times. This "trapping" seems to be effected by "fire from the sky (suggesting modern aerial warfare) at Carcassonne (a city in southern France on the Aude River) and in Comminges" (an ancient region east of Bigorre in France). "Foix, Auch and Mazeres" (three cities in southern France) also appear to be effected by this in some way. "The high ranking old man (possibly suggesting a general, a pope, a European leader, or someone else) escaped (due to aid) by people of Hesse (a region of central west Germany), Thuringia (a former state of central Germany) and some Saxons" (a region of northwestern Germany). Apparently during a future period, when France is being attacked by unnamed enemies, citizens form various parts of Germany will come to the assistance of the French during a time of crisis. We have no specific clues regarding the intended time-frame of this future tragedy.

CENTURY VI

	6 - 5	
Si grand famine par onde pestifère,		A very great famine caused by a pestilent wave through
Par pluie longue le long du pôle arctique:		long rain the length of the Arctic pole. In Samarobryn, one
Samarobryn cent lieues de l'hémi-sphère,		hundred leagues from the hemi-sphere; they will live without
Vivront sans loi exempt de politi-que.		law, exempt from politics.

A SPACE STATION VIEWS PESTILENCE ON EARTH

"A very great famine caused by a pestilent wave (perhaps created due to chemical warfare, atomic fall-out or a heat wave) through a long rain the length of the Arctic Pole (throughout the northern hemisphere -- North America, Europe and Asia). In Samarobryn (possibly the name of a space station or space colony) one hundred leagues from the hemisphere (300 statute miles above the surface of the Earth -- a common altitude for space shuttle missions); they (its occupants) will live without law, exempt from politics." Politics seem to affect the fate of Samarobryn.

"Samarobryn" appears to be an anagram. The present Russian space station is named *Mir*. And since there is no letter "i" in "Samarobryn", the Russian space station does not appear to be the intended topic here. If the word "Samarobryn" is an anagram intended to be a clue to the national identity of its creator, the forthcoming American inspired International Space Station might be intended here. In example, "Samarobryn" is an anagram for the name "Sam Rayborn" which could be an allusion to *Sam Rayburn* -- the famous American political figure who served 48 years in the U.S. House of Representatives. Speaker Rayburn, a Texan, was the senior democrat in Congress in 1958, and along with Senator Lynden Johnson, was instrumental in passing the bill which created NASA (House of Representatives Bill# 12575). This is a very fascinating prediction which is presently in the process of fulfillment. According to NASA, the final phase of the construction of the International Space Station should be completed in 1999 (or shortly thereafter).

Dresser copies pour monter à l'empire, Du Vatican le sang Royal tiendra: Flamans, Anglois, Espagne avec Aspire, Contre l'Italie et France contiendra.	6 - 12	To raise forces to ascend to Empire from the Vatican the Royal blood will hold fast. Flemish, English, Spain with Aspire: he will fight against France and Italy.

EUROPE WILL UNITE TO FIGHT OFF INVADERS

"To raise forces (suggesting military forces) to ascend to Empire (of or characteristic of the first Empire of France - 1804-1815, or a political unit comprising several nations ruled by a single supreme authority) from the Vatican (located in Rome, Italy) the Royal blood (pertaining to a king, queen, monarch, or in the service of a kingdom) will hold fast (suggesting these royal forces - perhaps Italians, hold their ground during combat). Flemish (the Belgians), English, Spain with Aspire (possibly representative of Germany, but unclear). He (identity unclear, possibly the third Antichrist or a Middle Eastern leader) will fight against France and Italy". All the nations listed here are N.A.T.O. members.

Quand ceux du pôle arctique unis ensemble, En Orient grand effrayeur et crainte: Élu nouveau, soutenu le grand tremble, Rodes, Bisance de sang Barbare teinte.	6 - 21	When those of the Arctic pole are united together, in the East will be great terror and dread. The newly elected one upheld, the great Rhodes, and Byzantium stained with Barbarian blood.

GREECE AND TURKEY BECOME BATTLE GROUNDS

"When those (nations) of the Arctic Pole (suggesting America and Russia - which almost touch one another in the Arctic region) are united together (as they more or less have been since 1989, or sometime afterwards) in the East (suggesting Asia and the Middle East) there will be great terror and dread (political and military concern). The newly elected one (a future world leader or a pope?) upheld (prevented from falling or sinking), the great Rhodes (a Greek island) and Byzantium (an allusion to the nation of Turkey) stained with Barbarian (an unnamed enemy's) blood". Based upon the first line of this quatrain, this prediction pertains to the near future. Could this be linked to quatrains #5-47, #5-86 and #5-90?

Gen. Colin Powell (Ret.) Chairman of the Joint Chiefs of Staff for the U.S. Army.

The U.S.S. San Jacinto fired volleys of cruise missiles into Iraq during the Gulf War.

Sa main dernière par Alus sanguinaire,	6 - 33	His final hand through Alus, he will be unable to protect
Ne se pourra par la mer garantir:		himself by sea. Between two rivers he will fear the
Entre deux fleuves craindre main militaire,		military hand, the black one, irate, will make him regret it.
Le noir l'ireux le fera repentir.		

OPERATION DESERT STORM; THE INVASION OF KUWAIT

"His final hand (Saddahm Hussien's final military advance) through Alus (an anagram for Saul, perhaps a fictitious name of an Iraqi commander), he (Saddahm) will be unable to protect himself by sea (Coalition naval forces bombed and shelled Saddahm's military assets by sea, followed by an amphibious assault of Kuwait). Between two rivers (in the geographic region between the Tigris and Euphrates Rivers, in Iraq) he (Saddahm) will fear the military hand (attack from Coalition forces). The black one, irate (perhaps a reference to General Colin Powell, commander of the Coalition forces and a gentleman with a self-admitted bad temper) will make him (Saddahm) regret it" (the invasion of Kuwait and the missile attacks on Israel and Saudi Arabia). Although this quatrain is vague in regards to specific names and precise geographic locations, it seems to fit some of the people and events associated with Operation Desert Storm in 1991. This quatrain appears connected to quatrains #3-61 and #8-70.

	6 - 42	
A Logmygon sera laissé le regne,		To Ogmios the kingdom of the great Selin will be left, who will do even more. Across Italy he will extend his banner, he will be ruled by a prudent deformed one.
Du grand Selin, qui plus fera de fait:		
Par les Itales étendra son enseigne,		
Regi sera par prudent contrefait.		

OGMIOS WILL RULE OVER ITALY AFTER WAR WITH THE THIRD ANTICHRIST

"To Ogmios (a Celtic Hercules, suggesting a future European general or freedom fighter, most likely a Frenchman, who will defend his nation during the war with the future third Antichrist) the kingdom of the great Selin (an allusion to a future Middle Eastern or Asian leader of a muslim nation --, perhaps the third Antichrist) will be left, who will do even more. Across Italy he (Ogmios) will extend his banner (the standard of a military commander, or the flag of a nation), he (Ogmios) will be ruled by a prudent deformed one" (meaning unclear). See quatrains #1-94, #4-77, #6-58, and #6-78 for additional references to Selin.

	6 - 44	
De nuit par Nantes l'Iris apparîstra,		By night the Rainbow appears near Nantes, the marine arts will stir up rain. In the Gulf of Arabia a great fleet will sink: in Saxony a monster will be born of a bear and a sow.
Des artz marins susciteront la pluie:		
Arabiq gouffre grande classe parfondra,		
Un monstre en Saxe naîtra d'ours et truie.		

NAVAL WARFARE IN THE MIDDLE EAST

"By night the Rainbow (meaning the various colors of flags on naval ships, an actual rainbow, an explosion, or something else?) appears near Nantes (a port city in western France). In the Gulf of Arabia (suggesting the Arabian Gulf, the Red Sea, Arabian Sea, or Persian Gulf, since there is no actual 'Gulf of Arabia') a great fleet (an unnamed powerful fleet) will sink (suggesting an American, European, or some other fleet?). In Saxony (a former region of northwestern Germany) a monster will be born of a bear (suggesting the Soviets, or someone else?) and a sow" (an unnamed piggish nation?). The meaning of "bear" and "sow" are unclear. This quatrain appears to be yet another reference to a Euro/Arabic conflict.

Entre les deux monarques éloignés, Lorsque le Sol par Selin clair perdue: Simulté grande entre deux indignés, Qu'aux Îles et Sienne la liberté rendue.	6 - 58	Distance between the two monarchs, when through Selin, the clear light of the Sun will be lost, between two indignant ones will be great hatred, liberty to be restored to the Isles and Siena.

EUROPEANS TO QUASH SELIN

"Distance between the two monarchs (two kings or leaders will be geographically separated from one another), when through Selin (due to the actions of Selin, a future Middle Eastern leader of an unnamed country), the clear light of the Sun will be lost (because of the actions of Selin, the direct light of the Sun will be veiled -- perhaps suggesting that an atmospheric disturbance results due to the use of nuclear weapons), between two indignant ones will be great hatred (Selin and his adversary will hate one another), liberty to be restored to the Isles (suggesting the British Isles -- the United Kingdom) and Siena" (a city in Italy, an allusion to the nation of Italy). It appears that Italy and the United Kingdom (and perhaps other European nations) will be negatively affected by the actions of Selin (see quatrains #1-94, #4-77, #6-42, and #6-78).

On ne tiendra pache aucun arrêté, Tous recevants iront par tromperie: De paix et trêve, terre et mer protesté, Par Barcelonne classe pris d'industrie.	6 - 64	They will not keep any peace agreed upon, all the receivers will go through deceit. In peace and truce, land and sea having protested, the fleet is seized with ingenious skill by Barcelona.

FALSE PEACE, A FLEET WILL BE SEIZED BY SPAIN

"They (suggesting unidentified nations) will not keep any peace agreed upon (apparently an international peace, agreed upon by several nations, will not be kept in good faith by the parties who make the agreement), all the receivers (of this false peace) will go through deceit. In peace and truce, land and sea having protested (suggesting war), the fleet (an unidentifed naval force, perhaps a foe) is seized with ingenious skill by Barcelona" (a region and city in Spain, suggesting the Spanish or forces located in Spain). We have no clues here regarding the intended time frame for this event.

Crier victoire du grand Selin croissant: Par les Romains sera l'Aigle clamé, Ticcin, Milan et Gennes n'y consent, Puis par eux-mêmes Basil grand réclamé.	6 - 78	To announce victory over the great expanding Selin, the Romans will demand the Eagle. Pavia, Milan, and Genoa refuse their consent thereto, then by themselves the grand King claimed.

ITALY THREATENED BY SELIN

"To announce victory over the great expanding Selin (in order to obtain a military victory over the future Middle Eastern leader Selin, apparently an Islamic expansionist), the Romans (suggesting the Italians) will demand the Eagle (an allusion to the United States, apparently Italy will request American assistance). Pavia, Milan, and Genoa (cities in Italy, an allusion to the nation of Italy) refuse their consent thereto (refuse their consent to the intentions of Selin?), then by themselves, the grand King (or captain) proclaimed" (or announced). This quatrain is connected to quatrains #1-94, #4-77, #6-42, and #6-58. Could "Selin" be the name Nostradamaus used as an allusion to the third Antichrist?

Pleurs, cris et plaintes, hurlements, effrayeur, Coeur inhumain, cruel noir et transi: Leman, les Îles de Gennes les majeurs, Sang épancher, frofaim à nul merci.	6 - 81	Tears, cries and wailing howls of terror, an inhuman cruel heart, black and cold. Lake Geneva, the Islands, the notable people of Genoa; blood to pour, an agricultural famine, mercy to none.

THE SWISS, BRITISH, & ITALIANS FIGHT ENEMIES

Apparently during a time of war and terror, "tears, cries and wailing howls of terror" are heard. "An inhuman, cruel heart, black and cold (a cruel individual, perhaps the third Antichrist or another enemy, seems to be responsible for these conditions). Lake Geneva (in southwestern Switzerland, the Swiss), the Islands (an allusion to the British Isles), the notable people of Genoa (the Italian people in the northwestern port city of Genoa, Italy), blood to pour (suggesting war), an agricultural famine, mercy to none" (during this horrible warfare). This appears to be a reference to a horrible future war involving Europe and an unnamed "inhuman, cruel, and black hearted" foe. Could this be a reference to the times of the so-called future third Antichrist?

La grande cité de Tharse par Gaulois Sera détruite, captifs tous à Turban: Secours par mer du grand Portugalois, Premier d'été le jour du sacre Vrban.	6 - 85	The great city of Tarsus by the Gauls will be destroyed, all the Turbans captive. Help from the sea from the great one of Portugal, the first day of summer, Urban's consecration.

FRANCE, WITH HELP FROM PORTUGAL, WILL ATTACK TROOPS LOCATED IN TURKEY DURING A TIME OF WAR

"The great city of Tarsus (a Turkish seaport city in the south of Turkey) by the Gauls (the French) will be destroyed, all the Turbans (the Moslem forces) captive (held as prisoners). Help from the sea from the great one (a powerful man or nation) of (who departs from) Portugal, the first day of summer, Urban's consecration" (Urban was a pope from 1088 - 1099). To "consecrate" something means to make it holy or sacred. Perhaps this event occurs near June 21 (the first day of summer) in an unknown year, during a time when a new pope will be in Rome.

L' ennemi docte se trouvera confus, Grand camp malade, et défait par embûches, Monts Pyrenees et Poenus lui seront faits refus, Proche du fleuve découvrant antiques cruches.	6 - 99	The learned enemy finds himself confused, his great army sick, defeated by ambushes, the Pyrenees and Pennine Alps will be denied to him, discovering near the river ancient urns.

AN ENEMY ATTACKS EUROPE

"The learned enemy (suggesting a powerful unnamed enemy) finds himself confused (will turn around), his great army (suggesting a large military force) sick (by chemical, atomic, or biological war, or disease?), defeated by ambushes (by unnamed European or other military forces), the Pyrenees (the European mountain range between France and Spain, extending for 260 miles between the Bay of Biscay and the Mediterranean Sea) and the Pennine Alps (a European mountain range of the Alps in southwest Switzerland on the Italian border) will be denied him (suggesting that European military forces repel the advancing invader), discovering near the river ancient urns" (near an unnamed river some party will discover vases containing the ashes of the cremated dead). Perhaps this refers to a future Euro/Arabic conflict.

CENTURY VII

Après de France la victoire navale, Les Barchinons, Saillinons, les Phocens, Lierre d'or, l'enclume serré dedans la balle, Ceux de Ptolon au fraud seront consens.	7 - 3	After a naval victory for France, the people of Barcelona, the Saillinons and those of Marseilles; the robber of gold, enclosed in the ball, the people of Ptolon will be party to the fraud.

A NAVAL VICTORY FOR FRANCE

"After a naval victory for France, the people of Barcelona (a city in Spain, an allusion to the Spanish) and Saillinons (an unknown place) and those of Marseilles" (a city in France, an allusion to the French) are somehow connected to "a robber of gold" (an enemy perhaps) who is "enclosed in the ball" (a mystery to me, perhaps suggesting an enemy is destroyed). "Enclosed in the ball" might suggest a "ball" of fire. "The people of Ptolon (Ptolon is an unknown location yet Garencières, a Nostradamus commentator from 1672, thought it referred to 'Toulon' in France) will be party to the fraud" (an unstated fraud).

Naples, Palerme, et toute la Sicille, Par main Barbare sera inhabitée: Corsicque, Salerne et de Sardeigne l'Îsle, Faim, peste, guerre, fin de maux intentée.	7 - 6	Naples, Palermo, and all of Sicily will be uninhabited through Barbarian hands. Corsica, Salerno and the isle of Sardinia, famine, plague, war, the end of extended evils.

ITALY TO BE UNINHABITED DUE TO BARBARISMS

"Naples, Palermo (cities in Italy) and all of Sicily (an Italian island south of the Italian mainland) will be uninhabited (suggesting an exodus of the masses, or their death?) through Barbarian hands (perhaps a Middle Eastern confederation, or another unnamed party). Corsica (a French island in the Mediterranean Sea, and birthplace of Napoleon Bonaparte), Salerno (an Italian seaport west of the Gulf of Salerno), and the isle of Sardinia" (an Italian island located south of the Italian mainland) appear to be affected by "famine, plague, and war". This action seems to mark the end of a period of "extended evils" (perhaps the end of a lengthy conflict).

Sur le combat des grand chevaux légers,
On criera le grand croissant confond:
De nuit tuer monts, habits de bergers,
Abîmes rouges dans le fossé profond.

7 - 7

Upon the struggle of the great light horses, it will be claimed that the great crescent was destroyed. Killing by night, in the mountains, dressed in shepherds garb. Red gulfs in the deep ditch.

THE GREAT CRESCENT TO BE DESTROYED

"Upon the struggle of the great light horses (suggesting a siege by infantry, cavalry, or light mechanized armor units?), it will be proclaimed that the great crescent (suggesting Turkish or other unidentified Islamic forces) was destroyed (these unidentified Moslem troops are apparently defeated in a future conflict). Killing by night (combat), in the mountains (location unknown); dressed in shepherds garb (apparently one of the warring parties disguises themselves as shepherds). Red gulfs in the deep ditch" (suggests blood in the waters of an unnamed body of water, which results from this future conflict). A reference is made to "light horses" in quatrain #5-91 in the Astrological chapter.

Florira, fuis, fuis le plus proche Romain,
Au Fesulan sera conflit donné:
Sang épandu, les plus grands pris à main,
Temple ni sexe ne sera pardonné.

7 - 8

Florence, flee, flee the approaching Roman, at Fiesole battle will be given: bloodshed, the greatest ones taken by the hand, neither temple nor sex will be pardoned.

DEVASTATION IN FLORENCE AND FIESOLE

"Florence (a cultural city on the Arno River in Tuscany, Italy), flee, flee the approaching Roman (suggesting that the citizens of Florence should flee from an unnamed person from Rome), at Fiesole (an Italian city northeast of Florence) battle will be given (between the "Roman" and those of Florence, or between the "Roman" and an unnamed party?): bloodshed (battle), the greatest ones (an unnamed party) taken by the hand (kidnapped or abducted?), neither temple (church buildings) nor sex (suggesting both genders) will be pardoned" (neither men, nor women, will escape the devastation of the battle or social turmoil, which will develop near Florence and Fiesole). This quatrain appears to be a reference to a future "revolution" of some type, rather than a foreign invasion (since we have citizens of Rome confronting citizens of Florence).

De Languedoc, et Guienne plus de dix Mille voudront les Alpes repasser. Grands Allobroges marcher contre Brundis, Aquin et Bresse les viendront rechasser.	7 - 31	From Languedoc and Guienne more than ten thousand men will want to cross the Alps again. The great Savoyards to march against Brindisi, Aquino and Bresse will come to repel them back.

10,000 MEN FROM FRANCE WILL CROSS THE ALPS TO ENGAGE THE INVADERS OF ITALY

"From Languedoc and Guienne (provinces in France) more than 10,000 men (Frenchmen or others?) will want to cross the Alps again (for a second time?). The great Savoyards (a region in France, an allusion to the French) to march against Brindisi (a city located on the eastern coast of Italy), Aquino and Bresse (which belonged to the Kingdom of the Two Sicilies, suggesting the cities of Sicily and Naples in Italy, or perhaps forces located in this region) will come to repel them" (the unidentified invaders of Italy).

Le conducteur de l'armée Francoise, Cuidant perdre le principal phalange: Par sus pavé de l'ovaine et d'ardoise, Soi parfondra par Gennes gent étrange.	7 - 39	The leader of the French army will expect to ruin the main phalanx. Upon the pavement of oats and slate the foreign nation will undermine themselves through Genoa.

THE FRENCH AND ITALIANS UNDERMINE AN ENEMY

"The leader of the French army (identity unknown) will expect to ruin the main phalanx (a formation of infantry of an unknown force). Upon the pavement of oats and slate (possibly suggesting trade and commerce) the foreign nation (identity unknown, a nation "foreign" to France) will undermine themselves (by some type of action) through Genoa" (a city in Italy, suggesting the Italians). This quatrain suggests that the French and Italians will be involved in combat with an unnamed invader of Europe.

CENTURY VIII

Apparaîtra temple luisant orné, La lampe et cierge à Borne et Bretueil: Pour la Lucerne le Canton détourné, Quand on verra le grand Coq au cercueil.	8 - 5	There will appear a glittering ornate temple, the lamp and candle at Borne and Breteuil. For the Canton of Lucerene turned aside, when one sees the great Cock in his tomb.

SWITZERLAND ATTACKED

"There will appear a glittering ornate temple (meaning unclear), the lamp and candle at Borne (a city in the Ardèche) and Breteuil (one Breteuil is located in Normandy, another in France). For the Canton of Lucerene (a city in Switzerland on Lake Lucerene) turned aside (suggesting this region will be devastated by an unnamed party), when one sees the great Cock (an allusion to France) in his tomb" (suggesting either the death of a French leader, or destruction in France).

Verceil, Milan donra intelligence, Dedans Ticin sera faite la plaie: Courir par Siene eau, sang, feu par Florence, Unique choir d'haut en bas faisant maye.	8 - 7	Vercelli, Milan will give the intelligence, the wound will be made within Pavia. To run in the Seine water, blood and fire through Florence, the unique one falling from high to low calling for help.

WAR IN ITALY AND FRANCE

"Vercelli (a city in Italy) and Milan (the second largest city in Italy) will give the intelligence (or information of some type, to an unknown party), the wound (suggesting some type of injury or plague) will be made within Pavia (a city in Italy). To run in the Seine water (the region surrounding the Seine River in northern France), blood and fire through Florence (a city in central Italy), the unique one (a pope or someone else?) falling from high to low (suggesting good times turning to bad) calling for help" (apparently the "unique one" will request assistance from friendly parties during a crisis).

Pendant que l'Aigle et le Coq à Sauone, Seront unis, Mer Levant et Ongrie: L'armée à Naples, Palerne, Marque d'Ancone, Rome, Venise par Barbe horrible cri.	8 - 9	While the Eagle is united with the Cock at Savona, Sea, Levant and Hungary. The army at Naples, Palermo, the march of Ancona, Rome and Venice, by the Barbarian a great outcry.

THE U.S.A. AND FRANCE UNITE IN ITALY AGAINST AN ENEMY

"While the Eagle (an allusion to America and its military) is united with the Cock (an allusion to France and its military) at Savona (in Italy), Sea (suggesting the Adriatic?), Levant (from Middle English *Levaunt* - "the Orient", possibly suggesting Turkey and countries bordering the eastern Mediterranean Sea) and Hungary (eastern Europe's newest N.A.T.O. member). The army (suggesting the American, French, and Italian armies, or their foes?) at Naples and Palermo (cities in Italy), the march (of troops, to or from) Ancona, Rome and Venice (cities in Italy); by the Barbarian (an unnamed invader) a great outcry". This suggests that the barbarian invaders of Europe (identity unknown) will take a whipping, losing in battle. Perhaps the invaders are from North Africa or the Middle East.

Les bien aisés subit seront désmis, Par les trois frères le monde mis en trouble, Cité marine saisiront ennemis, Faim, feu, sang, peste, et de tous maux le double.	8 - 17	The prosperous ones will suddenly be removed, the world put into trouble by the three brothers; their enemies will seize the marine city, hunger, fire, flood, plague, all evils doubled.

AMERICA AT WAR, HER ENEMIES WILL ATTACK BY SEA

"The prosperous ones (nations, leaders, or individuals?) will suddenly be removed (removed from what, and by whom?), the world put into trouble by the three brothers (the phrase "the three brothers" appears to be an allusion to the Kennedy brothers, and or America, thus this suggests that the United States will somehow be placed in a perplexing position and will respond to the unstated trouble); their enemies (suggesting America's enemies) will seize the marine city (an unnamed coastal city), hunger, fire, flood, plague, all evils doubled" (suggesting war, an escalation of war, or the worsening of various circumstances). This quatrain appears to reference a future plague, famine and war, possibly involving the United States and an unidentified adversary.

Le Bisantin faisant oblation,
Après avoir Cordube à soi reprise:
Son chemin long repos pamplation,
Mer passant proie par la Colongna prise.

8 - 51

The Byzantine makes an oblation after having taken back for himself Cordoba. A long rest on his road, the vines cut down, on the sea the passing prey captured by the Pillar.

TURKEY CAPTURES SOUTHERN SPAIN

"The Byzantine (suggesting a Turk) makes an oblation (a religious offering to a deity) after recapturing for himself Cordoba (a city in southern Spain). A long rest on his road, the vines cut down (possibly suggesting supply routes or electrical lines?), on the sea the passing prey (perhaps a naval fleet) captured by the Pillar" ("the pillar" possibly suggests the famous Straits of Gilbraltar located between Spain and Morocco). The Straits of Gibraltar is the gateway to the Mediterranean Sea from the Atlantic. We have very few clues to work from in this quatrain.

Par deux fois haut par deux fois mis à bas,
L'Orient aussi l'Occident faiblira:
Son adversaire après plusieurs combats,
Par mer chassé au besoin faillira.

8 - 59

Twice raised up and twice cast down, the East, also the West, will weaken. Its adversary, after several conflicts chased by sea, will fail at time of need.

TWICE THE ORIENT RISES AND FALLS, FAILING AT SEA

"Twice (on two separate occasions) raised up (elevated in some type of status - military, economic, social, etc...) and twice cast down (being lowered in status on two separate occasions), the East (Asia), also the West (the New World), will weaken (at some point in the future). It's adversary (the adversary of the West?) after several conflicts chased by sea will fail at time of need" (the forces of "the East" will fold during a future period of intense naval warfare).

Il entrera vilain, méchant, infame,
Tyrannisant la Mesopotamie:
Tous amis fait d'adulterine dame,
Terre horrible noir de physionomie.

8 - 70

He will enter ugly, wicked, infamous, tyrannizing over Mesopotamia: All friends through the adulterine lady. The land made horrible, black of physiognomy.

OPERATION DESERT STORM

In 1947, forty four years before the Gulf War, Roberts (a Nostradamus commentator) stated the following in regards to this quatrain, "the country near Babylon shall be terrorized by a person of the negro race". During Operation Desert Storm, in 1991, Coalition forces under the command of U.S. General Colin Powell (a distinguished gentleman of the black race) entered "Mesopotamia" (the ancient country between the Tigris and Euphrates Rivers -- modern-day Iraq) in a "wicked and infamous" manner (entering not as tourists, but as combat soldiers) conquering Iraq's military forces.

The "tyrannizing" mentioned in this quatrain could be interpreted several ways. It could suggest that the Coalition forces would militarily "tyrannize over Mesopotamia", or it may be a reference to the United Nations sanctions imposed upon Iraq as terms of their surrender ("tyranny" in the view of Iraq). An alternate interpretation might be "He (suggesting Saddahm Hussien) will wickedly tyrannize over Mesopotamia in an ugly and infamous manner". The meaning of "all friends through the adulterine lady" is unclear.

"The land made horrible" suggests a great destruction of people, land, buildings and oil fields which resulted from the Coalition's aerial bombardments and following land war.

The phrase "black of physiognomy" is a key phrase in this quatrain. The word "physiognomy" is defined as the art of judging human character based on human facial features. Thus the phrase "the land made horrible, black of physiognomy" might suggest that the face of the land of Mesopotamia (Iraq) will be made (temporarily) horrible (suffering great carnage) due to the actions of someone with black facial features (by a gentleman of the black race, possibly suggesting General Colin Powell, commander of Coalition forces in Iraq).

An alternate interpretation of line four could be "the face of the land made horrible and black". The oil fields of Kuwait certainly looked "horrible and black" after the retreating Iraqi army set fire to them on their way back to Iraq. As a result of these fires, the skies above Kuwait were also quite "blackened". This quatrain appears to be another amazing example of a recently fulfilled prophecy. See quatrains #3-61 and #6-33.

CENTURY IX

Voile Simacle port Massiliolique, Dans Venise port marcher aux Pannons: Partir du gouffre et sinus Illirique, Vast à Socille, Ligurs coups de canons.	9 - 28	The Allied fleet from the port of Marseilles, arrives in the port of Venice to march against Hungary. Leaving from the gulf and the bay of Illyria, devastation to Sicily, for the Ligurians cannon shot!

AN ALLIED FLEET SAILS FROM FRANCE TO ITALY TO ENGAGE AN ENEMY

"The Allied fleet (perhaps suggesting a N.A.T.O. fleet) from the port of Marseilles (a port city in France) arrives in the port of Venice (a port city in Italy) to march against the Pannons (suggesting that the N.A.T.O. forces arrive in Italy to attack the invaders occupying Hungary and the former Yugoslavia). Leaving from the gulf and the bay of Illyria (perhaps the N.A.T.O. fleet departs from the Adriatic Sea), devastation to Sicily (an Italian island south of the Italian mainland), for the Ligurians (Italians who occupy the northwest coast of Italy), cannon shot "(war and destruction!). We have no clues regarding the identity of the Allied fleet's adversary. If this is connected to quatrain #10-62, then perhaps the "invaders" are Arabic.

Au port de Puola et de sainct Nicolas, Périr Normande au gouffre phanatique, Cap. de Bisance rues crier hélas, Secours de Gaddes et du grand Philippique.	9 - 30	At the port of Pola and San Nicolo, Norman will perish in the Gulf of Quarnero: Capet in the streets of Byzantium crying alas, the help from Cadiz and the great Philip.

WARFARE IN THE BALKANS

"At the port of Pola and Saint Nicolo (Pola and St. Nicolo are located in the former Yugoslavia, Pola is on the west coast of the Istrian Peninsula in the Adriatic Sea, and San Nicolo is across the bay on the north end of the peninsula, some type of action occurs, most likely warfare), Norman (a Frenchman or Scandinavian, probably the French are inferred) will perish in the Gulf of Quarnero" (where Rijeka is, a seaport in northwestern Croatia on the Adriatic Sea). How they perish is unknown. "Capet (King of France from 987 - 996 A.D., maybe a fictitious name or perhaps a reference to a French leader) in the streets of Byzantium (an allusion to Istanbul, Turkey) crying alas (an expression of sorrow, grief, or an apprehension of danger), the help from Cadiz (a seaport in Spain, the Spanish or forces located there) and the great Philip" (Philip appears to be an allusion to Great Britain, but its meaning is unclear).

Summation: A French or Scandinavian naval force (or possibly a N.A.T.O. force) battle an enemy in the Gulf of Quarnero in the Adriatic Sea. The French or Scandinavian forces perish. The forces of Spain and the United Kingdom (if "Philip" represents the United Kingdom) arrive to assist the Norman (the French or Scandinavian) forces after their battle. This action seems to make the Turks (or forces located in Turkey) very uneasy.

L'entrée de Blaye par Rochelle et l'Anglois, Passera le grand Aemathien Non loin d'Agen attendra le Gaulois, Secours Narbonne déçu par entretien.	9 - 38	The entry at Blaye for La Rochelle and the English, the great Macedonian passes beyond. Not far from the Aegean the Gaul waits, help from Narbonne misled by a conversation.

WARFARE IN FRANCE

"The entry at Blaye (a seaport city in southwest France) for La Rochelle (a seaport in France on the Bay of Biscay, and allusion to the French military) and the English (military forces from the United Kingdom), the great Macedonian (an unnamed person from the ancient region consisting of parts of Greece, Bulgaria and Yugoslavia) will pass beyond (suggesting that he and his army will pass beyond some geographic point, or that they perish?). Not far from the Aegean (the sea between Greece and Turkey) the Gaul (a Frenchmen or perhaps an allusion to the French military) waits, help from Narbonne (a French city on the Mediterranean more than 200 miles southeast of the Aegean Sea) mislead (deceived or confused) by a conversation" (via a radio transmission or a face to face conversation?).

Migrez, migrez de Geneue trestous, Saturne d'or en fer se changera, Le contre RAYPOZ exterminera tous, Avant l'avent de ciel signes fera.	9 - 44	Leave, leave Geneva every single one of you! Saturn will turn from gold into iron. All who oppose RAYPOZ will be exterminated. Before the arrival the sky will show signs.

FUTURE DESTRUCTION IN GENEVA

Nostradamus warns the citizens (or occupants) of "Geneva" (a city in Switzerland on the Rhône River) to leave, "every one of you"! "Saturn (in astrology the planet of obstacles and punishment) turns from gold into iron (suggesting good luck turning to bad, or possibly commerce turning to war). "All who oppose RAYPOZ (either a person or thing) will be exterminated". The identity of "RAYPOZ" has remained a mystery over the years, yet since a future war seems inferred, one could wonder if it represents a nuclear device, some type of high-tech "Star Wars" ordnance, or some other type of weapon. Its meaning is unclear. "RAYPOZ" might be an anagram for someone's name. "Before the arrival (before the arrival of what?) the sky will show signs" (perhaps a reference to fighter planes, clouds of fall-out, or something else). UFO enthusiasts have hypothesized that this last line might be a reference to the UFO phenomena, though its meaning is unclear.

Arrivera au port de Corsibonne, Près de Rauenne, qui pillera la dame: En mer profonde légat de la Vlisbonne, Sous roc cachés raviront septante âmes.	9 - 54	There will arrive at Porto Corsini, near Ravenna, one who will wish to plunder the lady. The Legate from Lisbon in the deep sea, hidden under a rock they carry away seventy souls.

ENEMIES OF ITALY TO INVADE NEAR RAVENNA

"There will arrive (an enemy military force) at Porto Corsini (a city located eight miles north of Ravenna, in northern Italy, six miles inland from the Adriatic Sea), one who will wish to plunder the lady ("the lady" may suggest Italy, France, Lady Liberty, the Catholic Church, or something else). The Legate from Lisbon (a representative of the pope from Lisbon, Portugal) in the deep sea (perhaps suggesting that he is on a ship at sea), hidden under a rock (hiding beneath some rocks in an unnamed location) they (an unnamed party) carry away seventy souls" (apparently this unidentified "hidden" party takes seventy people hostage).

Conflit Barbare en la Cornette noire, Sang épandu, trembler la Dalmatie: Grand Ismael mettra son promontoire, Ranes trembler secours Lusitanie.	9 - 60	In a black head-dress the Barbarian fights, blood shed, Dalmatia trembles. The great Ismaël will establish his promontory, Frogs tremble under aid from Lusitania.

AN ARAB ARMY WILL INVADE CROATIA

"In a black head-dress (while wearing a black 'head-dress', perhaps an Arabic style head-dress) the Barbarian fights (a brutal insensitive military man, apparently an Arab), blood shed (suggesting warfare), Dalmatia trembles (the coastal region of Croatia along the eastern Adriatic Sea will be troubled by war). The great Ismaël (son of Abraham and Hagar, Patriarch of the Muslims, suggesting a powerful Arabic leader) will establish his promontory (a promontory is a high ridge of land jutting out into a body of water, thus this seems to suggest that the invading Arabic forces establish a foothold in Dalmatia), Frogs tremble (possibly suggesting an unnamed amphibious force or possibly an allusion to the French) under aid from Lusitania" (the ancient name for modern Portugal). Perhaps the Portuguese (or a force located there) provide military assistance to an unnamed ally combating the Arabic invaders of Dalmatia (possibly linked to quatrain #2-32).

Dedans le coin de Luna viendra rendre, Où sera pris et mis en terre étrange: Les fruits immûrs seront à grand esclandre, Grand vitupère, à l'un grande louange.	9 - 65	He will come to travel to the corner of Luna, where he will be captured, and put into a strange land. The unripe fruits to be subjects of great scandal, great blame, to one great praise.

THE SPACE RACE AND THE U.S. LANDING ON THE MOON

"He (mankind, the American astronauts) will come to travel to the corner of Luna ('Luna' suggests the Moon), where he will be captured (on film) and put into a strange land (outer space, the Moon, a mysterious and alien land). The unripe fruits (assets which take time to develop before reaching maturity, a reference to the space-race) to be subjects of great scandal (a reference to the Apollo 1 tragedy, the Apollo 13 incident, the Challenger disaster, the collision on space station Mir, and other American and Russian space related accidents), great blame (to unnamed parties), to one great praise" (perhaps a reference to the success of the American space program). This quatrain is a remarkable example of Nostradamus' uncanny ability to accurately forecast an amazing event which occurred in July 20th, 1969. This is one of the most demonstrative quatrains to be fulfilled in the 20th century.

It is fascinating that Nostradamus used "the Eagle" as an allusion to the U.S.A. in several quatrains, and the American lunar landing craft also happened to be named "the Eagle". Copernicus was the original mapper of the Moon, and considering that maps have four corners, the twisted phase "the corner of Luna" may be a salute to Copernicus. Oh, coincidentally, the American lunar landing craft landed near a rather large Moon crater named *Copernicus*!

Sept ans sera Philipp fortune prospère, Rebaissere des Arabes l'effort: Puis son midi perplexe rebours affaire, Jeune ogmion abîmera son fort.	9 - 89	Fortune will favor Philip for seven years. He will trample the vigorous efforts of the Arabs: Then during his noon a perplexing and contrary affair. The Young Ogmios will destroy his fortress.

A FUTURE MILITARY ACCIDENT IN EUROPE

"Fortune (prosperity and success) will favor Philip (possibly an allusion to a future British leader) for seven years (apparently Philip will enjoy a seven year period of success between two periods lacking in fortune). He (Philip) will trample (beat down or quash) the vigorous efforts (perhaps suggesting military efforts) of the Arabs (North African and Middle Eastern Muslims). Then during his Noon (suggesting the middle segment of his reign or term in office), a perplexing and contrary affair (occurs). Young Ogmios (an allusion to the future Celtic destroyer of the third Antichrist) will destroy his (Philip's) fortress." If "Philip" and "Ogmios" are allusions to future "persons", then in the opinion of the author, "Philip" will be British, and "Ogmios" will be French. The phrase "Young Ogmios" suggests that Ogmios (the person or thing that destroys Selin in quatrain #6-42) will be in the early phase of his development when he destroys "Philip's" fortress. Thus it appears that this quatrain might suggest that the French and British will be involved in a massive military accident of some type, at some point in the future.

L'horrible peste Perynté et Nicopolle, Le Chersonèse tiendra et Marceloyne, La Thessalie vastera l'Amphipolle, Mal inconnu, et le refus d'Anthoine.	9 - 91	The terrible plague at Perinthus and Nicopolis will over come the Peninsula and Macedonia; it will lay waste Thessaly and Amphipolis, an unknown evil, and refusal from Anthony.

CHEMICAL WARFARE IN GREECE AND MACEDONIA

"The terrible plague (suggesting disease by natural influences or by chemical, biological, or nuclear agents) at Perinthus (an ancient city in Thrace, modern Eski Eregli in Greece) and Nicopolis (an ancient Greek city, modern Perveza in western Greece) will overcome the Peninsula (suggesting the Greek peninsula) and Macedonia (a Balken region consisting of parts of Greece, Bulgaria, and the former Yugoslavia); it will lay waste Thessaly (a division of Greece along the Aegean Sea) and Amphipolis (located near modern Salonika, a Greek seaport and inlet of the Aegean Sea), an unknown evil (suggesting a new or mysterious plague or evil), and refusal from Anthony" (suggesting an Italian, Greek, or someone named "Anthony", perhaps a government leader or business man, who will consider this plague to be absolutely unacceptable). See quatrain #5-90.

De mer copies en trois parts divisées, À la seconde les vivres failliront, Désespérés cherchant champs Helisees, Premiers en brèche entrés victoire auront.	9 - 97	The forces of the sea divided into three sections, the second one to run out of supplies, in despair looking for the Elysian Fields, the first ones entering the breech will obtain victory.

NAVAL WARFARE

"The forces of the sea (unidentified naval forces) divided into three sections, the second one to run out of supplies, in despair looking for the Elysian Fields" (the Elysian Fields formed heaven in Greek mythology). This might suggest a territory in Greece, or some other location may be intended. "The first ones (an unidentified naval or land force) entering the breech (the rear of something, or possibly the first party to fire their guns) will obtain victory." The identity of the places and parties in this quatrain remain a mystery.

Navale pugne nuit sera superée, Le feu aux naves à l'Occident ruine: Rubriche neuve la grande nef colorée Ire à vaincu, et victoire en bruine.	9 - 100	A naval battle will be overcome at night. Fire in the ships, to the West ruin, a new trick, the powerful ship colored, anger to the vanquished and victory in a drizzle.

A WESTERN FLEET WILL BE DESTROYED

"A naval battle (involving unidentified parties) will be overcome (will transpire) at night (in an unnamed location). Fire in the ships, to the West ruin" (American, or naval ships from the New World, appear to be destroyed in this naval battle). Apparently, the Western fleet appears to fall prey to a "new trick" of some type, possibly involving a "re-coloring" of a powerful enemy naval ship. "Anger (hatred) to the vanquished (to the ruined ships of the West by their opponents), and victory in a drizzle" ("drizzle" is mentioned in several quatrains and appears to suggest a combination of rain and atomic fall-out which falls from the sky). Though we have no clues as to the time and location of this event, it seems to suggest doom for a Western fleet, followed by a victory. Since "drizzle" suggests a post - nuclear atmospheric condition, the "victory" mentioned here apparently occurs after a nuclear battle. See quatrain #5-35 in the United Kingdom chapter.

CENTURY X

Je pleure Nisse, Mannego, Pize, Gennes,
Sauone, Sienne, Capue, Modene Malte:
Le dessus sang et glaive par étrennes,
Feu, trembler terre, eau, malheureuse nolte.

10 - 60

I weep for Nice, Monaco, Pisa, Genoa, Savona, Siena, Capua, Modena, and Malta. For these places; bloody swords for the New Year's gift. The Earth will tremble, water, an unfortunate reluctance.

WAR, FLOODS, EARTHQUAKES IN EUROPE

Nostradamus "weeps for Nice (a city in France), Monaco (a European principality on the Mediterranean Sea), Pisa (a city in Italy), Genoa (a city in Italy), Savona (a city in northwestern Italy), Siena (in Italy), Capua (in Italy), Modena (in Italy), and Malta" (a British Commonwealth island in the Mediterranean Sea). These regions receive "bloody swords" (death by war) as a New Year's gift (around January 1st in an unknown year) by unnamed enemies. "The Earth will tremble (due to war, and or an earthquake?), water (suggesting flooding), an unfortunate reluctance". This suggests future trouble around Europe.

Près de Sorbin pour assaillir Ongrie,
L'hérault de Brudes les viendra avertir:
Chef Bizantin, Sallon de Sclauonie,
À loi d'Arabes les viendra convertir.

10 - 62

Near Sorbia in order to assail Hungary, the herald of Brudes travels to warn them. The Byzantine leader, Salona of Slavonia, he arrives to convert them to the laws of the Arabs.

ARABS TO INVADE SERBIA, CROATIA, & HUNGARY

"Near Sorbia (a former region of eastern Germany in Lusatia) in order to assail Hungary (a central European republic and new member of N.A.T.O.), the herald of Brudes (an unnamed envoy, perhaps from Buda, which was the capital of Turkish Hungary), travels to warn them (an unnamed party, perhaps suggesting the Hungarians). The Byzantine leader (a Turkish chief), Salona of Slavonia (a real, or fictitious name, of a future Croatian leader or general), he (an unnamed Arabic invader) arrives to convert them to the laws of the Arabs". It appears that Croatian and Turkish troops unite to confront an Arabic military invader as he approaches the region of Hungary. This quatrain references another Euro-Arabic conflict.

O vaste Rome ta ruine s'approche, Non de tes murs, de ton sang et substance: L'âpre par lettres fera si horrible coche, Fer pointu mis à tous jusqu'au manche.	10 - 65	O great Rome thy ruin draws near, not of your walls but of your blood and substance; the one who is harsh in letters will make so horrible a notch, pointed steel wounding all up to the hilt.

ROME ATTACKED BY ENEMIES

"O great Rome (the ancient capital of Italy and seat of the Vatican) thy (your) ruin draws near, not of your walls, but of your blood and substance" (suggesting injury to Italian citizens, their social customs, and their history and culture). The "one who is harsh in letters" (identity unclear, but perhaps a reference to an enemy) will take horrible actions, injuring the citizens. We have no clues regarding the time-frame of this awful future event.

L'armée de mer devant la cité tiendra, Puis partira sans faire longue allée: Citoyens grand proye en terre prendra, Retourner classe prendre grande emblee.	10 - 68	The army of the sea will stand before the city then depart without making a long passage. The great flock of citizens will be taken on land, a fleet returns to seize by great robbery.

NAVAL FORCES WILL PLUNDER A COASTAL CITY

"The army of the sea (naval and marine forces of an unnamed nation) will stand (will arrive) before the city (an unnamed city) then depart without making a long passage (a short voyage); the great flock of citizens (from which country?) will be taken on land (through some type of forced action), a fleet (of unknown identity) returns to seize (an unknown land) by great robbery". This is a very general quatrain with few specific clues.

	10 - 72	
L'an mil neuf cent nonante neuf sept mois,		In the year 1999, in the seventh month, from the sky will come
Du ciel viendra un grand Roi d'effrayeur:		the great King of Terror, bringing back to life the great
Ressusciter le grand Roi d'Angolmois,		King of the Mongols. Before and after, Mars to reign by good
Avant après Mars regner par bonheur.		fortune.

THE 1999 PROPHECY EXAMINED

The arrival of July, 1999, was a highly anticipated event by everyone familiar with the prophecies of Nostradamus. Most people expected the worst, but some people held a view of optimism regarding its outcome. Would it be the end of the world? Would it be the arrival of Nostradamus' so-called third Antichrist? Would a huge global war occur, or would nothing significant happen in 1999? All of these questions were fair to ask ourselves.

The following interpretation of this quatrain was written "before" July of 1999. However, on the next page, we have included some interesting commentary about this prophecy written "after" July of 1999 (see the notation for the *post facto* view).

"In the year 1999, in the seventh month (suggesting July, although the French word 'sept' might suggest the abbreviation for the English word September), from the sky (suggesting an aerial event, perhaps through means of aircraft, missiles or something else) will come the great (as in powerful) King of Terror (suggesting an unnamed leader of a nation who possess a powerful military, probably a foe of Europe and the West), bringing back to life (rebirthing) the great King of the Mongols (Genghiz Khan was the Mongolian king who conquered Asia in the 13th century, thus an Asian military leader seems to be suggested by this phrase). Before and after (some accident or military event in July of 1999), Mars (the symbolic planet of war in astrology) to reign by good fortune" (war appears to reign fortunate for an unnamed nation, or group of nations, "before and after" July of 1999).

If "the great King of the Mongols" is an allusion to Genghiz Khan, we should consider that by the year 1227 the Mongol empire of Khan stretched from the Pacific to the Black Sea. However, if the phrases "the great King of the Mongols" and "the great King of Terror" were both intended as allusions to present or future Asian military leaders, then there are many possibilities to consider.

It is also a possibility that "great King of the Mongols" is an allusion to the Mongol race (rather than a specific reference to the nation of Mongolia). The Chinese, Mongolians, Siberians, (and other oriental Asians) are all categorized as being members of this ethnic division of the human race. So in consideration of this fact, we could easily hypothesize that "the great King of the Mongols" is an allusion to China (the most economically and militarily powerful Mongol nation in 1999).

But could a war between North Korea and South Korea a possibility? They have been sworn enemies for four decades. Could there be more trouble in Iraq? Could there be trouble somewhere else in the Middle East or Europe? Could a future war between communist China and democratic Taiwan be referenced here? Could a war between India and Pakistan be a possibility here? Now that each of these two nations possess nuclear weapons the tension in Asia is rising.

Since July (or September) of 1999 is near the change of the millennium, and quatrains #2-46 and #10-74 suggest that warfare might possibly occur near the time of this change, one could wonder if these three quatrains could be connected with each other?

As of March of 1999, NATO nations began a grand aerial bombing campaign against the Yugoslavian military in Kosovo and Serbia. Although this event began four months before July (the "seventh" month), many of the parameters surrounding it appear to **fulfill** parts of this unique prophecy. In example, since this quatrain mentions war "before" July of 1999, would NATO's military campaign in Yugoslavia (which ended in June) qualify as the event referencing warfare <u>before</u> July of 1999?

In May, NATO air forces accidentally bombed the Chinese Embassy in Belgrade. Could this event be a reference to "bringing back to life the great king of the Mongols" (perhaps alluding to upsetting the Chinese)?

THE 2000 POST FACTO VIEW: Who, or what, was the great King of Terror (who came from the sky in July of 1999)? Was it an allusion to a person, or to something else? Over the last few decades this phrase has generally been interpreted as a reference, or allusion, to a human being (usually to a terrorist or Asian war lord). But that was speculation, and or assumption, on behalf of most Nostradamus authors (including myself).

Could the crash of John F. Kennedy Jr.'s airplane in July of 1999 fulfill the line "in the seventh month from the sky will come the great King of Terror"? Could the human fear of death and bodily injury be the intended definition of "the great King of Terror"? It might be possible! Since Nostradamus made several predictions about the death of President Kennedy (and Robert F. Kennedy), could a prediction about the death of John F. Kennedy Jr. fit into a familiar Nostradamian theme? It would certainly seem possible.

And in regards to China "the Great King of the Mongols", it should be noted that unknown to the public (until early August of 1999), China and Taiwan were involved in an aerial show-down during late July in the skies over the straits which separate the two nations. China, mad at NATO, was also upset with the Taiwanese for publicly suggesting that they were an independent state, free of Communist influence, with no plans of pursuing the "one China" policy of the main-land. Both nation's militaries were on a heightened state of alert as the Chinese captured a Taiwanese island and naval vessel. Due to this tension the air forces of both nations confronted each other in the skies over the strait. Fortunately, a full scale war was avoided.

In September of 1999, the Russian air force began an aerial bombing campaign in the break-away republic of Chechyna. Could this military campaign satisfy the second part of quatrain #10-72 referencing "war after July of 1999"? It would seem possible.

Could Nostradamus have intended July of 2000 (the completion of 1999 years and seven months)?

An révolu du grand nombre septième, Apparaîtra au temps jeux d'Hécatombe: Non éloigné du grand âge millième, Que les entrés sortiront de leur tombe.	10 - 74	The year of the great seventh number accomplished, it appears at the time of the games of slaughter, not far from the age of the great millennium, when the buried will come out of their graves.

WAR UNDERWAY BY THE YEAR 2001?

In light of the fact that the millennium is quickly approaching us, this is a very interesting quatrain. In the Preface, Nostradamus stated that all his prophecies would be fulfilled before the year 3797, thus the "millennium" mentioned here has to be a reference to either the year 2001 or 3001. The phrase "the year of the great seventh number accomplished" is unclear. However, if the millennium intended here is the year 2001, rather than 3001, then "the great seventh number" might be a reference to the years 2007 or 2017. "The games of slaughter" might suggest the Olympics, or it might be an allusion to warfare. "The buried" according to Nostradamus, will "come out of their graves" at this time (spooky sounding) which possibly suggests a period of war or flood, followed by mass death.

It is possible that the phrase "the great seventh number" might be an allusion to the seventh millenary mentioned in paragraph #5 in the Epistle, which is a reference to an unspecified period of time (speculated by some to begin in the year 2001). If Nostradamus intended this quatrain to be fulfilled around the year 2001 (rather than the year 3001), could this event be related to quatrain #10-72 or #2-46? This quatrain seems to suggest turmoil around the millennial change, however, the information it contains is somewhat ambiguous.

Pieds et Cheval à la seconde veille, Feront entrée vastient tout par la mer: Dedans le poil entrera de Marseille, Pleurs, cris, et sang, onc nul temps si amer.	10 - 88	Foot and horse at the second watch, they make an entry defeating all at sea. He will enter the port of Marseilles, tears, cries and blood, never were times so bitter.

AN ENEMY INVADES FRANCE

"Foot and horse at the second watch" (suggesting an infantry or cavalry attack during the 'second watch', an unknown time of day), they (an enemy of France) make an entry defeating all at sea (apparently this unidentified fleet will have just defeated an adversary at sea). He (an unnamed enemy of the French) will enter the port of Marseilles (a French seaport), tears (hardship), cries and blood (war), never were times so bitter" (for the French and possibly others).

À cité neuve pensif pour condamner, L'oiseau de proie au ciel se vient offrir: Après victoire à captifs pardonner, Cremone et Mantoue grands maux aura souffert.	1 - 24	The New City contemplates a condemnation. The bird of prey arrives and offers itself to the heavens. After the victory, the captives pardoned, Cremona and Mantua have endured great evil.

AMERICA WILL RESPOND TO AN INVASION OF ITALY

The following five quatrains pertain to "the New City", which appears to be an allusion to New (York) City, or in a broader sense, perhaps an allusion to the United States of America (or the New World). "The New City (New 'York' City, or the United States?) contemplates a condemnation (suggesting a military reprisal against an enemy?). The bird of prey (perhaps suggesting an eagle, an allusion to either a military power or a jet fighter) arrives (at an unidentified location) to offer itself to the heavens (departs on a military mission and commits itself to combat). After the victory (in a war involving the 'New City'), the captives pardoned (enemy prisoners of war released), Cremona (a city in northwestern Italy) and Mantua (a city in northern Italy) have endured great evil" (the evils associated with war). If "New City" is an allusion to America, and if "bird of prey" is a general reference to military might or military planes, this quatrain might suggest American involvement in a future war in Italy.

Ennosigée feu de centre de terre Fera trembler autour de cité neuve: Deux grands rochers longtemps feront la guerre, Puis Arethuse rougira nouveau fleuve.	1 - 87	Volcanic fire from the middle of the Earth will cause tremors around the New City. Two great rocks will war for a long time, and Arethusa reddens a new river.

EARTHQUAKES IN AMERICA FOLLOWED BY WAR?

"Volcanic fire from the middle of the Earth will cause tremors (suggesting earthquakes) around the New City". In a macro sense, "New City" could suggest the New World or America. In a micro sense it could suggest "New (York) City". Considering that three fault-lines exist on Manhattan Island a future earthquake in New York is a possibility (or the San Andreas or New Madrid fault lines). "Two great rocks (two great international powers) will war for a long time and Arethusa reddens a new river" (with blood?). An Arethusa is an orchid which is native to eastern North America, thus North America appears to be intended as one of the two great rocks. Arethusa is also an anagram for "EARTH, U.S.A.". This quatrain appears to suggest that a war involving two super powers will begin following earthquakes somewhere in North America. See quatrain #2-65 and #10-79.

Cinq et quarante degrés ciel brûlera, Feu approcher de la grande cité neuve: Instant grande flamme éparse sautera, Quand on voudra des Normans faire preuve.	6 - 97	At forty-five degrees the sky will burn, fire approaches the great New City. Instantly a huge scattered flame leaps up when they demand proof of the Normans.

AMERICA AND FRANCE ATTACKED

"At 45 degrees (of latitude north of the equator) the sky will burn, fire approaches the great New City (an allusion to New 'York' City, America, or the New World). Instantly (in the flash of a second) a huge scattered flame (a fire ball) leaps up (into the sky) when they (the Americans and other allies of France) will demand proof of the Normans" (the French), perhaps suggesting that France (and possibly other nations) will also be under attack, and the Americans will wonder if they too were hit by missiles (see quatrain #4-99). Another possibility is that other cities in western Europe along the 45th parallel (Lyons, Turin, Bordeaux, Milan, Naples and Genoa) might also be inferred. The state of New York, home to both "New (York) City" and the United Nations, has its southern boundary on the 40th parallel, and its northern boundary on the 45th parallel. France's southern boundary rests on the 41st parallel, and its northern boundary on the 50th parallel. Thus if New York City and France are the intended regions in the quatrain, the 45th parallel of latitude would certainly pass over these areas. Could this be connected to quatrains #4-99, #9-92, #10-72, or #10-79?

Le Roi voudra en cité neuve entrer, Par ennemis expugner l'on viendra: Captif libre faux dir et perpétrer, Roi dehors être, loin d'ennemis tiendra.	9 - 92	The King will wish to enter the New City, through his enemies they will arrive to subdue it, a captive freed falsely to speak and act, King to be outside, he stays far away from the enemy.

A PRESIDENT FLEES BEFORE AN ATTACK?

"The King (suggesting a king, president, or leader) will wish to enter the New City (suggesting New 'York' City, America, or the New World), through his enemies (the enemies of the King of the New City, possibly suggesting the enemies of the president of the United States), they (unnamed enemies of the New City) will arrive (by plane, ship, or via missiles?) to subdue it (to subdue the New City through means of terror and war), a captive freed falsely to speak and act (a hostage publically freed, but still under the control of his captors), King to be outside, he (the American president) stays far away from the enemy" (during the war). The key word phrase in this quatrain is "New City". Quatrain #6-97 seems to suggest a military attack on a great "New City". As previously stated, the New World, America, or New (York) City is indeed the meaning of "New City", then this quatrain might be a reference to events in America, during the war with the third Antichrist.

Perhaps the American president of this time will wish to visit New York City (or another region of America) after it is attacked by enemies. However, the president will be "outside" of American territory, perhaps located in a military secured zone, fortress, or underground command center of some type (far away from his enemies). Though it is possible that there is another intended meaning here, this interpretation follows the theme suggested by other quatrains.

Jardin du monde auprès de cité neuve, Dans le chemin des montagnes cavées: Sera saisi et plongé dans la Cuve, Buvant par force eaux soufre envenimées.	10 - 49	Garden of the world near the New City, in the road of the hollow mountains it will be seized and plunged in the tank, citizens forced to drink the waters poisoned with sulphur.

NEW YORK CITY'S WATER SUPPLY POISONED BY SULPHUR

"Garden of the world (a center of commerce) near the New City (New 'York' City) in the road of the hollow mountains (a 16th century description of streets in between modern day sky scrapers.), it will be seized (perhaps a water reservoir or pumping station) and plunged in the tank, citizens forced to drink the waters poisoned with sulphur." This seems to possibly suggest that terrorists dump toxic sulphur based chemicals into the water supply of New York City. Or, an alternate interpretation might be volcanic sulphurous gases mysteriously creep into New York City's (or another North American City's) water supply from beneath the ground, poisoning it. In alchemy, "sulphur" symbolized the flames of the lower world.

New York City

Senator Robert F. Kennedy

Le grand du foudre tombe d'heure diurne, Mal, et prédit par porteur postul'aire: Suivant présage tombe de l'heure nocturne, Conflit Reims, Londres, Etrusque pestifère.	1 - 26	The great man will fall in the day by lightning. Evil predicted by the bearer of a petition. According to the prediction another falls at night time. Conflict at Reims, London, plague in Tuscany. .

THE ASSASSINATION OF JFK AND RFK FORETOLD

The next three quatrains appear to pertain to the Kennedy brothers. "The great man (possibly suggesting President John Fitzgerald Kennedy, unquestionably a great man) will fall in daylight by lightning (falling by a rifle shot -- a flash followed by a thunderous sound). Evil predicted by the bearer of a petition" (refers to the uneasiness felt by the famous psychic/astrologer Jeane Dixon, who sent a letter to JFK through a mutual friend, warning him not to travel to the Southwest). Dixon also "predicted" the fall of "another" Kennedy, Senator Robert F. Kennedy, who "fell during the night time" at the hands of assassin Sirhan Sirhan in Los Angeles, California on June 6, 1968, while seeking the U.S. Presidency. The reference to "conflict at Reims (a city of northeastern France, the French), and London (the capital of England and of the United Kingdom), and plague in Tuscany" (a region of northwest Italy - the Italians), might apply to a time after this period, perhaps in the near future, but may suggest the sorrow felt worldwide by these senseless tragedies.

La mort subite du premier person-nage. Aura changé et mis un autre au regne: Tôt, tard venu à si haut et bas âge, Que terre et mer faudra qu'on le craigne.	4 - 14	The sudden death of the first personnage will have caused change and put another into sovereignty. Soon, but late come to so high a position, of young age, such by land and sea it will be necessary to fear him.

PRESIDENT KENNEDY, LBJ, THE CUBAN MISSILE CRISIS

"The sudden death (suggesting an assassination) of the first personnage (a leader of a nation, possibly suggesting President John F. Kennedy) will have caused change (suggesting the societal changes which occurred after the death of John F. Kennedy) and put another (suggesting Vice President Lyndon Johnson) into sovereignty (Johnson succeeding Kennedy as president). Soon, but late come to so high a position (the American presidency), of young age (John F. Kennedy became president at age 44), such by land and sea it will be necessary to fear him." This last line appears to be a general reference to the Cuban Missile Crisis of October, 1962. The Soviets and Cubans "feared" President Kennedy's show of military power, which successfully forced Soviet President Khrushchev, through an agreement, to remove the Soviet nuclear missiles from their launch sites in Cuba.

President John F. Kennedy

A view of the copse on the infamous grassy knoll in Dallas, Texas (Circa 1993).

L'oeuvre ancienne se parachevera, Du toit cherra sur le grand mal ruine: Innocent fait mort on accusera, Nocent caché taillis à la bruine.	6 - 37	The ancient work will be finished and from the roof; evil ruin will fall upon the great man. Being dead, they will accuse an innocent one of the deed, the guilty one hidden in the misty copse.

JFK, OSWALD, THE GRASSY KNOLL

"The ancient work (suggesting murder -- a work as ancient as the story of Able and Cain) will be finished from (will be made successful through the means of) the roof (suggesting the roof and upper floors of the Texas School Book Depository Building where Lee Harvey Oswald, the self described 'patsy' of the crime was located). Evil ruin (assassination) will fall upon the great man (President John F. Kennedy was unquestionably a great man). Being dead (Oswald was killed two days after his arrest by Jack Rubey during a prisoner transfer), they will accuse an innocent one (Lee Harvey Oswald) of the deed (the assassination), the guilty one (the true assassin) hidden in the misty copse" (a copse is a thicket of small trees or shrubs). This amazing quatrain appears to suggest that JFK's real assassin was hidden in the underbrush (in the misty copse) of the infamous grassy knoll, located just west of Dealy Plaza, and that Oswald would be the "fall-man". Great controversy still surrounds the November 22, 1963 assassination of American President John F. Kennedy, in Dallas, Texas. Nostradamus' description of this tragedy seems to parallel the views held by many experts on the conspiracy to assassinate President Kennedy.

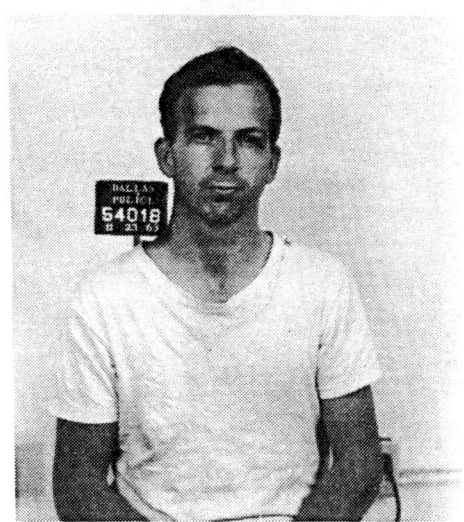
Lee Harvey Oswald was the alleged "lone assassin" who fired from the window, near the roof of the Texas School Book Depository.

Jack Ruby was the Dallas night club owner who shot Oswald while he was being transfered from the Dallas County Courthouse.

A view of Dealy Plaza (from the southwest, facing towards the northeast), circa 1963.

Un prince Anglois Mars à son coeur de ciel Voudra poursuivre la fortune prospère, Des deux duels l'un percera le fiel: Haï de lui bien aimée de sa mère.	3 - 16	An English prince, Mars in his heavenly heart, will pursue his prospering fortune. In one of his two duels, his pancreas is pierced, hated by him, yet well loved by his mother.

AN ENGLISH PRINCE WILL BE WOUNDED DURING COMBAT

And now the quatrains which pertain to Great Britain (The United Kingdom). This quatrain seems to apply to a future (or possibly present) member of the British Royal family during the time of a future war. "An English prince, Mars in his heavenly heart (which in astrological terminology could suggest 'war in his heart') will pursue his prospering fortune. In one of his two duels (an old fashioned duel, or modern combat?) his pancreas is pierced, hated by him (the English prince's enemy), yet well loved by his mother". Though Nostradamus uses the word "English", could Scottish be a possibility here? Could Prince William or Prince Harry (or their off-spring) be a possibility here? We have no clues regarding the intended time frame in this vague, yet interesting quatrain.

Sept fois changer verrez gent Britannique, Teints en sang en deux cent nonante ans: Franche non point appui Germanique Aries doute son pôle Bastarnan.	3 - 57	Seven times you will witness the British nation change, dyed in blood for 290 years. Free not through German support, Aries doubts his Polish pole.

CHANGES FOR BRITAIN

"Seven times you will witness the British nation (Great Britain or the United Kingdom) change (how and in what way?), dyed in blood (continually involved in military conflicts -- like colonization, conquest, domestic revolution, and defense against the attacks of foreign nations) for 290 years" (beginning on what date and ending on what date?). Free not through German support" (a reference to World Wars I and II). The phrase "Aries doubts his Polish pole" is unclear to me. However, Adolf Hitler was born under the astrological Sun sign of "Aries", and "Poland" was the first nation Germany invaded at the beginning of World War II in 1939. Though not specific (in terms of dates), this too is remains an interesting quatrain.

La grande Bretagne comprise d'Angleterre Viendra par eaux si haut à inonder La Ligue neuve d'Ausonne fera guerre, Que contre eux ils se viendront bander.	3 - 70	Great Britain, including England will be flooded by very deep waters. The new league in Ausonne will make war so that they will arrive to strive against them.

FUTURE FLOODING IN THE U.K.

"Great Britain, including England (the choice of words here 'Great Britain including England' suggests the modern day United Kingdom) will be flooded by very deep waters (suggesting a broad and massive flood). The new league (a political or military league?) in Ausonne (a city in Italy) will make war (against what nation?) so that they (an unnamed party) will arrive (where?) to strive against them" (who?). Could this quatrain be intended for some future time frame, during the era of the Great Flood, which Nostradamus mentions in the Preface? According to Nostradamus, the universal flood will occur sometime after the fall of the yet-to-arrive third Antichrist. Nostradamus commentator, Erika Cheetham, suggests that this quatrain pertains to British unification, and the flood of 1607.

Par cité franche de la grande mer Seline, Qui porte encore à l'estomac la pierre, Angloise classe viendra sous la bruine Un rameau prendre, du grand ouverte guerre.	5 - 35	For the free city of the great Crescent Sea, still carrying the stone in its stomach, an English fleet will arrive under the drizzle to seize a branch, war to be unfolded by the great one.

THE U.K. AND NAVAL COMBAT

"For the free city (suggesting a city under its own control, not yet attacked during a time of war?) of the great Crescent Sea (since there is no 'Crescent Sea', perhaps this is a symbolic reference to the seas or oceans near Turkey -- "the Crescent", or another Moslem nation), still carrying a stone in its stomach (perhaps suggesting that the intended region in the quatrain has endured pain through war, or some other type of hardship), an English (the United Kingdom's) fleet will arrive under the drizzle ('drizzle' appears to be a combination of rain and atomic fall-out which falls from the sky) to seize a branch (a peninsula or piece of land?), war to be unfolded by the great one" ("the great one" could suggest the U.K., one of her powerful allies, or perhaps a powerful unnamed opponent). See quatrain #9-100.

Au chef Anglois à Nimes trop séjour,
Devers l'Espagne au secours Aenobarbe:
Plusieurs mourront par Mars ouvert ce jour,
Quand an Artois faillir étoile en barbe.

5 - 59

The English chief stays too long at Nimes, towards Spain Aenobarbe arrives to the rescue. Many will die through war opened on that day, when a bearded star falls in Artois.

THE U.K., FUTURE WAR IN FRANCE AND SPAIN

"The English chief (an unnamed British leader) stays too long at Nimes (a city in southeast France), towards Spain Aenobarbe ('Aenobarbe', as stated in quatrain #5-45, appears to be an allusion to Charles De Gaulle, as stated in this quatrain "Aenobarbe" might be an allusion to the French military, whatever its meaning is, he or it) arrives to the rescue (of Spain). Many will die through (the) war opened on that day, when a bearded star (suggesting a comet, or possibly a rocket or missile?) falls in Artois" (a region of northern France). If comet is intended as the meaning of "bearded star" rather than a meteorite or rocket, then the years of 2061/62 would be the next time Halley's Comet returns. The Hale-Bopp comet passed near the Earth in early 1997, so this appears to be an unfulfilled prophecy.

Le tremblement de terre à Motara,
Cassich sainct George à demi perfondrez,
Paix assoupie la guerre éveillera,
Dans temple à Pâsques abîmes enfondrez.

9 - 31

The trembling of the Earth at Mortara, the tin island of St. George half sunk to the bottom; drowsy with peace, war will awaken at Easter, in the temple abysses will rip open.

THE U.K. AT WAR DURING EASTER

"The trembling of the Earth at Mortara (a city in Italy, approximately thirty-five miles southwest of Milan), the tin island of St. George (an allusion to the United Kingdom, or a literal reference to the British island of Mortara in the West Indies?) is half sunk to the bottom (suggesting that it is flooded, or damaged by war); drowsy with peace (this action seems to occur unexpectedly during a time of peace), war will awaken at Easter (a Christian festival commemorating the resurrection of Christ, celebrated on the first Sunday following the full Moon that occurs on, or next, after March 21). In the temple (suggesting a place of worship), abysses (a bottomless pit, hell, a profound void) will rip open". This quatrain seems to suggest that a massive earthquake will occur in Italy, followed by flooding in the U.K., resulting in war.

	9 - 74	
Dans la cité de Fertsod homicide, Fait, et fait multe bœuf arant ne macter: Retour encore auz honneurs d'Artemide, Et à Vulcan corps morts sepulturer.		Homocide within the city of Ferstod. The deed, many oxen not plowing a sacrifice. Once again returning to the honors of Artemis. To Vulcan, the bodies of dead ones to bury.

THE DEATH OF PRINCESS DIANA?

"Homocide (suggesting murder) within the city of Ferstod (which according to Nostradamus commentators Torné and Chavigny, is an allusion to the city of Paris). The deed (suggesting the deaths of Princess Diana, Dodi Al Fayed, and their driver), many oxen not plowing a sacrifice (obscure poetry). Once again returning to the honors of Artemis (Artemis, in Greek mythology, is the goddess of the hunt and the moon, and identified with the Roman goddess Diana, thus it appears to be an allusion to Princess Diana). To Vulcan (the Roman mythological god of fire) the bodies of dead ones (suggesting Princess Diana, Dodi, and their driver) to bury (suggesting the funerals of Princess Diana, Dodi, and their limo driver).

The key words here are homocide, Ferstod, and Artemis. If Chavigny and Torné's "Ferstod" indeed alluded to Paris, that would be interesting. Artemis is clearly an allusion to Princess Diana. The word "homocide" adds an element of mystery. Could this suggest the alleged negligence of the pursuing Paparazzi, the actions of the elusive Fiat, or some unknown mysterious assailant?

	10 - 22	
Pour ne vouloir consentir au divorce, Qui puis après sera connu indigne; Le Roi des Îles sera chassé par force, Mis à son lieu qui de roi n'aura signe.		For not wanting to consent to divorce, which afterwards will be recognized as unworthy, the King of the Islands, by force, will be driven out, and one put in his place who has no mark of kingship.

KING EDWARD VIII AND MRS. SIMPSON

This quatrain seems to be a reference to the conditions surrounding the relationship of King Edward VIII of Great Britain (the Duke of Windsor) and his deep sincere love for Mrs. Simpson, an American divorcee. King Edward (the "King of the Islands") abdicated the British throne to marry Mrs. Simpson (the Duchess of Windsor) and this action was not viewed as popular among the British people. The "one put in his place" is a reference to George VI, who was forced to accede to the British throne as King. It is interesting that Nostradamus used the phrase "who has no mark of kingship" as a description of King Edward VIII's replacement because many British citizens of that era felt that George VI lacked the leadership skills necessary to be successful as a king. This is one of the rare quatrains where Nostradamus deals with the subjects of love, marriage, and relationships.

Le chef de Londres par regne l'Americh, L'Île d'Escosse tempiera par gelée: Roi Reb auront un si faux Antechrist, Que les mettra trestous dans la mêlée.	10 - 66	The London chief through the realm of America, will soften the Island of Scotland by frost. King Reb facing an Antichrist so false, that he places them in conflict all together.

THE U.K. AND THE THIRD ANTICHRIST

"The London Chief (the British prime minister or perhaps the king) through the realm of L'Americh (apparently an allusion to America), will soften the Island of Scotland (placing it in a precarious situation) by frost (through something cold, or a "cold deal" of some type). King Reb (possibly an allusion to Rob Roy, the legendary Scottish leader, considered a "rebel" by the English, possibly suggesting that the British King referenced in this quatrain will be of Scottish descent), facing an Antichrist so false that he places them in conflict all together" (the third Antichrist will force America and the United Kingdom to unite as allies in a war against him). I should point out that some translations of line three read "Reb the King", "King Reb", "King and Reb", and "King and Rebel". *Roi Reb* is left to your interpretation. However you interpret line three, America and the U.K. are affected by a condition in Scotland, and the two nations will be faced by an Antichrist (the yet-to-arrive third Antichrist?) who leads them into a conflict. Though this quatrain "might" apply to World War II, it seems intended for future times.

Le grand empire sera par Angleterre, Le pempotam des ans plus de trois cents; Grandes copies passer par mer et terre, Les Lusitains n'en seront pas contents.	10 - 100	A great empire will be in England, the all powerful for more than 300 years. Great forces pass by land and sea. The Luistanians will not be satisfied.

ENGLAND WILL BE ALL POWERFUL FOR 300 YEARS

There is no doubt that England (or Great Britain, or the United Kingdom) is a powerful land with a great history. Allied soldiers made it a base in World Wars I and II (the reference to "great forces pass by land and sea"). How the Portuguese (the Luistanians) fit into this quatrain is not very clear. Could this be a reference to a future war situation which results between the United Kingdom and an enemy, which somehow involves forces occupying Portugal, or is there another meaning here? As in quatrain #3-57, we have no clues regarding the dates of the beginning (or end) of this 300 year period. What is your guess?

Par l'univers sera fait un Monar-Mue,
Qu'en paix et vie ne sera longuement:
Lors se perdra la piscature barque,
Sera régie en plus grand détriment.

1 - 4

In the world there will be a monarch who will have no peace and a short life: At this time the fishing bark will be lost, governed to its greater detriment.

THE THIRD ANTICHRIST TO VEX THE VATICAN

The next thirteen quatrains appear to pertain to the yet to arrive third Antichrist. Though this quatrain has been attributed to the Napoleonic era, or to the conditions of World War II, it may have been intended for the future times of the third Antichrist.

De l'Orient viendra le coeur Punique
Fâcher Hadrie et les hoires Romulides,
Accompagné de la classe Libyque,
Trembler Melites et proches îles vides.

1 - 9

From the Orient will arrive the Punic heart, to vex "Adria" and the heirs of Romulus, accompanied by the Libyan fleet, the temples at Malta will be trembling while the neighboring isles empty.

THE THIRD ANTICHRIST

"From the Orient (suggesting eastern Asia, or possibly the Middle East) will arrive the Punic heart ('Punic' infers ancient Carthage or Phoenia, the Romans considered the Carthaginians to be treacherous in character, thus "treacherous heart" may be suggested here, perhaps a reference to the third Antichrist), to vex Adria (of the Adriatic Sea, suggesting Italy) and the heirs of Romulus (the son of Mars in Roman mythology, suggesting the Italians), accompanied by the Libyan fleet (the naval forces of this Middle Easterner or Asian man will be allied with, and accompanied by, the Libyan fleet), the temples at Malta (a British Commonwealth island south of Sicily in the Mediterranean Sea) will be trembling while the neighboring isles empty" (inhabitants of the islands in the Mediterranean Sea leave in a mass exodus to avoid the combat). This quatrain appears to be a reference a future naval (and possibly land) conflict which involves an alliance of Asian (or Middle Eastern) nations and Libyan forces, against Italian and European nations, somewhere in the Adriatic and Mediterranean Seas. Perhaps this event pertains to the times of the third future Antichrist.

L'Oriental sortira de son siège,
Passer les monts Apennins voir la Gaule:
Transpercera le ciel, les eaux et neige,
Et un chacun frappera de sa gaule.

2 - 29

The man from the East will leave his seat and will cross the Apennines to see Gaul. He will cross through the sky, the seas and the snows and will strike everyone with his rod.

ANTICHRIST III WILL JOURNEY TO FRANCE

"The man from the East (from the Middle East or Asia?) will leave his seat (departing from his homeland) and will cross the Apennines (a mountain range in Italy) to see Gaul (the ancient name for France). He will cross through the sky (suggesting travel by plane), the seas (suggesting ocean travel), and the snows (land travel during the winter) and will strike everyone (along his route) with his rod" (an allusion to his powerful his war machine). As in quatrain #1-9, an Asian leader travels from "the East" to Europe (from his unnamed homeland to Italy and then to France) and makes war upon every nation he passes through in route to France. The "East", as used here, is non-specific and could suggest either the Middle East, central Asia, or the Orient. This quatrain could easily be a reference to the future third Antichrist.

Un qui des dieux d'Annibal infernaux
Fera renaître, effrayeur des humains
Onc plus d'horreur ni plus pire journaux
Qu'avint viendra par Babel aux Romains.

2 - 30

A man who rebirths the infernal Gods of Hannibal, the terror of all mankind. Never more horror nor worse of times in the past than will come to the Romans through Babel.

THE THIRD ANTICHRIST WILL INVADE ITALY

"A man (an unnamed individual) who rebirths (brings back to life) the infernal (relating to hell or the dead) Gods of Hannibal (Hannibal was the notorious Carthaginian general from 218 B.C. who left North Africa and crossed over the Alps with elephants to make war on his Roman enemies in Europe), the terror of all mankind (which might suggest the third Antichrist). Never more horror nor worse of times in the past will come to the Romans (an allusion to the Italians) through Babel" (an ancient city in Mesopotamia, now Iraq). This is a reference to a conflict involving Italy and a militant North African or Middle Eastern leader, and/or perhaps with the future third Antichrist. It is unclear if the unnamed man responsible for this rebirth of terror is a native of from Babel.

L'aîsné vaillant de la fille du Roi, Repoussera si profond les Celtiques, Qu'il mettra foudres, combien en tel arroi Peu et loin, puis profond és Hesperique.	4 - 99	The brave eldest son of a King's daughter will hurl the Celts back far. He will cast thunderbolts, so many in such an array, both near and distant, then deep into the "the Lands of the West".

EUROPE AND THE NEW WORLD ATTACKED

"The brave eldest son of a king's daughter (identity unknown) will hurl the Celts (the people of western and central Europe, including the Britons and the French) back far (suggesting great damage through war). He (the eldest son of the unnamed king) will cast thunderbolts (suggesting missiles or futuristic weaponry), so many and in such an array (suggesting a large quantity in a pre-arranged order), both near and distant (throughout Europe and elsewhere) then deep into the Lands of the West" (suggesting America, Canada, and the New World). This quatrain is most likely pertains to the war with the future third Antichrist. As in quatrain #4-99, it appears that France and Britain will be attacked first, then shortly afterward, the New World. Since Europe is closer to the Middle East and Asia than the New World is, from a military perspective, this would make sense.

Du pont Exuine, et la grand Tartarie, Un Roi sera qui viendra voir la Gaule, Transpercera Alane & l'Armenie, Et dedans Bisance lairra sanglante gaule.	5 - 54	From beyond the Black Sea and great Tartary, there will be a King who will come to visit Gaul. He will penetrate through Alania and Armenia and inside Turkey, he will leave his bloody rod.

THE THIRD ANTICHRIST WILL DEVASTATE TURKEY

"From beyond the Black Sea and great Tartery (western Asia) there will be a King (perhaps the third Antichrist?) who will come to visit Gaul (the ancient name of France). He will penetrate (or tear) through Alania (a region of southwestern Russia near the Caucasus Mountains, north of Georgia and to the west of Chechnya) and Armenia (a country bordering Russia, Turkey, and Iran) and inside Turkey he will leave his bloody rod" (suggesting the out-break of war followed by a military occupation). This is an interesting quatrain from a military perspective since it reveals a land route of a future invasion of Europe. If this "King" begins his journey in Alania, perhaps he's Russian. If he passes <u>through</u> Alania, perhaps he is from Iran, or another country in the Middle East or Asia. This quatrain duplicates the theme of quatrain #2-29 (a man from the East who travels to France with a rod).

De Fez le regne parviendra à ceux d'Europe, Feu leur cité, et lame trenchera: Le grand d'Asie terre et mer à grande troupe, Que bleus, pers, croix à, mort dechassera.	6 - 80	From Fez the realm will reach out to the people of Europe. Cities blazing, the sword will cut; the powerful one of Asia with a great troop by land and sea so that "blues" and "bluishgreens", the cross will pursue to death.

THE THIRD ANTICHRIST AND HIS NORTH AFRICAN ALLIES ATTACK EUROPE

"From Fez (a city which is the religious center of the country of Morocco in North Africa), the realm (various unnamed provinces of North Africa) will reach out to (attack) the people of Europe (the nations of N.A.T.O.). Cities blazing (due to war), the sword will cut (suggesting warfare); the powerful one of Asia (the future third Antichrist, or someone else?) with a great troop (armed forces), by land and sea (will attack Europe) so that blues and bluishgreens (possibly a reference to the helmet color of the future invaders of Europe), the cross (suggesting Christian forces from various nations, who in return) will pursue (the invading enemy) to (their) death". As in quatrains #1-9, 2-29, and 5-54, a powerful man from "the East" (the Middle East or Asia) united with North Africans (as in quatrain #1-9) arrives to trouble Europe.

L'antechrist trois bien tôt annihilés, Vingt et sept ans sang durera sa guerre: Les hérétiques morts, captifs, exilés. Sang corps humain eau rougie grêler terre.	8 - 77	By the Antichrist three very soon annihilated, twenty seven years his war will last. The heretics are dead, and the captives exiled; human blood to hail on land and sea.

THE THIRD ANTICHRIST AND HIS 27 YEAR WAR

"By the Antichrist (suggesting the future third Antichrist) three very soon annihilated (suggesting that the third Antichrist goes to war with three other nations?), twenty seven years his war will last (the war with the future third Antichrist will last for the duration of twenty seven years). The heretics (persons who dissent from the dogmas of Christianity) are dead (due to war?) and the captives exiled (prisoners freed); human blood to hail on land and sea" (due to this futuristic 27 year long war). This appears to be a demonstrative reference to the future third Antichrist. For what it may be worth, an alternate translation of line one could be "Antichrist three very soon annihilated".

	9 - 51	
Contre les rouges sectes se banderont, Feu, eau, fer, corde par paix se minera: Au point mourir ceux qui machineront, Fors un que monde surtout ruinera.		Against the red ones sects will unite, through fire, water, steel, the rope will weaken through peace. Those who plot at the point of dying, except one who above all, will ruin the world.

ANTICHRIST III WILL PLOT AGAINST THE CHURCH

Regional sects will unite against "the red ones" (possibly an allusion to Catholic cardinals, the pope, the Vatican, or Christian nations). "Through fire, water, steel (war and flooding?) the rope (suggesting military might, or Christianity?) will weaken through peace (through actual peace, or through a falsely constructed peace?). Those who plot (against the "red ones"?) at the point of dying, except one (the future third Antichrist's nation?) who above all (above all the other powers plotting with him) will ruin the world" (will plunge the world into dark chaos). An interesting quatrain which appears to spell trouble for the future of Christian nations.

	9 - 73	
Dans Fois entré Roi ceiulee Turban, Et regnera moins évolu Saturne: Roi Turban blanc Bizance coeur ban, Sol, Mars, Mercure près la hurne.		The Blue Turban King will enter Foix, he will reign for less than a revolution of Saturn; White Turban King, Turkish heart banished, when the Sun, Mars and Mercury near Aquarius.

THE THIRD ANTICHRIST?

"The Blue Turban King (which might suggest the third Antichrist) will enter Foix (a city in France), he (the third Antichrist) will reign for less than a revolution (or perhaps evolution) of Saturn (which is 27.5 years); White Turban King (identity unclear, perhaps a Turkish Muslim), Turkish heart banished (perhaps the White Turban King is a Turkish leader who leaves Turkey due to war), when the Sun, Mars, and Mercury near Aquarius" (see the astrological tables for the many dates this transit occurs). If the Blue Turban King is indeed an allusion to the third Antichrist, he appears to affect Turkey on his route to France (as mentioned in quatrain #2-29 and 5-54). Could Selin (mentioned in quatrains # 1-94, #4-77, #6-42, #6-58, and #6-78) be the same person as the "Blue Turban King"?

Tache de meurtre, enormes adultères, Grand ennemi de tout le genre humain: Que sera pire qu'aieuls, oncles ni pères, En fer, feu, eaux, sanguin et inhumain.	10 - 10	Stained with murder and enormous adulteries, great enemy of all humanity, he will be worse than his forefathers, in hell, fire and waters, inhuman and bloody.

THE THIRD ANTICHRIST

The third of Nostradamus' so-called Antichrists will be "worse" than any Antichrist before him. Due to modern technology, the third Antichrist's killing ability will be exponentially greater than was Napoleon's and Hitler's.

Le chef de Londres par regne l'Americh, L'Îsle de l'Escosse tempiera par gelee: Roi Reb auront un si faux antechrist Que les mettra trestous dans la mêlée.	10 - 66	The London chief through the realm of America will soften the island of Scotland by frost. King Reb facing an Antichrist so false, that he places them in conflict all together.

THE U.K. AND THE THIRD ANTICHRIST

"The London Chief (the British prime minister or perhaps the king) through the realm of L'Americh (apparently an allusion to America), will soften the Island of Scotland (placing it in a precarious situation) by frost (through something cold, or a "cold deal" of some type). King Reb (possibly an allusion to Rob Roy, the legendary Scottish leader, considered a "rebel" by the English, possibly suggesting that the British King referenced in this quatrain will be of Scottish descent), facing an Antichrist so false that he places them in conflict all together" (the third Antichrist will force America and the United Kingdom to unite as allies in a war against him). I should point out that some translations of line three read "Reb the King", "King Reb", "King and Reb", and "King and Rebel". *Roi Reb* is left to your interpretation. However you interpret line three, America and the U.K. are affected by a condition in Scotland, and the two nations will be faced by an Antichrist (the yet-to-arrive third Antichrist?) who leads them into a conflict. Though this quatrain "might" apply to World War II, it seems intended for future times.

Tant attendu ne reviendra jamais, Dedans l'Europe en Asie apparaîtra: Un de la ligue issu du grand Hermés, Et sur tous Rois des Orients croîtra.	**10 - 75**	Long awaited he will never return in Europe, he will appear in Asia; issued from the great league of Hermes, he will rise above all the Kings in the Orient.

THE THIRD ANTICHRIST TO BE BORN IN ASIA

"Long awaited he (the third Antichrist?) will never return (be born again) in Europe, (as were Antichrists I and II), he will appear (will be born the next time) in Asia, issued from the great league of Hermes (in Greek mythology Hermes was the god of commerce, cunning, and theft -- he was also the conductor of 'the dead' to Hades). He (the third Antichrist or someone else?) will rise above all the other kings (or leaders) of the Orient" (suggesting Asia). Though China and eastern Asia are perhaps suggested here, during the era of the Renaissance, Europeans considered the "Orient" to consist of the lands and regions east of the Mediterranean Sea (which includes central Asia and the region we refer to in modern times as the Middle-East).

Nul de l'Espaigne, mais de l'antique France	5 - 49	Not from Spain but from ancient France, he will be elected for the trembling papacy. He will make a promise to an enemy who creates a cruel plague in his realm.
Ne sera élu pour le tremblante nacelle,		
À l'ennemi sera faite fiance,		
Qui dans son regne fera peste cruelle.		

A FUTURE POPE WILL BE FROM FRANCE?

Now the quatrains which pertain to the Catholic Church. This is an interesting chapter considering the fact that there are over 100 million Catholics in the world. "Not from Spain, but from ancient France, he (an unnamed future pope) will be elected for the trembling papacy (elected as pope during a period of confusion). He (this futuristic pope) will make a promise (of some type) to an enemy (an unnamed enemy) who creates a cruel plague (a pestilence or calamity) in his realm" (apparently this unnamed futuristic enemy of the Church will be responsible for creating havoc in the 'realm' of Christendom). According to Nostradamus commentator John Hogue, Poland (the birth place of Pope John Paul II) was once part of ancient France, thus, in his opinion, Pope John Paul II is the pope suggested in this quatrain. Another possibility is that the pope after Pope John Paul II will be French. Some have speculated that the present Cardinal of Paris, His Eminence Jean' Marrie Lustiger, might possibly be the future *De Gloria Olivae* (as described in the quatrain below).

Par le trépas du très-vieillard Pontife	5 - 56	Due to the death of a very old pope, will be elected a Roman of young age. It will be said of him that he weakens the Seat, but long will he sit and in biting activity.
Sera elu Romain de bon âge:		
Qui sera dit que le siège débiffe,		
Et long tiendra et de piquant ouvrage.		

A FUTURE POPE WILL BE ITALIAN?

"Due to the death of a very old pope (possibly suggesting Pope John Paul II, or his successor), will be elected a Roman (possibly suggesting an Italian) of young age (a young man). It will be said of him that he weakens the Holy Seat (the Papacy), but long will he sit and in biting activity". It appears that this future pope will be criticized for some of his actions and possibly accused of weakness or negligence, but in reality, this pope will hold a strong reign over the Catholic Church and will occupy the papacy for many years. Could this quatrain pertain to the future times of *De Gloria Olivae* (Of the Glory of the Olive Tree) or to *Petrus Romanus* (Peter the Roman) who St. Malachi, a 12th century Irish Catholic priest, prophesied would be the last popes of the Roman Catholic Church (after Pope John Paul II)? According to St. Malachi, who prophetically nick-named every future pope of the Catholic Church (according to their personal spiritual attributes), there will only be "two" more popes. Peter the Roman (according to Catholic prophecy) will feed his flock through tribulation and persecution, after which the seven-hilled city will be destroyed, and the judge will judge.

Persécutée sera de Dieu l'Eglise, Et les saints Temples seront expoliez, L'enfant la mère mettra nue en chemise, Seront Arabes aux Pollons ralliés.	5 - 73	The Church of God will be persecuted, and the church buildings will be pillaged; the child will put his mother out in her shift. The Arabs will be allied with the poles.

CHRISTIANS PERSECUTED, FUTURE POLAR SHIFT

This is a clear warning that "the Church of God" (an allusion to the Christian religion and its followers) will be heavily persecuted at some point in the future, and "the church buildings (holy temples) will be pillaged (by unnamed parties). The child will put his mother out in her shift" (is perhaps a reference to a polar shift, or a symbolic reference to something new replacing something old, or something which gives birth to something new). The final line, if "Saudi" Arabia is inferred, may suggest the political alliance that existed during Operation Desert Storm in 1991. Saudi Arabia and the nations of the Arctic pole (the United States and Russia) were generally "allied" with one another during Operation Desert Storm.

Could "the child" in line three, be a clever allusion to *El Nino* (the massive pool of warm water from the equatorial Pacific which alters global weather patterns due to its affect on trade winds and the jet stream)? Peruvian fisherman named this weather phenomena after the Christ child, since it arrived near Christmas time ("el nino" means male child in Spanish). Could future western expansion of *El Nino* act as a catalyst for a futuristic polar shift at some point in the 21st century or beyond?

Après le siége tenu dix sept dix-sept ans, Cinq changeront en tel révolu terme: Puis sera l'un élu de même temps, Qui des Romains ne sera trop conforme.	5 - 92	After the See has been held for seventeen years, five will change within the same time frame. Then a man will be elected during this time who will not be very comforting to the Romans.

THE ARRIVAL OF A NEW POPE

"After the See (suggesting the papacy) has been held for 17 years (has been occupied by one pope for a 17 year period), five (somethings or someones -- probably popes) will change within the same time frame. Then a man will be elected (as a pope, or as the leader of some nation?) during this time who will not be very comforting (agreeable) to the Romans (suggesting the citizens of Italy or the citizens of the Vatican?). This "newly elected man" is probably a reference to a pope. Pope Pius XII held the papacy for 19 years (not 17 years). From 1958 to 1975, (17 years after the death of Pope Pius XII, only two popes were elected. So popes does not fit here. Could the "change of five" be a reference to unnamed elected officials? The exact meaning here is unclear.

L'union feinte sera peu de durée,   6 - 20   The feigned union will last a short time, some changed, the greater part reformed. In vessels people will sustain injuries, then Rome will have a new Leopard.
Des uns changés réformés la plupart:
Dans les vaisseaux sera gent endurée,
Lors aura Rome un nouveau Léopard.

NAVAL WARFARE, A PAPAL TRANSITION

"The feigned union (some type of make-believe union involving unnamed parties) will last a short time (the unnamed parties involved in this feigned union do not remain allied for very long). Some changed, the greater part (of some conditions or lands are) reformed (in some unknown way). In vessels (naval vessels?) people will sustain injuries (due to war?), then Rome (the capital of Italy, and seat of the Vatican) will have a new Leopard" (suggesting a new pope?). It appears that during a time of naval warfare, a new pope (if "Leopard" is indeed an allusion to a pope) will arrive in the Vatican. Could this "feigned union" be a reference to the friendship between Russia and the United States, or is another "feigned union" of unnamed parties intended here? Could this prophecy pertain to furture political conditions which might exist when a new pope is elected after the death of Pope John Paul II? Or does this prophecy pertain to the pope who will one day replace Pope John Paul II's successor?

Par les déserts de lieu libre et farouche,   6 - 82   Through the deserts of the free wild place, the nephew of the powerful Pope will wander. Killed by seven with a heavy club, by those who later occupy the Chalice.
Viendra errer neveu du grand Pontife:
Assomé à sept avec lourde souche,
Par ceux qu'après occuperont le Cyphe.

A POPE'S NEPHEW

"Through the deserts of the free wild place (an unnamed geographic region), the nephew (an unnamed male person) of the powerful pope (an unnamed future pope) will wander (why and for what reason?). Killed by seven with a heavy club (the powerful pope, his nephew, or something else, appears to die due to the actions of seven people or seven somethings), by those (the 'seven' or some other group) who will later occupy the Chalice (a cup for the consecrated wine of the Eucharist, as used here, possibly a symbolic reference to the Papacy and/or the Vatican). Though this is a vague quatrain, it appears to suggest that an enemy of the Church will one day occupy the Vatican after a period of conflict. One could wonder if the term "nephew" was intended literally or symbolically?

Pol mensolee mourra trois lieues du rosne, Fuis les deux prochains tarasc destrois: Car Mars fera le plus horrible trône, De Coq et d'Aigle de France frères trois.	8 - 46	He will pass on at St.Paul-de-Mausole three leagues from the Rhône, the two nearest flee the oppressed monster. When Mars will take up his horrible throne, the Cock and the Eagle, France and the three brothers.

THE PASSING OF A POPE?

"He (suggesting a pope, or a world leader?) will pass on (die) at St.-Paul-de-Mausole (which according to Leoni, is a convent in Saint Rémy in France) three leagues from the Rhône (approximately 9 miles from the Rhône River). The two nearest (nations or individuals?) flee the oppressed monster (an unnamed enemy). When Mars (suggesting war) will take up his horrible throne, the Cock (France) and the Eagle (the U.S.A.), France and the three brothers" (the "three brothers" might refer to the three Kennedy brothers, which is an allusion to their homeland -- the U.S.A.). Some believe this quatrain might be a reference to the present pope, Pope John Paul II (due to the inclusion of the word 'Pol' in line 1 of the quatrain). Pope John Paul VI died three miles (but not three leagues) from Rome (but not the river Rhône) in 1978. The "he" character in this quatrain is thought to represent a pope, since according to Nostradamus commentator Edgar Leoni, "Pol mensolee" is a reference to St.-Paul-de Mausole, a Catholic convent in France. Perhaps this event occurs during a period when France and the United States will be involved in some type of military event.

Des gens d'Église sang fera épanché, Comme de l'eau eu si grande abondance: Et d'un long temps ne sera retranché, Ve ve au clerc ruine et doléance.	8 - 98	Of the church men the blood will be poured forth as abundant as water. For a long time it will not be restrained, woe, woe, for the clergy, ruin and grief.

THE FUTURE PERSECUTION OF CHRISTIANS

At some point in the future, Nostradamus sees an unrestrained ruin and grief for the clergymen (suggesting a lengthy period of persecution for Christians and their clergy). Could this be linked to a Euro/Arabic conflict, a social or religious revolution, or to the times of the third Antichrist (as referenced in paragraph #33 of the Epistle)? This certainly appears to be a serious warning, yet we have no clues as to a date associated with this horrible time. In the Epistle, Nostradamus states that a persecution of this nature will occur when Aquilon (Russia) is allied with the Easterners (unnamed orientals, Asians or Middle Easterners). This quatrain is very similar to quatrain #5-73.

Par la puissance des trois Rois temporels, En autre lieu sera mis le saint Siège: Où la substance et de l'esprit corporel, Sera remise et reçus pour vrai siège.	8 - 99	Through the powers of three temporal kings, the holy seat will be moved to another place, where the substance of the body and the spirit will be restored and received as the true see.

ONE DAY THE VATICAN WILL RELOCATE

"Through the powers of three temporal kings (suggesting three unnamed short lived leaders from unnamed regions), the holy seat (the papal government and residence of the pope -- presently located near Rome) will be moved to another place (to a new unnamed location) were the substance (the spiritual substance) of the body and spirit (of Christ) will be restored and received as the true See" (the new true seat of the Catholic Church). We are not told how or why these three unnamed kings are temporal. Perhaps their reigns will be cut short due to a future war. Nostradamus fails to provide us with a clue as to the future location of the Vatican. "Temporal kings" are also mentioned in the Epistle.

La grande étoile par sept jours brûlera, Nuée fera deux soleils apparoir: Le gros mâtin toute nuit hurlera Quand grand pontife changera de terroir.	2 - 41	The great star will burn for seven days and the cloud will make the Sun appear double. The big mastiff will howl all night when the great pontiff changes his countries.

A POPE WILL FLEE THE VATICAN DURING WAR

"The great star will burn for seven days and the cloud will make the Sun appear double (possibly suggesting that a nuclear explosion will burn in an unnamed geographical area for seven days after exploding, or this might be a reference to a future astrological event). The big mastiff (an allusion to "the dogs of war") will howl all night (suggesting that a battle is opened during the night-time hours) when the great pontiff (an unnamed future pope -- perhaps the future popes *Of the Glory of the Olive Tree*, or *Peter the Roman*?) changes his countries" (suggesting that the future unnamed pope will flee from one geographic territory, from the Vatican City in Rome, Italy, to another country, in order to avoid unnecessary exposure to some type of danger). Perhaps this is a reference to future trouble during a Euro/Arabic conflict or the war with the third Antichrist. This quatrain is consistent with the theme of quatrain #8-99 above -- a future change of location for the Vatican (the official residence of the pope, and seat of the Roman Catholic Church).

THE ASTROLOGICAL QUATRAINS

As an exercise in prudence, assumptive (and premature) judgements regarding the quatrains have purposely been avoided, and or minimized in this book. However, at some point we had to decide whether or not Nostradamus included planetary positions in some quatrains as a means to provide us clues as to when various prophecies might be fulfilled, or whether he included them as a ploy to confuse our interpretation. With this question in mind, it was decided that Nostradamus included astrological data for our guidance.

The study of the positions and aspects of heavenly bodies and how they effect human life, came to be known as *astrology*. The word comes from *astra*, the Latin word for stars, and *logos*, which relates to logic and words. It means "speaking the language of the stars" or "searching for the logic of the stars".

At one time astrologers were held in very high regard and were often employed by kings and queens who called upon their advice in guiding their kingdoms.

Astrology is the mother (or precursor) of the modern science of astronomy. However, in ancient times and up until the end of the Renaissance, learned men considered astrology to be a science. In this regard, astrology is actually one of the oldest sciences (or pseudosciences -- depending upon your point of view) on Earth.

Astrology should not be misperceived as a religion. This is grossly incorrect and any astrologer will tell you this if asked. Astrology does not constitute a "worship" of the stars as some uninformed people might believe. That would be analogous to saying biologists "worship" the frogs that they dissect. Astrology consists of a "study" (not a worship). In reality, astrology is an interpretative *fine art* based upon the "science" of astronomy. It consists of correlating celestial cycles (and positions) with terrestrial events and experiences.

We are neither advocating the fine art of astrology in this book, nor are we attempting to denounce it. Considering that Nostradamus was both a physician, as well as an astrologer, it would have been senseless for us to have left this topic unaddressed. To delve too deeply into the definition of astrology, as well as all the parameters which effect it, would require another book entirely. Thus we are providing readers who may have little knowledge of this subject with a brief overview.

Simply stated, at the moment of your birth the planets were at a place and time that they will never occupy again. This "moment in time" at your birth is where astrologers begin your personal astrological clock. This birth information is required to construct a natal chart. A natal chart can be made for any person or object (i.e., airplanes, houses, cars, etc.). Even intangible things like nations, and political movements, can have charts cast for them if an exact time and place of birth (or creation) can be determined.

There are many different parts to an astrological chart. A chart is split into twelve different compartments and each of these compartments is called a "house". Each "house" represents a part of your life where things happen. There are houses that rule your home, children, wealth, travel, etc.. For example, your ascendent (or rising sign) is one of the boundaries of the first house, which rules your inner self.

When we place all your planets on your chart, they aspect each other. For instance, if two planets are directly opposite of each other, this aspect would be given the name "opposition". Some of the various aspects include sextile, semi sextile, square, trine, opposition, and conjunction.

In the opinion of astrologers, the movement and positions of the planets affect events in your life. Each planet has meaning. For example, Mars is related to energy, pain, fire and war. Venus is related to love and comfort. Jupiter is usually associated with money and fortune. Mercury is associated with the mind, thought and communication. Unique attributes exist for all the ten planets of our solar system (including our Sun and Moon). The signs the planets are in tell us what action or "energy" the planets are trying to make, which in turn, theoretically impact the events in our daily lives.

Astrology is very intricate. There are asteroids, nodes, mid points, and many additional facets to a chart. Unlike the simplistic information contained within astrology columns of daily newspapers (which only pertains to one's Sun sign), a properly constructed natal chart reveals a more complete (and complex) view of the individual (or thing).

In addition to utilizing standard methods of astrology, Nostradamus may have used Horary astrology. This is the casting of a chart using a question of any sort, i.e.:

"Where is my billfold?"

"Will taxes rise?"

Using the exact time the question was asked, the question can supposedly be answered. You can make a chart for the future, the past, or even to just ask a question. Because of the perfection of the movement of the stars and planets, astrologers can attempt to pinpoint events and answer startling questions.

A book known in astrology as an ephemeris, provides us with tables which tell us the coordinates of all the planets at all times of the year. These tables provide us with the times that these planetary positions (referred to as "transits" in astrology) occur. This is how we derived the specific dates stated in the quatrains (and astrological tables) included in this chapter.

Some of the quatrains included in this chapter may be intended to be fulfilled in the 20th or 21st centuries and some of them may not be, some may be intended for the 22nd century or beyond. Bearing this in mind, we have looked up the stated planetary positions (or transits) to see when these positions will occur exactly, and when they "come close" to occurring. Most of the dates when these transits occur "exactly" are listed in my interpretations under the quatrains. The astrological tables in the back of this chapter list both the exact dates these positions occur, as well as the dates these positions "come close" to occurring. My research began with the year 1994 and ended with the year 2050.

Thus if Nostradamus did in fact include planetary positions in the quatrains as a means of guidance, and if some of these quatrains were intended by Nostradamus to be fulfilled during the time span between 1995 and 2050, then the dates listed in the interpretations should be the dates when these events could most likely occur, or at least have the potential to occur, if they were intended to be fulfilled before the year 2050. The dates when these positions occur "exactly" should in theory, be more relevant to us than the dates when these planetary positions occur "almost exactly", or not at all.

These alternate dates (the dates when some of these transits occur "almost exactly") are included as a back up, in order to provide readers with a complete listing of all the dates that the planets mentioned in any particular quatrain come close to aspecting one another as stated.

Bear in mind that just because we were able to determine the dates of a transit listed in a quatrain, it does not necessarily mean that the stated event will occur on the date listed. What it means is that the prophesied event has the potential to be fulfilled on one of these dates, if Nostradamus intended for that particular quatrain to be fulfilled before 2050 (which is a "major" unknown parameter).

Other parameters to consider include the possibility that Nostradamus might have accidentally made errors in his astrological calculations, or he included astrological information as a ploy to throw us off course, rather than as a means to guide us (though unlikely).

Over the last four centuries most Nostradamus commentators have failed to thoroughly address the subject of astrology in their literary endeavors. However, the author chose to focus on this overlooked area because astrological transits can be a useful tool to provide us with possible dates and other information, regarding future events. Though not an astrologer myself, the basic fundamentals of astrology are clear enough to me to recognize why Nostradamus included planetary positions in some quatrains, and this book is unique in this regard.

Based upon historical accounts, as well as his own writings, Nostradamus was very knowledgeable (and ahead of his time) as an astrologer. The influence his great-grandfather had upon him as a child, is perhaps one of the reasons for his mastery of this subject. Even as a young man, Nostradamus supported the Copernican concept that the Earth was round and circled the Sun, a century before the famous Galileo formed his revolutionary beliefs on the subject.

As another example of his celestial foresight, Nostradamus mentioned "the light of Neptune" in relation to four other planets in our solar system in quatrain #4-33:

Iupiter joint plus Venus qu'à la Lune Apparaissant de plénitude blanche: Venus cachée sous la blancheur Neptune De Mars frappée par la granée blanche.	4 - 33	Jupiter joined more to Venus than to the Moon, appearing in white fullness: Venus hides beneath the whiteness of Neptune. Struck by Mars through the white gravel.

THE DISCOVERY OF NEPTUNE

"Jupiter joined more to Venus than to the Moon (a poetic line referencing the fifth and second planets of the solar system, in relation to the Moon) appearing in white fullness (suggesting that the planet Jupiter is shining brightly in the night sky). Venus hides beneath the whiteness of Neptune (an astronomically poetic line). Struck by Mars (Mars, the 4th planet of the solar system somehow poetically strikes, or affects in some way, the planet Venus) through the white gravel" (perhaps an allusion to the stars and planets in the Milkey Way Galaxy -- which could resemble shiny white pieces of gravel strewn into the night sky). At first glance, this quatrain appears to be esoteric astrological (or astronomical) poetry. It appears to resemble other quatrains which contain astrological planetary positions. However, the third line of this quatrain is actually quite amazing.

The planet Neptune was not "officially" discovered until September, 1846 (280 years after Nostradamus' death). The discovery of this planet, located 2,800 million miles from the Sun, was credited to the French astronomer Jean Joseph Leverrier, and to the English mathematician John Couch Adams (with most credit going to Leverrier). According to the 20th century Italian astronomer Giogigio Abetti, "the fact that it was possible to predict not only the existence of an unknown planet beyond Uranus, but also its position, was a real triumph for celestial mechanics." So apparently, this was not an easy discovery to make. Did the ancient Hebrew astrologers know more about our solar system than they are credited with, or is this just another example of Nostradamus' uncanny prophetic ability? Due to the facts surrounding this prophecy, we could ask ourselves if credit for the discovery of Neptune should be given to Michel Nostradamus, rather than to Leverrier and Adams.

Le parc enclin grande calamité. Par l'Hesperie & Insubre fera: Le feu en nef peste et captivité, Mercure en l'Arq Saturne fanera.	2 - 65	The sloping park, great calamity through "the Lands of the West" and Lombardy. The fire in the ship, plague and captivity; Mercury in Sagittarius, Saturn fading.

FUTURE DISASTER IN ITALY AND THE NEW WORLD

"The sloping park (suggesting shifting ground?), great calamity (suggesting earthquakes, war or what?) through l'Hesperie (the 'Lands of the West', the New World, more specifically, possibly America) and Lombardy (a region of northern Italy). The fire in the ship (suggesting naval warfare), plague (through war?) and captivity" (a military occupation of an unnamed nation due to war). The astrological position stated in line four occurs next on November 25, 2015, November 23, 2016, and again on December 7, 2044. Could 2015 or 2016 be the years of a future military conflict involving the United States? Could 2015 or 2016 be the year of a major earthquake in the United States and/or Italy? According to the forecasts of some of the leading geologists in America, a major earthquake could strike the San Francisco Bay area any day now. An even greater danger exists in the New Madrid fault zone in the central-southern region of the United States. See quatrain #10-79.

Mars et Mercure, et l'argent
    joint ensemble,
Vers le midi extrême siccité:
Au fond d'Asie on dira terre
    tremble
Corinthe, Ephese lors en per-
    plexité.
	3 - 3	Mars, Mercury and the Moon in
		conjunction, towards the south
		there will be a vast drought. An
		earthquake occurs in the depths
		of Asia, both Corinth and
		Ephesus then in perplexity.

A MAJOR EARTHQUAKE WILL STRIKE ASIA

If this quatrain is intended to be fulfilled in the 20th or 21st century, then the next dates that this astrological transit occurs (before 2050) is on February 11, 2013 (almost exact) and on January 18, 2026 and again January 27, 2028 (see table 3-3 on page 179 for additional dates that this transit occurs in the future). This earthquake will strike in the heart of Asia. Corinth is a Greek city located fifty miles west of Athens, and Ephesus is an ancient city of Greece. Perhaps Greece and eastern Europe are affected in some way (either by warfare, the depletion of their resources, or because of some other circumstances) due to the disaster in Asia. The "south" may infer the southern region of the northern hemisphere, which appears to endure a vast drought. The last time this astrological position occurred "exactly" was on December 23, 1995 (eleven months after the January 17, 1995 earthquake in Kobe, Japan which killed 5000 people). It is a noteworthy fact that this prophesied event occurred in the same year as the tragic earthquake in Japan. Could this be a reference to the *impending Tokai* (the overdue earthquake experts predict will one day strike Tokyo)?

	5 - 23	
Les deux contents seront unis ensemble, Quand la plupart à Mars seront conjoint: Le grand d'Affrique en effrayeur tremble, DUUMVIRAT par la classe déjoint.		The two contented ones are united together when for the most part the planets are conjunct with Mars. The powerful one from Africa trembles in terror. The twin alliance disjoined by the fleet.

A TWIN ALLIANCE WILL BE DEFEATED BY A FLEET

"The two contented ones (two groups or nations?) are united together (allied, or in agreement in some way with one another) when for the most part the planets (of our solar system) are conjunct (in conjunction) with Mars (the planet Mars). The powerful one (a mighty leader or nation) from Africa trembles in terror (for an unknown reason). The twin alliance (a military alliance between two unnamed nations or parties - perhaps between the 'two contented ones') disjoined (separated) by the fleet" (of an unnamed nation). Though we are lacking in clues here, the astrological transit listed above occurs every 200 years or so (occurring last in January 6, 1994). This quatrain is most likely intended for a time in the distant future.

	5 - 24	
Le regne et loi sous Venus élevé, Saturne aura sus Iupiter empire: La loi et regne par le Soleil levé, Par Saturnins endurera le pire.		The realm and law raised under Venus, Saturn will dominate Jupiter. Law and realm raised by the Sun, suffering the worst through those of Saturn.

CHRISTIANITY WILL ENDURE SUPPRESSION

"The realm and law raised under Venus (harmony, love, beauty, feminine values, brotherhood), Saturn (cold rulership not based on sympathy or generosity like Jupiter), will dominate Jupiter (generosity, easy fortune, expansion, travel, widening horizons). Law and realm raised by the Sun (can represent benevolent leadership, egotistical rulership, high office, government affairs and perhaps symbolizes Christianity) suffering the worst through those Saturn" (control, domination, rules, the "letter" of the law). This quatrain appears to symbolically represent the on-going struggle between Christianity and Islam. Nostradamus is saying that the Sun-style "Law and Empire" such as the U.S.A. and Europe, eventually proves longer lasting and endures through the worst times, while Saturn-style governments cave in from their own stagnant rules.

	5 - 25	
Le Prince Arabe Mars, Sol, Venus, Lion,		An Arab Prince, Mars, the Sun, Venus and Leo, the rule of the
Regne d'Eglise par mer succombera:		Church will be overwhelmed by sea. Towards Persia very nearly
Devers la Perse bièn près d'un million,		a million men, the true serpent will invade Egypt and
Bisance, Egypte, ver. serp. invadera.		Byzantium.

EUROPE, TURKEY, AND EGYPT TO BE INVADED

"An Arab Prince (identity unknown), Mars, Sun, Venus and Leo, the rule of the Church (the Christian Church) will be overwhelmed by sea (possibily suggesting naval combat followed by a land invasion of Italy and Europe). Towards Persia (Iran) very nearly a million men (possibly troops gathered on the Turkish/Iranian border?), the true serpent (possibly suggesting the enemies of humanity and Christianity) will invade Egypt and Byzantium" (suggesting that Egypt and Turkey--as alluded to by the word 'Byzantium', will be invaded by unnamed military forces). The dates this astrological position occurs next is Aug. 1 - 6, 2000, Aug. 10 - 23, 2015, July 29 - Aug. 18, 2019, and Aug. 16 - 23, 2030. Apparently, Iran (and her allies) will one day attempt to invade Egypt and Turkey (as well as parts of Europe). See quatrains #1-73, #2-96, #3-64, #4-39, #5-27, #5-47, #5-86, and #6-21. Could this "Arab Prince" be a reference to the third   Antichrist?

	5 - 91	
Au grand marché qu'on dit des mensongers,		At the great market, called that of the liars, of the entire Torrent
Du tout Torrent et champ Athenien:		and the field of Athens: they will be astonished by the light
Seront surpris par les chevaux légers,		horses, by the Albanians, when Mars is in Leo, and Saturn in
Par Albanois Mars, Leo, Sat. un versien.		Aquarius.

WAR IN GREECE IN 2021?

Could "the great market called that of liars" be a reference to a national, or international stock exchange? The identity of "Torrent" remains a mystery. The English word "torrent" is defined as a raging flood or deluge. It may possibly suggest a flood of water, or an overwhelming of troops (though complete speculation on my part). It appears that Athens (the capital of Greece) will be overrun (if "they" suggests Greece) by Albanian armored units or infantry forces (which might explain "the light horses"). If this is the intended meaning, this astrological position occurs next on June 11, 2021, and again in 2051. Could this quatrain be connected to quatrain #4-98 or #5-46?

Mars et le sceptre se trouvera conjoint, Dessous Cancer calamiteuse guerre: Un peu après sera nouveau Roi oint, Qui par longtemps pacifiera la terre.	6 - 24	Mars and the scepter in conjunction under Cancer, a disastrous war. A short time afterwards a new King will be anointed who pacifies the Earth for a long time.

WAR TO BREAK OUT IN 2002, 2013, OR 2038?

This astrological transit occurs next on July 2, 2002. The next three times it occurs after 2002 is on July 23, 2013; May 21st, 2038; and June 12, 2049 (see the astrological tables for other dates when this transit comes close to occurring.) Nostradamus states that "a disastrous war" develops, followed by a long period of peace under a new King or ruler. Though the astrological data provides us with possible dates, we have no clues as to parties or regions involved here. Perhaps this pertains to the rise and fall of the third Antichrist or another disastrous event.

Condon et Aux et autour de Mirande, Je vois du ciel feu qui les environne. Sol Mars conjoint au Lion, puis Marmande Foudre, grand grêle, mur tombe dans Garonne.	8 - 2	Condon and Auch and around Mirande, I see fire from the sky which will encompass them. Sun and Mars conjoined in Leo, then at Marmande, lightning, great hail, the walls fall into the Garonne.

AERIAL WARFARE IN FRANCE

"Condon and Auch and around Mirande (all cities in France), I see fire from the sky (aerial combat or atomic fire?) which will encompass them. Then at Marmaude (a city in France fifty miles north of Condon, Auch, and Marmaude) lighting, great hail, the walls fall into the Garonne" (a river in southwestern France). Another reference to aerial combat and warfare within France. The transit "Sun, and Mars cojoined in Leo" occurs exactly on August 11, 2002; August 1, 2017; and again on August 19, 2034.

Parmi les champs des Rodanes entrées Où les croisés seront presque unis, Les deux brassières en pisces rencontrées, Et un grand nombre par déluge punis.	8 - 91	Surrounded by the fields next to the Rhône where the Crusaders will be nearly united, the two strands in Pisces encounter each other and a great number punished by the flood.

FLOODS OCCUR DURING WARTIME BETWEEN FEBRUARY 20, AND MARCH 20, IN AN UNKNOWN YEAR

A general quatrain describing a situation involving the occupiers of the Rhône River (a river in France) where "the crosses" or "the Crusaders (soldiers from Christian nations?) will be nearly united" during the astrological Sun sign of Pisces (February 20 - March 20) in an unknown year. The flood mentioned here appears to drown or ruin many people. The reference to "the two strands" eludes me.

L'horrible guerre qu'en l'Occidents' apprêste, L'an ensuivant viendra la pestilence Si fort horrible que jeune, vieux, ni bête, Sang, feu Mercure, Mars, Iupiter en France.	9 - 55	The horrid war which is being prepared in the West, the pestilence will arrive the following year, so dreadful that neither young, nor old, nor animal will survive. Blood, fire, Mercury, Mars, Jupiter in France.

THE WEST WILL PREPARE FOR WAR

Perhaps Nostradamus sees the nations of the West (suggesting the nations of the New World), defensively preparing themselves for a war. The year (an unstated time) after this preparation is made, "the pestilence" (war and disease) indeed arrives. It will be "so dreadful that neither the young, nor old, nor the animals will survive" in the areas where these future battles will take place. The astrological information here is vague, however, the positions of Mercury, Mars and Jupiter dates this quatrain to possibly be fulfilled on December 13, 2006, or February 17, 2009. Other dates Mars transits Jupiter (and the planet Mercury) are listed in the astrological tables.

	9 - 73	
Dans Fois entré Roi ceiulee Turban, Et regnera moins évolu Saturne: Roi Turban blanc Bizance coeur ban, Sol, Mars, Mercure près la hurne.		The Blue Turban King will enter Foix, he will reign for less than an evolution of Saturn; White Turban King, Turkish heart banished, when the Sun, Mars and Mercury near Aquarius.

THE THIRD ANTICHRIST

"The Blue Turban King (which might suggest the third Antichrist) will enter Foix (a city in France), he (the third Antichrist) will reign for less than an evolution (or perhaps revolution) of Saturn (which is 27.5 years); White Turban King (identity unclear, perhaps a Turk and or a Muslim), Turkish heart banished (perhaps the White Turban King is a Turkish leader who leaves Turkey due to war), when the Sun, Mars, and Mercury near Aquarius" (see the astrological tables for the many dates this transit occurs). If the Blue Turban King is indeed an allusion to the the third Antichrist, he appears to affect Turkey on his route to France (as mentioned in quatrain #2-29 and 5-54). Could Selin (mentioned in quatrains #4-77, #6-42, #6-58, and #6-78) be the same person as the "Blue Turban King"?

	10 - 67	
Le tremblement si fort au mois de Mai, Saturne, Caper, Iupiter, Mercure au boeuf: Venus aussi Cancer, Mars en Nonnay, Tombera grêle lors plus grosse qu'un oeuf.		A very great trembling in the month of May, Saturn in Capricorn. Jupiter and Mercury in Taurus, Venus also Cancer, Mars in Virgo, then hail falls larger than eggs.

CALAMITY IN MAY OR APRIL, 2048?

If this unclear event was intended to occur before 2050, then it may refer to the date of April 14, 2048. The year 2048 corresponds to the transit of "Saturn in Capricorn" and "Jupiter and Mercury in Taurus". We were unable to locate the other astrological positions mentioned here, which might suggest that this calamity is intended for the distant future. Could this be a reference to an earthquake or a polar shift?

THE ASTROLOGICAL TABLES

ASTRONOMICAL FOOTNOTE
(CENTURY #2-15)

Castor, "the Horseman", is the 23rd brightest star in the sky; magnitude 1.59. Castor and its twin star Pollux, form a prominent pair just 4 1/2° apart. Castor is the northern star and the slightly fainter of the two, shining with a diamond whiteness, in contrast to the bright golden tint of Pollux. Since ancient times, this sparkling pair have suggested the concept of Heavenly twins. In Greek legend they were the sons of Leda and Zeus, Pollux was the immortal twin brother of the mortal Castor. Both were later placed in the sky as the constellation Gemini. They are referred to in various writings as the *"Twin Laconian Stars"* or the *"Spartan Twins"*.

The Heavenly Twins are depicted frequently on coins of the ancient Greek and Roman world. Arabian astronomers called them *Al Tau 'aman*, or the Twins. Castor is located at a distance of 45 light years from Earth, and has a total luminosity of about 36 times that of our Sun.

Quatrain #2 - 65

Description of Planetary Positions:	Dates	Notes
Mercury & Saturn conjunct in Sagittarius Note: Sun at 3° Sag. on same date	Nov. 15, 2015	at 6° Sag.
Mercury & Saturn conjunct in Sagittarius	Nov. 23, 2016	at 16° Sag.
Mercury in Sagittarius, Saturn Fading	Dec. 7, 2044	

Quatrain #3 - 3

Description of Planetary Positions	Date Begin	Placement
Mars, Mercury & Moon conjunction (EXACT)	Dec. 23, 1995	17° Capricorn
Mars, Mercury & Moon conjunction	Mar. 29, 1998	19-21° Aries
Mars, Mercury & Moon conjunction	July 2, 2000	10-17° Cancer
Mars, Mercury & Moon conjunction	Sept. 23, 2006	10-17° Libra
Mars, Mercury & Moon conjunction	Sept. 1, 2008	3-8° Libra
Mars, Mercury & Moon conjunction	Jan. 25, 2009	22-26° Capricorn
Mars, Mercury & Moon conjunction	Dec. 7, 2010	0-5° Capricorn
Mars, Mercury & Moon conjunction	Apr. 30, 2011	14-21° Aries
Mars, Mercury & Moon conjunction (EXACT)	Feb. 11, 2013	7-8° Pisces
Mars, Mercury & Moon conjunction	July 15, 2015	11-13° Cancer
Mars, Mercury & Moon conjunction	Sept. 18, 2017	7-9° Virgo
Mars, Mercury & Moon conjunction	July 4, 2019	1-4° Leo
Mars, Mercury & Moon conjunction	Dec. 12, 2023	8-12° Sagittarius
Mars, Mercury & Moon conjunction	Oct. 23, 2025	21-22° Scorpio
Mars, Mercury & Moon conjunction (EXACT)	Jan. 18, 2026	25° Capricorn
Mars, Mercury & Moon conjunction (EXACT)	Jan. 27, 2028	18° Aquarius
Mars, Mercury & Moon conjunction	July 25, 2036	22-23° Leo
Mars, Mercury & Moon conjunction	Nov. 26, 2038	26-27° Scorpio

Quatrain #3 - 3 Continued

Description of Planetary Positions	Date Begin	Placement
Mars, Mercury & Moon conjunction	Oct. 8, 2040	5-7° Scorpio
Mars, Mercury & Moon conjunction	Dec. 14, 2042	8-12° Sagittarius
Mars, Mercury & Moon conjunction	Mar. 12, 2043	12-18° Pisces
Mars, Mercury & Moon conjunction ●Mercury turns direct the next day	May 8, 2043	0-1° Taurus
Mars, Mercury & Moon conjunction	June 5, 2043	22-23° Taurus
Mars, Mercury & Moon conjunction	Feb. 18, 2045	10-16° Pisces
Mars, Mercury & Moon conjunction	July 23, 2047	12-21° Cancer
Mars, Mercury & Moon conjunction	Sept. 25, 2049	15° Virgo

Quatrain #5 - 25

Description of Planetary Positions:	Date Begin	Date Ending
Sun, Venus & Mars in Leo	Aug. 1, 2000	Aug. 6, 2000
Sun, Venus & Mars in Leo	Aug. 10, 2015	Aug. 23, 2015
Sun, Venus & Mars in Leo	July 29, 2019	Aug. 18, 2019
Sun, Venus & Mars in Leo	Aug. 16, 2030	Aug. 23, 2030

Quatrain #5 - 91

Description of Planetary Positions:	Year	Date Begin	Ending
Mars in Leo when Saturn is in Aquarius	1993	Apr. 27th	May 11th
Mars in Leo when Saturn is in Aquarius	2021	June 11th	July 29th
Mars in Leo when Saturn is in Aquarius	2051	Feb.-Sept.	Approximately

Quatrain #6 - 24

Description of Planetary Positions:	Year	Date Begin	Position
Mars conjunct Jupiter	2002	July 2nd	22° Cancer
Mars conjunct Jupiter ●Opposed by Pluto at 9° Capricorn	2013	July 23rd	6° Cancer
Mars conjunct Jupiter ●Pluto at 24° Capricorn	2020	Mar. 20th	22° Capricorn
Mars conjunct Jupiter	2022	May 30th	4° Aries
Mars conjunct Jupiter ●Moon in oppostion at 16° Sagit	2024	Aug. 14th	16° Gemini
Mars conjunct Jupiter	2026	Nov. 15th	25° Leo
Mars conjunct Jupiter	2029	July 20th	19° Libra
Mars conjunct Jupiter ●Saturn and Uranus conjunct in Gemini (Gemini is opposite Sagittarius)	2031	Sept. 30th	22° Sagittarius
Mars conjunct Jupiter	2033	Dec. 19th	29° Aquarius
Mars conjunct Jupiter	2036	Feb. 17th	13° Taurus
Mars conjunct Jupiter ●Uranus nearby at 21° Cancer	2038	May 21st	25° Cancer
Mars conjunct Jupiter	2040	Aug. 18th	2° Libra
Mars conjunct Jupiter	2042	Oct. 31st	5° Sagittarius
Mars conjunct Jupiter	2045	Jan. 5th	11° Aquarius
Mars conjunct Jupiter	2047	Mar. 18th	23° Aries
Mars conjunct Jupiter	2049	June 12th	7° Cancer

Quatrain #8 - 2

Description of Planetary Positions		
During these dates, both Sun & Mars were in the sign Leo:	Date of Exact Conjunction	Place in Zodiac:
August 5th - Aug. 23rd, 2047	None	
July 23rd - Aug. 5th, 2036	None	
July 23rd - Aug. 23rd, 2034	Aug. 19th 2034	19° Leo
July 23rd - Aug. 23rd, 2017	Aug. 1st 2017	8° Leo
Aug. 9th - Aug. 23rd, 2015	None	
July 23 - Aug. 10th, 2004	None	
July 24th - Aug. 24th, 2002	Aug. 11th 2002	18° Leo
Sun-Mars aligned throughout period		
Aug. 1st - Aug. 22, 2000	None	

Quatrain #9 - 55

Description of Planetary Postions:	Year	Date of Conjunction	Position of Mars/Jupiter	Position of Mercury
Mars conjunct Jupiter ●Saturn at 18° Pisces is square●	1996	Nov. 15th	18° Sagit.	18° Scorpio
Mars conjunct Jupiter	1998	Jan. 20th	26° Aquarius	10° Capricorn
Mars conjunct Jupiter	2000	April 6th	10° Taurus	20° Pisces
Mars conjunct Jupiter	2002	July 2nd	22° Cancer	19° Gemini
Mars conjunct Jupiter	2004	Sept. 27th	00° Libra	27° Virgo
Mars conjunct Jupiter **●Mercury near conjunction●** (Sun almost conjunct PLUTO in Sagittarius)	**2006**	**Dec. 13th**	**04° Sagit.**	**07° Sagit.**
Mars conjunct Jupiter **●MERCURY near conjunction●** ●also North Node at 9° Aquarius Mercury, Mars, Jupiter in early Aquarius Sun, Neptune, Chiron in late Aquarius ●Feb 26th-total lunar eclipse at 06° Aquarius	**2009**	**Feb. 17th**	**09° Aquarius**	**03° Aquarius**
Mars conjunct Jupiter	2011	May 2nd	22° Aries	15° Aries
Mars conjunct Jupiter ●Opposed by Pluto at 9° Capricorn	2013	July 23rd	6° Cancer	13° Cancer
Mars conjunct Jupiter	2015	Oct. 16th	12° Virgo	05° Libra
Mars conjunct Jupiter ●Pluto at 24° Capricorn	2018	Jan. 7th	18° Scorpio	24° Sagit.
Mars conjunct Jupiter	2020	March 20th	22° Capricorn	02° Pisces
Mars conjunct Jupiter	2022	May 30th	4° Aries	26° Taurus
Mars conjunct Jupiter	2024	Aug. 14th	16° Gemini	00° Virgo

Quatrain #9 - 55 (cont'd)

Description of Planetary Postions:	Year	Date of Conjunction	Position of Mars/Jupiter	Position of Mercury
Mars conjunct Jupiter	2026	Nov. 15th	25° Leo	05° Scorpio
Mars conjunct Jupiter	2029	July 20th	19° Libra	08° Leo
Mars conjunct Jupiter	2031	Sept. 30th	22° Sagittarius	11° Libra
Mars conjunct Jupiter	2033	Dec. 29th	29° Aquarius	26° Scorpio
Mars conjunct Jupiter	2036	Feb. 17th	13° Taurus	06° Aquar.
Mars conjunct Jupiter ●Saturn at 18° Pisces is square●	2038	May 21st	25° Cancer	16° Taurus
Mars conjunct Jupiter	2040	Aug. 18th	02° Libra	00° Virgo
Mars conjunct Jupiter	2042	Oct. 31st	05° Sagittarius	05° Scorpio
Mars conjunct Jupiter	2045	Jan. 5th	11° Aquarius	27° Sagit.
Mars conjunct Jupiter	2047	March 18th	23° Aries	00° Pisces
Mars conjunct Jupiter	2049	June 12th	7° Cancer	28° Taurus

Quatrain #9 - 73

Description of Planetary Positions	Year	Date Begin	Ending	Sun at	Mars at	Mercury at
Sun, Mercury, Mars near Aquarius	1994	Jan. 28th	Feb. 1st	8-12° Aquarius	0-3° Aquarius	24-29° Aquarius
Sun, Mercury, Mars near Aquarius	1996	Jan. 21st	Feb. 14th	0-26° Aquarius	10-29° Aquarius	29° Cap., 0° Aq.
Sun, Mercury, Mars near Aquarius	1998	Jan. 28th	Jan. 29th	8° Aquarius	2° Pisces	22° Capricorn
Sun, Mercury, Mars near Aquarius	2009	Feb. 15th	Feb. 19th	26-29° Aquarius	0-4° Aquarius	8-9° Aquarius
Sun, Mercury, Mars near Aquarius	2011	Feb. 4th	Feb. 19th	15-20° Aquarius	0-24° Aquarius	14-26° Aquarius
Sun, Mercury, Mars near Aquarius	2013	Jan. 20th	Feb. 2nd	0-13° Aquarius	1-23° Aquarius	19-29° Aquarius
Sun, Mercury, Mars near Aquarius	2024	Feb. 17th	Feb. 20th	26-29° Aquarius	0-2° Aquarius	2-4° Aquarius
Sun, Mercury, Mars near Aquarius	2026	Jan. 25th	Feb. 6th	5-17° Aquarius	7-29° Aquarius	0-10° Aquarius
Sun, Mercury, Mars near Aquarius	2028	Jan. 21st	Feb. 10th	0-20° Aquarius	18-4° Aquarius	13-29° Aquarius
•Pluto at 3° Aquarius					retrograde	
•Moon's North Node at 2°						
Sun, Mercury, Mars near Aquarius	2041	Feb. 1st	Feb. 19th	12-29° Aquarius	19-7° Aquarius	0-14° Aquarius
•Pluto at 26° Aquarius					retrograde	
Sun, Mercury, Mars near Aquarius	2043	Feb. 10th	Feb. 18th	21-29° Aquarius	0-12° Aquarius	23-29° Aquarius
•Pluto at 29° Aquarius						

La grande famine que je sens approcher,
Souvent tourner, puis être universelle,
Si grande et longue qu'on viendra arracher,
Du bois racine, et l'enfant de mamelle.

1 - 67

The great famine I sense approaching will arrive (in various regions) then turn, and then it becomes universal. It will be so great and long lasting that one will pluck roots from the trees and babies from the breast.

VAST GLOBAL FAMINE FORECASTED

The following quatrains pertain to Earth Changes, floods and famines. "The great famine (a drastic and wide-reaching shortage of food resulting in hunger, starvation, and perhaps mass death) I sense approaching will arrive in various regions (will manifest itself periodically in various geographical areas of the planet) then turn (later vanishing), and then it becomes universal (following a period of intermittent famine, a world wide famine will develop, perhaps due to reversals of environmental conditions or war). It will be so great and long lasting that one will pluck roots from the trees and babies from the breast" (the world wide famine will be so vast and of such a lengthy duration, that people will eat the roots of trees, and some may even resort to human cannibalism). No clues were given as to the possible time frame of this horrendous futuristic famine.

Ennosigée feu du centre de terre
Fera trembler autour de cité neuve:
Deux grands rochers longtemps feront la guerre,
Puis Arethusa rougira nouveau fleuve.

1 - 87

Volcanic fire from the middle of the Earth will cause tremors around the New City. Two great rocks will war for a long time, and Arethusa reddens a new river.

EARTHQUAKES IN AMERICA FOLLOWED BY WAR?

"Volcanic fire from the middle of the Earth will cause tremors (suggesting earthquakes) around the New City". In a macro sense, "New City" could suggest the New World or America. In a micro sense it could suggest "New (York) City". Considering that three fault-lines exist on Manhattan Island a future earthquake in New York is a possibility (or the San Andreas or New Madrid fault lines). "Two great rocks (two great international powers) will war for a long time and Arethusa reddens a new river" (with blood?). An Arethusa is an orchid which is native to eastern North America, thus North America appears to be intended as one of the two great rocks. Arethusa is also an anagram for "EARTH, U.S.A.". This quatrain appears to suggest that a war involving two super powers will begin following earthquakes somewhere in North America. See quatrain #2-65 and #10-79.

Le parc enclin grande calamité Par l'Hesperie et Insubre fera: Le feu en nef peste et captivité, Mercure en l'Arc Saturne fanera.	2 - 65	The sloping park, great calamity through "the Lands of the West" and Lombardy. The fire in the ship, plague and captivity; Mercury in Sagittarius, Saturn fading.

DISASTERS IN ITALY AND THE NEW WORLD

"The sloping park (suggesting shifting ground?), great calamity (earthquakes?) through l'Hesperie (the 'Lands of the West' - the New World) and Lombardy (a region of northern Italy). The fire in the ship (suggesting naval warfare?), plague (an affliction, or the spread of disease) and captivity (suggesting a military occupation through war?); Mercury in Sagittarius, Saturn fading" (is an astrological position which occurs next on Nov. 25, 2015, then on Nov. 23, 2016, and again on Dec. 7, 2044). Could 2015 or 2016, be years that major earthquakes strike the New World and Italy? Could 2015/16 be the years of a future military conflict involving Italy and her allies in the New World? "If" the United States was one of the regions intended in this quatrain, it should be noted that according to the forecast of many geologists, a major earthquake could strike the San Francisco Bay at any time. An even greater danger exists in the New Madrid fault line located in the central region of the United States. In the early 1800's, this area of the U.S. experienced earthquakes so devastating that it reversed the tide of the mighty Mississippi River, and the trembling of the Earth could be felt as far away as Washington D.C.!

La voix ouïe de l'insolite oiseau, Sur le canon de respiral étage: Si haut viendra du froment le boisseau, Que l'homme d'homme sera Anthropophage.	2 - 75	The voice of the rare bird being heard on the chimney stack; bushels of wheat will rise so high that man will eat and devour his fellow man.

A FAMINE WILL OCCUR DURING A TIME OF WAR

"The voice of the rare bird being heard on the chimney stack (may suggest future times of very high-tech aircraft); bushels of wheat (agricultural goods, grains and produce) will rise so high (will become so scarce and will rise so high in price) that man will eat and devour his fellow man" (suggesting that the combination of war, natural disasters, or extreme environmental changes, will create a shortage of food, resulting in human cannibalism). We have no clues as to the time-frame or location of this horrid event.

Mars et Mercure, et l'argent joint ensemble, Vers le midi extrême siccité: Au fond d'Asie on dira terre tremble, Corinthe, Ephese lors en perplexité.	3 - 3	Mars, Mercury and the Moon in conjunction towards the south there will be a vast drought. An earthquake occurs in the depths of Asia, both Corinth and Ephesus then in a perplexed state.

A MAJOR EARTHQUAKE WILL STRIKE IN ASIA

If this quatrain is intended to be fulfilled in the 20th or 21st century, then the next dates that this astrological transit occurs (before 2050) is on February 11, 2013 (almost exact) and on January 18, 2026 and again January 27, 2028 (see table 3-3 on page 179 for additional dates that this transit occurs in the future). This earthquake will strike in the heart of Asia. Corinth is a Greek city located fifty miles west of Athens, and Ephesus is an ancient city of Greece. Perhaps Greece and eastern Europe are affected in some way (either by warfare, the depletion of their resources, or because of some other circumstances) due to the disaster in Asia. The "south" may infer the southern region of the northern hemisphere, which appears to endure a vast drought. The last time this astrological position occurred "exactly" was on December 23, 1995 (eleven months after the January 17, 1995 earthquake in Kobe, Japan which killed 5000 people). It is a noteworthy fact that this prophesied event occurred in the same year as the tragic earthquake in Japan. Could this be a reference to the *impending Tokai* (the overdue earthquake experts predict will one day strike Tokyo)?

Par la tumeur de Heb. Po, Tag. Timbre, et Rosne Et par l'etang Leman et Aretin, Les deux grands chefs et cités de Garonne, Pris, morts, noyés: Partir humain butin.	3 - 12	Due to the overflow of the Ebro, Po, Tagus, Tiber and Rhone and because of the Lakes of Geneva and Arezzo, the two great chiefs and cities of the Garonne captured, dead, drowned. Human booty to be divided.

EUROPE WILL BE FLOODED DURING A TIME OF WAR

"Due to the overflow of the Ebro (the longest river in Spain flowing 575 miles from the Cantabrain mountains, southeast to the Mediterranean Sea), the Po (a river rising on the slope of Mt. Viso in northwestern Italy, flowing 418 miles to the Adriatic Sea), the Tagus (a long river rising in east-central Spain flowing northwest, then southwest to the Atlantic near Lisbon, Portugal), the Tiber (a river in central Italy rising in the Apennines and flowing 251 miles south past Rome to the Tyrrhenian Sea), and the Rhone (a river rising in central Switzerland flowing 505 miles west, then south to the Mediterranean Sea near Arles, France), and because of the Lakes of Geneva (a lake near Geneva, in southwestern Switzerland, occupying

225 square miles with its southern shore in eastern France) and Arezzo (a city on the Arno River, in central Italy, which flows 150 miles to the Ligurian Sea near Pisa), the two great chiefs (suggesting two unnamed leaders) and cities of the Garonne captured, dead, drowned (possibly suggesting that the major cities located on the Garonne River -- Bordeaux and Toulouse in France, might be captured in a military campaign, after or during a devastating flood). Human booty to be divided" (the possessions of the dead or captured citizens will be divided among the unnamed invaders or survivors).

This quatrain very specifically names the European regions which Nostradamus indicates will be affected by a future flood. It is unclear if this quatrain is a reference to "the great global flood", mentioned in the Preface, or if it is simply a reference to a large futuristic flood in Europe.

In 1993 and 1995, Europe endured the worst flooding to occur in over a century.

Sol vingt de Taurus si fort terre trembler, Le grand théâtre rempli ruinera: L'air, ciel et terre obscurcir et troubler, Lors l'infidèle Dieu et saints voguera.	9 - 83	The Sun in twenty degrees of Taurus, a mighty trembling of the Earth; the great theater full up will be ruined. To darken and trouble the air, sky and land, causing the infidel to call upon God and the Saints.

AN EARTHQUAKE IN TAURUS (APRIL 21 - MAY 21)

"The Sun in twenty degrees of Taurus (suggesting May 10th - the twentieth day of the Sun sign of Taurus), a mighty trembling of the Earth" (possibly suggesting a mighty earthquake, polar shift, or natural disaster). "The great theater filled up will be ruined" is perhaps a reference to mass gatherings of people who will witness (and be involved in) this event, or remotely it may be a reference to Hollywood, California, the location of film studios for "the great theaters", which is located on a major fault line. Or, "the great theater" may be an allusion to the old Roman theaters in Rome, or perhaps its a reference to a military theater. This event (possibly the eruption of volcanos combined with earthquakes) "darkens and troubles the air and sky and land" (could nuclear blasts be a remote possibility here?). Due to this calamitous event "the infidel (one who has no religious beliefs, or is an unbeliever in Christianity or Islam) will call upon God and the Saints" (for spiritual guidance during this turmoil). Nostradamus gives us no specific clues as to the geographical region intended here.

Les vieux chemins seront tous embellis,
L'on passera à Memphis somentrée:
Le grand Mercure d'Hercules fleur de lis,
Faisant trembler terre, mer et contrée.

10 - 79

All the old roads will be improved, one will travel down them to modern Memphis: the grand Mercury of Hercules fleur-de-lys, causing the land, sea, and country to tremble.

FUTURE COLLAPSE OF THE NEW MADRID FAULT LINE

"All the old roads will be improved (this places us in at least the 20th century), one will travel down them (by automobile?) to modern Memphis (possibly suggesting Memphis, Tennessee): the grand Mercury (Mercury was the Roman god of travel, commerce, and thievery, who served as a messenger to the other gods and was a common figure in alchemy) of Hercules (the mythological immortal son of Zeus who was a hero of extraordinary strength) fleur-de lys ("fleur-de-lys" is associated with the Bourbons -- a French royal family, perhaps Nostradamus is making an esoteric allusion to himself in this line), causing the land (the geographic region of the central-southern United States), sea (possibly suggesting the Gulf of Mexico and the Atlantic Ocean), and country (an allusion to the United States of America) to tremble (suggesting an earthquake will occur, perhaps in the region comprising the New Madrid fault line, which will be so powerful in the magnitude of its destruction that it will affect the central and southern states along the Mississippi River, as well as the southeastern coastal areas of the United States).

The first line of this fascinating quatrain appears to allude to the creation of the *Tennessee Valley Authority* (the U.S. government corporation created in 1933 to "improve" the roads of the Tennessee Valley, and to build dams, hydroelectric plants, and flood control works throughout the region).

The second line of this quatrain is especially demonstrative. There are only two cities of major significance in the world named *Memphis*. One of them is located twelve miles south of Cairo, and was the ancient capital of Egypt. The other one, "the modern *Memphis*" is located in southwestern Tennessee on the Mississippi River. Thus, the American *Memphis* appears to be the city alluded to in this quatrain.

This quatrain appears to predict a major earthquake in the geographic area comprising the New Madrid fault line (which includes parts of Tennessee, Arkansas, Missouri, and Illinois). Geologists with the U.S.G.S. have stated that they predict a quake in this region before 2018. In 1809, this area experienced an earthquake so devastating that it temporarily reversed the tide of the mighty Mississippi River. See quatrain #1-87 and #2-65.

THE EPISTLE TO KING HENRY II

An epistle is defined as a letter, especially a formal one, a verse letter of the genre invented by Horace (a Latin poet whose Latin name was Quintus Haratius Flaccus, 65 ~ 8 B.C.).

The Epistle to King Henry II of France, which Nostradamus wrote in 1558, is a fascinating work of prophetic literature. At first glance, the Epistle appears to be a confusing and rambling personal letter, in which Nostradamus praises his king. In reality, however, the Epistle is full of important information. The messages and clues it contains (as in the quatrains) are for the greater part, veiled in symbolism.

The Epistle serves many purposes. Besides revealing information regarding wars, religion, and natural disasters, it also provides a rough chronology of various events (both past and future) which pertain to the regions of France, Europe, the Mediterranean, Asia, the Middle East, Africa, and the New World.

An interesting dimension of the Epistle is the chronological aspect of the information it appears to contain (especially as related to future events). It contains several brief chronologies of events, yet their linear chronological sequence is not always clear since Nostradamus divided his chronologies of events into separate groups throughout the Epistle.

By cross-referencing information in the quatrains with information contained in the Epistle one can obtain a clearer view of both past and future events.

Some of the paragraphs in the Epistle seem to reinforce (and verify) Nostradamus' accuracy regarding prophesied events which have now come to pass. In paragraphs #1 through #10, Nostradamus provides us with a general overview of *The Prophecies*. In paragraph #10 Nostradamus provides us with an interesting chronograph of Biblical figures, yet many scholars disagree with this particular chronograph of Biblical history.

Within paragraphs #11 and #12 Nostradamus states his views on prophecy, and in a very humble manner, he suggests that he would never claim the personal title of a prophet.

From paragraph #13 to #22 Nostradamus, uses a great deal of allusions and symbology to provide us with an historical overview of the history of France (beginning with the era of the French Revolution, and ending with the post World War II era).

Paragraphs #23 through #38 seem to pertain to the future and describe events paralleled in language found in various unfulfilled quatrains (references to Euro/Arabic conflicts, the war with the third Antichrist, famine and pestilence, religious matters and natural disasters).

In paragraph #23 Nostradamus appears to suggest that the future third Antichrist will begin his rise to power in Iran and in the former region of Attila (the Hun). Paragraph #24 makes a reference to "the grand translation", which appears to be a massive futuristic natural disaster of some type (possibly global earthquakes or a polar shift).

Paragraph #33 mentions a future persecution of Christians and the arrival of a pestilence which will remove two-thirds (67%) of the world's population. In paragraphs #34 and #35, Nostradamus makes a reference to the Holy Land and a future invasion of Israel by Muslim forces. It appears that military forces from the West (perhaps American forces) will defeat the invaders and desolate their cities.

Within Paragraphs #36 through #38 he provides us with what appears to be a description of the future war with the third Antichrist. It appears that military forces for the West, from America and other nations in the New World, will ally themselves with Russian forces, to defeat the evil third Antichrist of Asia. In paragraph #39 Nostradamus states that his predictions will not fail, and if he had wanted to, he could have provided us with a date of fulfillment for each of his quatrains.

Paragraph #40 contains another Biblical chronograph which mentions Noah, Isaac, Solomon, and Jesus Christ. Paragraph #41 contains detailed astrological information. In paragraph #43 a reference is made to Napoleon and the French Revolution.

In paragraphs #43, #44, and #45, Nostradamus describes the military events leading up to the end of World War II. Paragraph #46 pertains to the Antichrists and appears to make an allusion to Napoleon Bonaparte. In paragraphs #47 and #48, a reference is a made to a future global flood, and future combat in the Holy Land involving Russia.

Within paragraphs #48 through #55, additional information is provided to us regarding the future persecution at Christmas, which appears to be brought about in an era when Russia is united with Easterners (perhaps suggesting China and/or other unnamed Asian nations).

In his closing (paragraphs #56 through #59) Nostradamus stated that a golden age will begin after the great future war and a state of peace on Earth will endure for a period of 1000 years.

The definitions of various terms, allusions and geographical locations contained in the text of the Epistle are listed in the Sub-Glossary. As a courtesy to the reader the terms are listed in the order in which they appear within the body of the text.

Most parenthetical text consists of alternate English translations of the original text.

The footnotes in the Epistle contain brief commentaries on the text as well as some additional definitions of terms and allusions. Readers should note that any words typed in *italics* indicates that the original text was written in Latin.

Though jumbled chronologically, penetrating the symbolism contained in the Epistle, as well as the events it references, might prove to be some of the most interesting clues Nostradamus has left us regarding the future.

SUB-GLOSSARY (THE EPISTLE)

PLUTARCH, (46-120 B.C.) a patriotic Greek biographer and philosopher known as "the Prince of Ancient Biographers", author of the famous book Parallel Lives.
MINERVA, in Roman mythology the goddess of wisdom, the arts, and invention.
VARRO, (116-27 B.C), Roman scholar and encyclopedist.
CHALDEAN, an ancient Semitic people who ruled in Babylonia, a person versed in occult learning.
SARACENS, a member of a pre-Islamic nomadic people of the Syrian-Arabian deserts, an Arab.
ENIGMATIC, puzzling.
THE GREAT LADY, an allusion to the Queen of France.
TWO PRINCIPAL CHILDREN, an allusion to the two surviving children of Marie Antoinette.
SHE BEING IN GREAT DANGER, an allusion to the danger faced by the monarchy during the French Revolution.
EIGHTEENTH YEAR, an allusion to the end of the Eighteenth Century (the year 1792), which marked the end of the French monarchy.
THE THIRTY SIXTH, an allusion to the thirty-sixth king of France (from King Hugues Capet to King Charles X).
THREE MALES, an allusion to Louis XVIII, Charles X, and Louis-Philippe I, the three males who would become kings of France after Louis XVII.
ONE FEMALE, an allusion to Madam Royale (daughter of Marie Antoinette).
TWO CHILDREN, an allusion to two emperors, the first being Napoleon Bonaparte, the second being Napoleon III.
THREE BROTHERS, an allusion to Louis XVI, Louis XVIII, and Charles X.
THE TREMBLING OF 3/4 OF EUROPE, an allusion to the Napoleonic wars which shook Europe following the French Revolution.
THE PARTIES, the political parties associated with the French Revolution.
ARABS DRIVEN BACK, an allusion to Napoleon's conquests of the East and the French conquest of Algeria (which began in 1830).
KINGDOMS CREATED, an allusion to Napoleon's creation of kingdoms in Europe.
NEW LAWS PROMULGATED, an allusion to the Napoleonic Codes of French Civil Law.
THE OTHER CHILDREN, an allusion to Napoleon Bonaparte's brothers.
THE FURIOUS CROWNED LIONS, an allusion to the many nations of Europe containing a lion in its coat-of-arms.
THE SECOND ONE IN AGE, an allusion to Napoleon III.
THE SECOND TREMBLING, an allusion to Napoleon II's invasion of Italy.
THE THIRD INUNDATION OF BLOOD, an allusion to World War I (1914-18).
MARS, a general allusion to modern warfare.
THE DAUGHTER, an allusion to the Third Republic of France.
HER DOMINATOR, an allusion to the powerful Czar of Russia.
THE 1ST CHILD OF THE DAUGHTER, the French Chamber of Deputies.

THE PAGAN SECT OF NEW INFIDELS, an allusion to the Russian Communist Party.
THE 2ND CHILD OF THE DAUGHTER, the French Chamber of the Senate.
THE UNFAITHFUL SON, French-Nazi collaborators, Fascism, Nazism, and the Spanish revolution.
THE THREE REGIONS, an allusion to Germany, Italy, and Spain during the 1930's and 40's.
THE 50TH TO THE 52ND DEGREE OF LATITUDE NORTH, in Europe this would include central Germany.
NORTH OF THE 40TH DEGREE OF LATITUDE, this would include most all of Europe.
WHAT WAS BROUGHT ABOUT BY UNION AND DISCORD, an allusion to the alliances of Germany and Italy, which resulted in World War II and the Spanish Revolution.
THEY, an allusion to the nations of Germany, Italy, and Spain.
VERY DIFFERENT IN FAITH, an allusion to the ideological difference between the Allies, and the nations of Germany, Italy, and Japan during World War II.
THE STERILE LADY (more powerful than the second), an allusion to the Republic of France after World War II.
MYRMIDONS, one of a legendary Greek warrior people of ancient Thessaly who followed their king Achilles on the expedition against Troy in Asia Minor.
ATTILA, leader of the barbaric Asiatic nomads who ravaged Europe in the fourth and fifth centuries.
THE NEW XERXES, Xerxes was a Persian king who unsuccessfully invaded Greece (485-465 B.C.). Thus, the New Xerxes is an allusion to a futuristic Iranian Warlord.
THE GRAND TRANSLATION, apparently a deadly massive natural disaster, i.e., global earthquakes, a polar shift, or world wide flooding. In physics, "translation" is defined as the motion of a body in which every point of the body moves parallel to, and the same distance as, every other point of the body; nonrotational displacement. This could suggest that this disaster might occur due to a gravational effect upon the Earth, resulting from an alignment of some of the planets in our solar system. In theology, "translate" means to convey to heaven without natural death.
BABYLON, ancient capital of Babylonia, situated in Mesopotamia on the Euphrates River in modern day Iraq. Any city of great luxury and corruption.
HOLOCAUST, a sacrificial offering consumed by flames, total destruction by fire.
THE FURIOUS ONE, an allusion to Satan.
POTENTATE, a leader who has the power and position to rule over others.
THE STERILE DAME, an allusion to the Third French Republic.
GREAT CHAIN OF THE PORT, possibly an allusion to Marseille, France.
THE ABODE OF ABRAHAM, Jerusalem and the surrounding areas such as Ur, Haran, Shechem, Bethel, and Hebron. After Abraham left Ur, he lived within 25 miles of Jerusalem for the remainder of his life. The City of Schechem is located approximately 30 miles from Mount Megiddo (Armageddon).
JOVIALISTS, pertaining to Jupiter, possibly a reference to the followers of Antiochus Epiphanes, a Syrian king of ancient times, an allusion to the Syrians.

THRASIBULUS, the Athenian general who fought the Peloponnesian War in 431 B.C. and restored democracy in ancient Greece. As used in the context of "war followed by democratic liberation", this might be an allusion to the French leader, Charles De Gaulle.
THE THREE SECTS, an allusion to three religions (in order): Hebrew, Christianity, and Islam.
EASTERNERS, Middle Easterners, Asians, or Orientals.
DOG AND DOHAM, possibly an allusion to "Gog and Magog" in the Bible (Revelation 20:1).
CITY OF THE SUN, an allusion to Rome, and/or the Vatican.
PORT OF THE MARINE OX, Marseilles, France.
SIERRA MORENA, a reference to an old region of Spain.
ACHEM, an anagram for Salem, the ancient name for Jerusalem.
SEPULCHRE, the tomb of Christ, in Jerusalem.
CALAMITOUS AFFLICTION, an allusion to holy wars which affect the nations of Christianity and Israel.
TRIUMVIRATE, a group of three governing nations or bodies.
TRUE ECCLESIASTICS, an allusion to the followers of Christianity.
AQUILON, an allusion to Russia and possibly other former Soviet states and other northern regions of Asia.
HORRIBLE TEMPORAL KING, an allusion to an enemy of France and her allies. This horrible temporal (or temporary) king will be an ally of the regions comprising Aquilon.
PHILISTINES, members of the ancient country of Philistia on the southwestern coast of Palestine.
ECCLESIASTICAL, pertaining to a church, churchly, a reference to Christians.
OGMIOS, an allusion to a Celtic (French) Hercules, a European leader (or dynasty) who helps to conquer the third Antichrist's army.
EASTERN CHIEF, an allusion to an Asian leader, possibly the third Antichrist. It is possible that "the East" suggests "the Middle East", rather than the Orient.
NORTHERNERS, an allusion to the people of Aquilon (the citizens of Russia, and possibly other former Soviet states).
WESTERNERS, an allusion to the citizens of the New World (North and South America).
GREAT EARTHQUAKES, a reference to earthquakes which seem to occur after the war with the future third Antichrist.
HORRIBLE PESTILENCE, an allusion to war and disease.
LATIN REGIONS, Western Europe (excluding France).
COUNTRIES OF THE SPANISH, an allusion to America and possibly other nations of the Old Spanish New World (such as Mexico, some of the nations of Central and South America, and some of the islands of the Caribbean).
VICAR OF THE HOOD, an allusion to a pope.
HOLY OF HOLIES, possibly an allusion to Christian churches and Jewish temples.
KINGDOMS OF CHRISTIANITY, an allusion to the nations of the Earth who embrace Christianity (nations in Europe, the New World, and elsewhere).
THOSE GIVEN TO CENSURE, an allusion to critics, skeptics, detractors, or non-believers of Nostradamus' writings and prophecies.

[Epistle]

**To the Most Invincible
Most Powerful and Most Christian
Henry, King of France the Second:
Michel Nostradamus,
his very humble and very obedient servant and subject,
Wishes Victory and Happiness.**

1) Because of that sovereign sight, O most Christian and victorious King, my face, which was clouded for a while, finally presented itself before the immeasurable deity of your Majesty. Since then I have remained perpetually dazzled and continue to honor and worship the day, which I presented myself before a majesty so singular and so humane. I have sought for an occasion which would allow me to manifest the goodness and stout courage of my heart, so that I could extend my acquaintance toward your most serene Majesty. But I realized that it was impossible for me to declare myself.

2) While overwhelmed with the desire to be suddenly removed from my long obscurity and be transported before the illuminating presence of the greatest Monarch of the world, I spent a great deal of time deciding who I would dedicate these last three Centuries of my Prophecies to, which make the complete one thousand. After a lengthy meditation upon such an audacious act, I decided to address your majesty. Unlike those mentioned by the great author Plutarch, as in the Life of Lycurgus[1], I have remained undaunted by the astonishing expense of the gifts and offerings brought as sacrifices in the temples of heathen gods, that they dared to present anything at all. Witnessing your royal splendor, combined with your unparalleled humanity, I address myself to you, not as one did to those Kings of Persia whom are unapproachable.

3) It is to a very wise and prudent prince that I have dedicated my nocturnal and prophetic calculations to. They are composed more by a natural instinct and poetical furor, rather than in accordance to the strict rules of poetry. Most of them were integrated with astrological calculations which correspond to the years, months, and weeks of the (geographical) regions, countries, and cities of Europe; as well as Africa and Asia, where most (but not all) of these future events will transpire. They (the prophecies) were composed in a natural fashion.

---

[1] An early Spartan king who lived about 800 years before Christ. Though uncertain, most historians think Lycurgus lived before the creation of the Olympic Games, others claim that Lycurgus was the one who persuaded the Greeks to cease all warfare during the Olympic Games. Some say he was a contemporary of Homer, and Homer may have known Lycurgus personally. Most credit him with introducing the *Iliad*, and the *Odyssey*, into Sparta.

4) Some may reply (who has a great need to blow his nose)[2], that the rhythm is as easily understood, as the sense is difficult. Therefore most humane king, most of the prophetical quatrains are so difficult (to understand) that there is no way to interpret them.[3]

5) Nevertheless, it was my wish to leave in writing, a record of the cities and regions where most of my prophecies shall occur, especially those of 1585 and 1606; beginning from the present time which is March 14, 1557, and extending far beyond the events which will occur at the beginning of the seventh millenary[4], when (according to my astronomical calculations and other knowledge indicate) the adversaries of Jesus Christ (and his Church) shall begin to greatly multiply.

6) During the choice hours of well disposed days, *when Minerva[5] was free and favorable*, I composed and calculated as accurately as I could, the events which will occur, for as long a period of time to come, as which has already passed. By these it will be known (in all regions) what will transpire in the course of time, just as it is written, with nothing superfluous (extra) added. Though some people might say *"there can be no truth entirely determined, for certain, concerning the future"*.

7) It is true, Sire, that my natural instinct[6] was inherited from my progenitors, (forebears) who disbelieved in the art of predicting. I adjusted my innate instinct and combined it with lengthy calculations (while freeing my mind, heart, and soul of all care and vexation). These prerequisites for presaging were achieved partly through the means of *the brazen tripod*.[7]

8) Though there are some (people) who would attribute to me, that which is not mine at all, and it is to the eternal God alone, the thorough searcher of human hearts, pious, just and merciful, who is the truest judge, and it is to him that I pray to defend me from the calumny (intentional fraud) of evil men.[8] These wicked people, in their slanderous manner, likewise would wish to inquire how all your ancient forebearers, the Kings of France, cured the scrofula[9], how other nations cured the bites of poisonous snakes, how others possessed the special instinct for foretelling events of the future, and of other things too numerous to mention here.

---

[2]This is an unusual line to be included here. Perhaps it is intended as a humorous personal message to an unnamed person (or persons).

[3]An apparent contradiction to language found in paragraph #30 of the Preface.

[4]Millenary pertains to "one thousand", or relates to the doctrine of the *Millenarians*. The actual date intended by Nostradamus is unclear and subject to debate.

[5]See the sub-glossary, identified with the Greek goddess Athena, also called "Pallas Athena".

[6]Innate wisdom.

[7]A device made of brass, which rests upon three legs, used in the magic rituals of Alchemy which allowed Nostradamus to see into the future.

[8]Nostradamus apparently foresaw that some persons would intentionally (not accidentally) attribute to him, various prophecies which he did not make, and had nothing to do with at all. This premeditated fraud, on behalf of others, apparently upset Nostradamus (i.e., Joseph Goebbels the Nazi Propaganda Minister).

[9]Also called "truma", a heath condition affecting the tissues in the young characterized by predisposition to tuberculosis, lymphatism, glandular swellings, and respiratory catarrhous.

9) Notwithstanding those whom the malignancy of the evil spirit shall not be contained, as time passes (after my bodily death) it is my hope that my work (or writings) will be held in a higher degree of esteem than it was when I was alive.[10] However, if I have made any errors in my calculations of dates and times, or find that I am unable to satisfy everyone, I request that your most imperial Majesty will forgive me.[11] Before God and his saints, I protest that I did not purposely intend to insert anything in my writings (in the present Epistle) that would be considered contrary in nature to the true Catholic faith,[12] during the process of consulting the astronomical calculations, in accordance with my learning (and to the best of my abilities).

10) The expanse of time past (of our fathers who came before us) is as such, subjecting myself to the correction of the most learned men, that the first man Adam arrived 1242 years before Noah, not by the computation of time according to the Gentile records as Varro did, but in accordance to the Sacred Scriptures, as best my understanding and astronomical calculations can comprehend them. 1,080 years after Noah[13] and the universal flood, arrived Abraham[14], who some say was a gifted astrologer and the inventor of the Chaldean alphabet. Some 515 or 516 years later, came Moses.[15] Between the time of Moses and David[16], 570 years elapsed. From the time of David to the birth of Jesus Christ[17] our Savior and Redeemer (born of the Virgin Mary[18]), 1,350 years elapsed (according to some chronographs).[19] Some may disagree with my calculations here and think them false, since they differ from those of Eusebius.[20] From the time of the human redemption to the hateful apostasy (or

---

[10] Nostradamus hopes (and possibly foresees) that the substantive nature of his prophetic writings will "carry more weight" in future times than during the era of his own life. Seemingly, as per his hope, this has indeed been the case (especially during the twentieth century). As time passes, one can see the past from a clearer perspective.

[11] In part, this is a contradiction to language in paragraph #16 in the Preface.

[12] In general terms, nothing which is contrary to the Christian religion, more specifically, nothing which is contradictory to the doctrines (or canons) of the Catholic Church.

[13] The patriarch God chose to build the ark in which Noah and his family (and pairs of animals) were saved from the universal flood (Genesis 5:9).

[14] The first patriarch (and progenitor) of the Hebrew people; father of Issac (Genesis 11:25).

[15] The law giver who led the Israelites out of Egypt.

[16] The second king of Judah and Israel and successor to Saul, the father of King Solomon (the reputed author of many of the Psalms).

[17] The son of Mary and founder of Christianity; regarded by Christians as the son of God and the Messiah.

[18] The wife of Joseph, who through immaculate conception, gave birth to Jesus Christ in the town of Bethlehem (where David once lived).

[19] Many scholars disagree with Nostradamus' chronology here and it contradicts the lengthy chronology he lists again in paragraph #40 of the Epistle.

[20] An ecclesiastical historian and Bishop of Caesarea (which is located on the northwest coast of Israel). Eusebius lived from 260-340 A.D.

heresy) of the Saracens, 621 years, or there about, passed. Now, it is easy to gather from this, the amount of time which has come to pass.

11) Though my calculations may be not good and available for all nations, they have however been calculated by celestial movements combined (as associated in my case) with an emotion which "steals over me at certain hours", resulting from an emotional tendency which I inherited from my ancestors. But the dangers of our times, O most serene Sovereign, requires that such secret events (prophecies) should not be bared (or manifested) except in enigmatic sentences, having but one sense and only one meaning, with nothing ambiguous or amphibological added. Instead they (were written) under a veiled obscurity, emanating from the same natural emotional outflow which resembles the sentential delivery of the 1002 Prophets that have existed since the Creation of the world, as per the calculations and Punic Chronicle of Joel: *I will pour out my spirit upon all flesh, and your sons and daughters will prophesy.*[21] But such prophecy did proceed from the mouth of the Holy Spirit, who was the sovereign and eternal power, in conjunction with the celestial bodies, which has inspired a great number of people to predict great and marvelous events.

12) As for myself, I set up no claim to such a title -- never, God forbid. I can honestly profess that "all" proceeds from God, and in return for that, I render him thanks, honor, and immortal praise. I have intermingled therewith, no divination which proceeds from fate, but from God and nature. Most of it is combined with the movement and course of the celestial (heavenly) bodies, as if we were looking into a burning mirror[22] and saw, with clouded and obscured vision, the great events (some sad and sinister) and calamitous occurrences which are about to fall upon the principal worshipers.[23] Firstly, upon the temples of God. Secondly upon those who, sustained by the Earth, this decadence draws near, and a thousand other calamitous incidents which will be known to occur in the course of time.

13) God will take notice of the long bareness of the Great Lady, who will conceive two principal children. But, she being in great danger, adjoined to her by the temerity of the hour of death, will decline in her 18th year, and it being impossible to outlive the 36th, will leave three males and one female, and he will birth two (children) who will not have the same father.

14) The three brothers will be quite different, then united and agreed, and 3/4 of Europe will tremble. Through a shorter period, the Christian monarchy shall be augmented and sustained. The parties shall be elevated, then suddenly cast down. The Arabs driven back, kingdoms will be created and new laws promulgated.

15) With the other children, the first shall rule the furious crowned Lions, holding their paws upon the intrepid escutcheon (shield).

---

[21] A reference to Joel (2:28), from the old testament of the Holy Bible.
[22] Or possibly "lens"
[23] A reference to Christians (the "principal worshipers" of Jesus Christ)

16) The second one in age (the second brother), will penetrate so far into Italy that a second trembling (and furious descent) shall be made, descending the Great St. Benard Pass to ascend the Pyrenees, which will not however, be transferred to the French Crown, and a third inundation (an overflowing) of human blood will result and for a long time Lent will not include Mars.

17) The daughter will be given for the preservation of the Christian Church. Her dominator shall fall into the Pagan sect of new infidels. She will give birth to two children. One shall be faithful, the other child an infidel, by the confirmation of the Catholic faith.

18) The other (the unfaithful child), to his great confusion and tardy repentance, will have wished to ruin her. He will have three regions (which extend over a vast area), namely the Roman (Italy), Germany, and Spain, which will create sects and will entail a great intricacy of military handling. This will stretch from the 50th to the 52nd degree of latitude (north), who will be left behind.

19) They (the three regions of Italy, Germany, and Spain) will render the homage of ancient religions to the more distant region of Europe north of the 40th degree of latitude, who at first (in a vain timidity) will tremble, followed by the regions of the west, south, and east (who will also tremble). The power (of the west, south, and east) will be such in nature, that what has been brought about by union and concord will prove to be insurmountable by warlike conquest.

20) They will be equal in their nature, yet very different in faith.

21) After this, the sterile Lady, now more powerful than the second, will be received by two nations. By the first nation made obstinate by he who had power over the others.

22) By the second and third (nations), whose forces shall extend forces towards the circuit to the east of Europe. There in the Pannonias, his forces (standards) will be stopped and slaughtered, but by sea, he will run to Trinacria[24] and the Adriatic with his myrmidons. The Germans shall fail (wholly) and the Barbaric sect (disquieted), shall be driven back by the whole Latin race.

23) Then shall begin the "grand Empire of Antichrist" (or the great Empire of the Antichrist) in the region of the former empire of Attila. This new Xerxes[25] descends (or "will arrive in force") with large and countless multitudes, so that the coming of the Holy Ghost, proceeding from the 48th degree,[26] shall make a transmigration,[27] driving away the abomination (the vile hatred) of the Antichrist that made war upon the royal Pope (vicar of Jesus Christ) and His Church (the Catholic Church), whose reign will be *for a time, and to the end of time.*

---

[24]Ancient name for Sicily, an Italian Island in the Mediterranean Sea.

[25]Attila was the leader of the Huns, the 5th century Asiatic invaders of Europe. Xerxes was the Persian king who unsuccessfully invaded Greece in the 5th century B.C..

[26]Of latitude north, this includes the geographic regions of Russia, China, and Mongolia.

[27]The passing of the human soul at death, from one body to another (metempsychosis), i.e., "transmigration of souls". This was a doctrine taught in ancient Greece and Egypt.

24) This will be preceded by a solar eclipse, more dark and gloomy than has ever occurred since the creation of the world, up to the death (and passion) of Jesus Christ and from then until now. It will be in the month of October that the "grand translation" (or great revolution) will occur (will be made), such that one will think that the libation[28] (gravity) of the Earth (the Earth's gravity) has lost its natural movement in (or passing into) the abyss of perpetual darkness.

25) In the spring-time there will be seen precursive signs (warning signs), and afterwards extreme changes; the reversal of kingdoms[29] and mighty earthquakes. All this will be accompanied with the procreations of the New Babylon[30], a miserable prostitute enlarged by the abomination of the first holocaust. It will only last for seventy three years and seven months.

26) Then, from the stock which had remained barren for so long a time, there will be issued (proceeding from the 50th degree[31]), one who will renovate the entire Christian Church. Then great peace, unity, and concord (results) between some of the children of races long opposed to one another, separated by diverse realms. Such will be the peace established, that the instigator and promoter of military faction, through means of the "diversity of religions", shall be tied to the bottom of the deepest pit, and united to the kingdom of "the furious one", who counterfeits the sage.

27) All the countries, cities, towns, and provinces who have abandoned their old customs to free themselves, will in fact enthrall themselves even deeper, and will secretly become weary of their liberty (their true religion lost), will begin to strike to the left, to return more than ever to the right.

28) In the place of holiness, so long desecrated, as with their former writings (circulating slanders), afterwards will come the great dog, as an irresistible mastiff who will destroy everything, even that which may have been prepared in times past, their Churches will be restored as before and the clergyman reinstated to his original position, till it lapses back into whoredom and luxury, committing (and perpetrating) a thousand crimes.

29) And upon the eve of another desolation, when she[32] will be atop her highest and most sublime point of dignity, the potentates and generals will rise up against her and will take away her two swords and leave her nothing but the insignia whose curvature attracts them. The people will cause it to go straight and will not be willing to submit themselves to those of the opposite extreme, whose hands, held in an acute angle, toucheth the ground they shall provoke.[33]

---

[28]Librate means to balance, to hang balanced, to vibrate as does a balance. Perhaps this is an allusion to a futuristic polar shift of the Earth or some other type of massive geo-magnetic fluctuation.
[29]Suggesting a reversal of fortune for nations damaged by futuristic earthquakes and/or war and famine.
[30]An allusion to a new version of the ancient city of Babylon (any rich, but vicious city).
[31]Suggesting the 50th degree of latitude north.
[32]An allusion to France.
[33]An allusion to the Nazis and their swastika emblem (the "insignia" of the Nazis).

30) Until there will be born, unto the branch a long time sterile, a person[34] who will rescue the French people from the "benign slavery"[35] which they voluntarily submitted to[36], placing himself under the protection of Mars[37], and stripping Jupiter[38] of all his dignities and honors, establishing himself in the free city in another scant Mesopotamia. The chief and governor[39] shall be tossed from the midst and hung in the air, ignorant of the conspiracy of the ones who conspired with the second Thrasibulus, who for a long time directed (or prepared) all of this.

31) Then, all the impurities and abominations will be, with the greatest of shame, set forth (and manifested) to the darkness of the veiled light[40], ceasing near the end of the change in reign, and the leaders of the Church[41] shall exhibit little of the love of God, while many of them will apostatize (abandon or stray away from) the truth faith.[42] Of the three sects, that which is positioned in the middle, upon the actions of its own partisans (or worshipers) will be thrown into a little decadence.[43] The first one will be exterminated throughout Europe, and the major part of Africa, by the third one, who through the means of the poor-in-spirit, by madness brought into existence by lustful desires, will adulterate.

32) The people will collapse the pillar and chase off those who adhered to the legislators and it will seem, from the kingdoms weakened by the Easterners, that God-the-Creator has unleashed Satan from the prisons of hell[44] making room for the great Dog and Dohan, which will produce such a great and injurious breach in the Churches, that neither the reds nor the whites (without their eyes and hands) will be able to judge the situation, and their power shall be taken (away) from them.

33) And then shall commence, a persecution of the Church[45], the likes of which has never been seen before. And while this is occurring, so great a pestilence shall arise that it will remove two thirds of mankind[46]. This will proceed to such a degree that one will be unable to distinguish (or recognize) the fields and houses, and grass (or

---

[34]Possibly an allusion to the French general (and leader) Charles De Gaulle.

[35]Possibly an allusion to Nazism.

[36]Possibly an allusion to the collusion between certain members of the French government and the German government at the beginning of World War II.

[37]In astrology the planet Mars is symbolic of war. In mythology Mars was the god of war, so this is perhaps an allusion to French and Allied generals of World War II.

[38]In Roman mythology, Jupiter was the supreme God, a supporter and defender of the Roman state, perhaps an allusion to Mussolini or Hitler.

[39]Possibly an allusion to Hitler and Mussolini.

[40]Possibly an allusion to the exposure of the atrocities committed by the Nazis during World War II (the Holocaust).

[41]Christianity

[42]Preaching a doctrine opposite of the truth faith (or word of God).

[43]Perhaps placing us in our modern "decadent" times, as per the chronological symbology of this section of the Epistle.

[44]Perhaps an allusion to the "yet-to-arrive" third Antichrist and his war.

[45]The Christian nations will receive great injury due to war with unnamed eastern Asian nations. Might China (or other Asian nations) be responsible?

[46]An "as-yet-to-occur" global pestilence which will occur during a period of future conflict resulting in the death of 66.6% of the world's population. Could there be a correlation between this event, and the number of the beast (666)?

weeds) will grow knee high in the streets of cities. The clergy[47] will face total ruin, military men (or warlords) will usurp (seize and hold power by force) what is returned from the City of the Sun, from Malta[48], and the Islands of Hières[49] and the great chain of the port, which takes its name from the marine ox, shall be opened.

34) From the maritime shores, a new incursion (invasion) will be made to liberate the Sierra Morena from its capture by the Mahometans. Their assaults shall not be in vain. The region which was once the abode of Abraham shall be assailed by those who hold the Jovialists[50] in reverence. The city of Achem[51] will be surrounded and attacked on all sides (from every direction) by a great force of armed troops. Their maritime forces (the naval and marine troops of the invaders of Israel) will be weakened by the Westerners[52] and upon this kingdom a great desolation will occur and the great cities will be depopulated. Those who enter within ("this kingdom" and "its great depopulated cities") will fall under the vengeance of the wrath of God[53].

35) The Holy Sepulchre[54], for a long period an object of great veneration, will remain exposed under the stars of heaven, the Sun and the Moon. The holy place[55] will be converted into a stable for cattle, and used for other base purposes. Oh what a horrible time it will be for pregnant women.

36) Then the "Sultan of the East"[56] will be defeated (vanquished) by the Northern[57] and Western[58] men, who will overthrow and kill him, putting the rest (of his

---

[47] Christian men (and possibly women) ordained for religious service.

[48] Malta, a former British Colony (island) located just south of Sicily in the Mediterranean Sea.

[49] Islands located near Marseilles, France.

[50] Originally, Jovialist meant "born under the influence of Jupiter". In astrology the planet Jupiter is regarded as the source of happiness. In the opinion of author Spike James, the term "Jovialists" is a reference to the followers of the ancient Syrian king Antiochus Epiphanes, who invaded Jerusalem, tore down their walls, robbed its temples and constructed a statue of Jupiter in their holiest of temples. They tried to force the Jews to worship it, but they refused. Thus the term "Jovialists" might be an allusion to the Syrians, who respected (or venerated the Jovialists of ancient times).

[51] "The modern nation of Israel (according to the American author Edgar Leoni, "Achem" is probably a Hebraic anagram for Shechem, an ancient capitol city of the Kingdom of Israel).

[52] "Westerners" appears to be an allusion to military forces from the New World (probably suggesting American troops).

[53] Paragraph thirty-four references a military invasion of Israel. It does not appear to be a reference to the war of 1967 (because although American naval forces were in the region during the conflict they failed to interact in it). Therefore this seems to reference a future military event.

[54] The sacred burial vault of Jesus Christ.

[55] This might suggest the city of Bethlehem (birth place of Jesus Christ).

[56] Perhaps an allusion to the third Antichrist, or to another powerful Middle Eastern or Asian leader. "Sultan", from Medieval Latin *Sultanus*, is defined as a ruler of a Moslem country. Could this "Sultan of the East" be an allusion to Selin?

[57] Here Nostradamus uses the word "Northern" (not Aquilon). Therefore, as used in this context, this could suggest troops from Russia, or Europe, or North America (which are located north of Israel and the Equator).

[58] Another allusion to military forces from the New World (Probably an American military force).

followers) to flight. His children (the Sultan's children), the offspring of many women, will be imprisoned. Then will be fulfilled the prophecy of the Royal Prophet,[59] "*let the sighing of the prisoner come before thee, to release the children of death*".[60]

37) Oh what great oppression will then fall upon the princes and rulers of kingdoms, even to those who are maritime and Oriental, whose languages intermingled with all the nations of the Earth - the languages of the Latin nations (and of the Arabs, via the Phoenicians).[61] All the Eastern kings will be overthrown, exterminated, and driven away, not altogether by the kings of Aquilon[62] and because of the drawing near (to the end of our age), through the three secretly united who seek out death, ambushing one another. This Triumvirate renewed, will endure (or last) seven years and its renown will spread around the world and the sacrifice of the holy wafer[63] will be upheld.

38) Then two lords of Aquilon (the Northern land)[64] will conquer the Orientals,[65] and so great an explosive and tumultuous warfare will be produced by these, that "all" the East will tremble at the noise of these two brothers of Aquilon (the North), who are yet not brothers.

39) And Sire, by this disclosure I (almost) introduce an element of confusion into these predictions (as to the time when each event shall take place). For the detailed chronology of time (which follows) conforms very little (if any at all) to what I gave above, that indeed could not err, determined by astronomical rules and in accord with the Holy Scriptures themselves. If I had wished to state the detailed date (for the occurrence) of every quatrain, I could have easily done so,[66] but it would not have been very agreeable to all, and still less agreeable to those interpreting them, until Sire, you granted me full power to do so, in order not to grant calumniators the opportunity to injure me.

40) I have reckoned the number of years, since the creation of the world to the birth of Noah as 1506 years. From the birth of Noah to the completion of the construction of the ark (at the time of the universal deluge), 600 hundred years passed (let the years be solar, lunar, or mixed). I believe the Scriptures take them to be solar years. At the end of this 600 years, Noah entered into the ark to escape

---

[59]Perhaps an allusion to Jesus Christ. The war alluded to here seems to suggest that American, European, and Russian troops combine forces to conquer an eastern oriental sultan.

[60]From the Biblical passage (Ps. lxxviii. 11).

[61]Phoenicians suggests the people of various North-African nations.

[62]A reference to future unnamed "Northern" leaders of Aquilon (Aquilon suggesting Russia, and or other nations of the former U.S.S.R.).

[63]A reference to holy communion.

[64]A reference to two powerful "northern" military leaders, perhaps one from Russia, and the other from another nation formerly of the U.S.S.R.

[65]From the East (from the "far East" presumably), i.e., China or other nations of eastern Asia. This might suggest that two powerful nations, formerly of the U.S.S.R., will make war against China and her Asian allies. Perhaps a reference to the future war with the third Antichrist (or another conflict).

[66]Nostradamus states very plainly that he could have stated the intended "date of fulfillment" for each of his quatrains if he had wanted to.

the flood. The flood was universal (covering all the Earth), and lasted for one year and two months. From the end of the flood, to the birth of Abraham, 295 years passed. From the birth of Abraham to the birth of Isaac, 100 years passed. And from the birth of Isaac to that of Jacob, 60 years passed. From the time Jacob entered Egypt, until he left, 130 years passed. Between the time that Jacob entered into Egypt, and to that of the Exodus, 430 years elapsed. And from that point, to the construction of the Temple by Solomon (during the fourth year of his reign), there elapsed 480 years. From the construction of the temple, until the birth of Jesus Christ (according to the computations of the holy writings), 490 years passed. Thus by my calculations, collecting it from the sacred writings, comes to about 4173 years and 8 months (more or less).[67] Due to the diversity of opinions, I refuse to go beyond Jesus Christ.

41) I have calculated the present prophecies in accordance with the "order of the chain" which contains the revolution, and all of it by astronomical rules, combined with my personal hereditary instincts.[68] After a period of time I found the time that Saturn turns to enter on April 7 till August 25; Jupiter from June 14 to October 7th; Mars from April 17 to June 22; Venus from April 9 to May 22; Mercury from February 3 to February 24.[69] After that from June 1 to June 24, and from September 25 to October 16, Saturn in Capricorn, Jupiter in Aquarius, Mars in Scorpio, Venus in Pisces, Mercury for a month in Capricorn, Aquarius, and Pisces, the Moon in Aquarius, the Dragons Head[70] in Libra in her opposite sign[71]. Following the conjunction of Jupiter and Mercury with a quadrin (quadrature) aspect of Mars and Mercury, and the head of the Dragon shall be with a conjunction of Sol (the Sun) with Jupiter. The year shall be peaceful without an eclipse.[72]

42) Then will begin a period (that will comprehend in itself), that which will long endure.[73] And during the first year (of this period), there will be a great persecution of the Christian Church, fiercer than that in Africa[74]. This will burst out in the year 1792.[75] They will comprehend this, and think it to be, a renovation of time.

---

[67] Many scholars disagree with this chronology and it differs from the chronology contained in paragraph ten of the Epistle.

[68] Nostradamus is stating that he used standard astronomical methods for calculating his planetary positions, but modified them slightly according to his instinct (a blend of "science and art").

[69] A personal astronomical observation of the times of year which various planets enter their given orbits.

[70] The Dragon's Head is an astrological reference to the Moon's north node.

[71] Apparently an astrological transit, but one we could not pinpoint the dates of.

[72] An eclipse occurs somewhere on Earth at least two times each year. As Nostradamus is aware there is no such thing as "a year without an eclipse". Perhaps he is suggesting that peaceful years are a scarce thing.

[73] The beginning of the French Revolution (followed by the birth of democracy and the creation of the first Republic of France).

[74] According to Ward, this is a reference to the persecution of the Vandals (the Germanic people who overran Spain, Gaul, Northern Africa, and Rome, in the 4th and 5th centuries A.D.).

[75] The fourth year of the French Revolution (1789-1799) and the year the Christian Calendar was abolished in France (though later it was restored under Napoleon I).

43) Following this, the people of Rome will begin to reestablish themselves. They will chase away obscurity and recoup a share of their ancient glory, yet not without great change and continual division. Venice[76] (afterwards) will be a powerful force, raising her wings quite high, not too short of the power of ancient Rome.

44) During the time great Byzantium[77] sails, associated with the Piedmontese,[78] and by the aid and power of Aquilon, will so impede them that the two Cretans[79] will find that they are unable to sustain their faith. Arks constructed by the ancient warriors will accompany them to the waves of Neptune.[80] In the Adriatic (Sea) such discord will arise, that what was united will be separated. That will be reduced to a house (which was before) a great city, including the Pampotamia[81] and Mesopotamia[82] of Europe at 45°, and others at 41°, 42°, and 47 degrees[83].

45) In this time (and in those countries) the infernal[84] power will set the power of its adversaries against the Church of Jesus Christ. This will constitute the second Antichrist,[85] who will persecute the Church (and its true vicar) through the means of the power of the temporal kings[86], who (in their ignorance) shall be reduced by tongues, which will cut deeper than any sword in the hands of a madman.

46) The said reign of (the) Antichrist[87] shall only last to the death of him (who was born near the beginning of the age) and of the other one of Lyons[88] associated with the elected one of the house of Modena and of Ferrara,[89] upheld by the Adriatic Piedmontese (or possibly Liguarians) and the proximity of the great Sicily. Then the Great St. Bernard will be passed.[90]

---

[76] An Italian port city at the head of the Adriatic Sea (possibly an allusion to the Italian conquest of Europe and North Africa during the 1930's and the World War II era).

[77] An allusion to "Great Britain" and her powerful naval forces in the Mediterranean Sea during World War II.

[78] A region of northwestern Italy, an allusion to the nation of Italy and her citizens.

[79] One afflicted with cretinism (an idiot), perhaps an allusion to Hitler and Mussolini.

[80] In Roman mythology, Neptune was the god of the oceans. This line appears to make reference to the naval power of the American and British fleets during World War II.

[81] An allusion to Panpotam (Sicily).

[82] An allusion to a "European" Mesopotamia (perhaps suggesting Italy).

[83] The nations of Europe located on the 41st, 42nd and 47th degrees of latitude north, which were affected by the events of World War II.

[84] Relating to hell (or to "the world of the dead" in classical mythology).

[85] An allusion to Adolf Hitler (and World War II).

[86] As used here, temporary leaders who hold absolute authority (as do kings) in their given kingdoms. This is perhaps an allusion to Hitler, Mussolini, and the Japanese Emperor of World War II.

[87] An allusion to Adolf Hitler (the so-called second Antichrist of modern Europe).

[88] A city in France at the confluence of the Saône and Rhône rivers. As used here, perhaps an allusion to Napoleon Bonaparte, Nostradamus' first so-called Antichrist of Europe).

[89] A reference to the lavish courts of renaissance Italy. Napoleon's first invasion of Italy occurred in the year of 1795.

[90] The land pass through the Alps mountain range, between France and Italy, also known as Mont Jovis. This appears to be a reference to Napoleon's crossing of the Great Saint Bernard Pass in 1800, during a French invasion of Italy.

47) The Gallic Ogmios[91] will be accompanied by such a great number (of men) that from afar the Empire will be presented with its great law. Then (and for some time afterwards) "the blood of the innocent" will be shed quite profusely by the guilty ones, who will have been recently elevated to a position of power. Then, due to great floods,[92] the memory of things (contained in such instruments) will suffer an incalculable loss -- even to the alphabet itself[93]. This will happen to the Northerners (Aquiloners)[94].

48) By the Divine Will (of God), Satan will once again be bound and universal peace will be established among all of mankind.[95] The Church of Jesus Christ will be delivered from all tribulation, though the Azostains (the Philistines)[96] will desire to "mix with the honey", the malice of their pestilent seduction. This will occur near the seventh millenary[97] when the sanctuary of Jesus Christ will no longer be down trodden by the infidels[98] who come from the North (Aquilon). The world will then be approaching its great conflagration.[99] Though according to my calculations (contained in my prophecies) the course of time stretches much further on.

49) In the epistle[100] that some years ago I dedicated to my son Caesar Nostradamus, I openly declared some points (without presage). But here, Sire, I have included many great (and marvelous) events to come, which those who follow after us (in time) shall witness.

---

[91] The Gallic Ogmios is an allusion to a powerful man from Gaul (suggesting France). This might be an allusion to Napoleon. However, if "the Gallic Ogmios" was intended to be an allusion to a futuristic leader, it may suggest that a powerful Frenchman will one day cross the Great Saint Bernard Pass with a mighty army, engaging the future invaders of Italy. There could easily be a double meaning to this line.

[92] A reference to a massive futuristic global flood.

[93] This "great flood" will be so devastating, that some countries will lose their languages.

[94] Apparently the Northerners (the Aquiloners) will be hard hit by this flood. This seems to suggest that Russia, as well as possibly other former Soviet states, might face more destruction by flooding than other areas of the world. It seems that this great flood occurs "after" the war with the future third Antichrist.

[95] A universal peace seems to follow the futuristic "great flood".

[96] An ancient country on the southwestern coast of Palestine.

[97] An uncertain date.

[98] One who is a "non-believer" with respect to some religion, especially Islam (and in some cases Christianity).

[99] A distantly futuristic period of mass destruction on the Earth by fire. One could wonder if this conflagration is a man-made event, or if it is something which results due to activity within the core of the Earth, or if it is an event thrust upon the Earth from the heavens (i.e., a great meteor shower, an asteroid or comet strike, or the passing of a comet too close to the earth). Could global warming, resulting from the decay of the Earth's ozone layer, possibly be a factor in this future conflagration?

[100] We know this as the Preface (which is located at the beginning of this book).

50) During the said astrological supputation[101], harmonized with the Holy Scriptures, the persecution of the Ecclesiastical folk[102] will originate its power through the kings of the North (Aquilon), united with the Easterners. This persecution will last for eleven years (or a little less), at which time the main Northern king will pass away[103].

51) Then later, a Southern king will persecute the clergy of the Church still more fiercely. This persecution will last for three years, by the "Apostolical seduction"[104] of one who takes away the absolute power from the Church Militant[105], and the holy people of God who observe its rituals. The entire order of religion will be so heavily persecuted, that the blood of true Ecclesiastics will float everywhere.

52) One of these horrible temporal kings will be told by his adherents, as a form of great praise, that "he will have shed more human blood of innocent Ecclesiastics, than anyone could spill of wine". Against the Church, this king will commit incredible crimes! Human blood will flow in the public streets and churches, like water flows after a heavy rain storm, and will "crimson with blood" the nearby rivers. And during another naval war, the sea will redden to such an extent that one king will comment to another king, *"the sea has blushed red with the blood of naval fights"*.

53) In this same year (and those following) there will ensue "the most horrible and astonishing pestilence".[106] This will be made even worse due to the famine which will have preceded it. Such distress and great affliction will have never been witnessed before. Nothing even approaching this situation will have ever occurred, since the first foundation of the Christian Church. This pestilence will occur throughout all the Latin regions and will leave traces in all the countries under Spanish rule.[107]

54) Then the third King of the North (Aquilon) addressing the petitions of the complaining citizens from whom he derives his main title,[108] will raise a mighty army and defy the precedent of his predecessors and ancestors and will restore almost everything back into its original condition. The great Vicar of the Cope[109] will be

---

[101] Which supputation, the one in paragraph #41 or another one?

[102] A reference to a futuristic persecution of Christians in Europe (and perhaps other regions too).

[103] Nostradamus "back-tracks" in time here from the events stated at the end of paragraph #48. It seems that the third Antichrist might originate his power in Russia (or in another former Soviet state) while united with the Easterners. The term "Easterners" is non-specific, thus it is unclear if the "Easterners" are "Middle Easterners" or "Orientals", or possibly both.

[104] Edgar Leoni speculated that this could be an allusion to some type of "Anti-Pope".

[105] An unclear allusion to future militant behavior by the Christian Church (or its representatives).

[106] A reference to the spread of an epidemic disease (or fatal chemical or biological agent) during an era of intense warfare.

[107] Suggesting various regions of the New World (once under Spanish dominion).

[108] This passage seems to suggest that the King of Aquilon derives his position of power from the citizens, which in a liberal sense, suggests that this "King" (or leader) will be elected by "the people" (as in a democracy).

[109] In the Roman Catholic Church a "vicar" is a deputy or representative for an ecclesiastic. A "cope" is a long ecclesiastical vestment worn over an alb or surplice. This seems to suggest a pope.

restored to his former state. But desolated, and abandoned by everyone, he will return to the sanctuary,[110] which was destroyed by paganism when the Old and New Testament were thrown out and burnt.[111]

55) After that Antichrist[112] will come the infernal prince.[113] Upon this final epoch[114], all the kingdoms of Christianity (including those of the infidels) will tremble for a period of twenty five years. The wars and battles will create great grief. Towns, cities, castles, and all the other buildings will be desolated, burnt, and destroyed with a great pouring of vestal blood. Married women, and widows, will be raped and violated. Breast fed babies will be thrown, and broken against the walls of cities. So many evil deeds will be committed (through means of Satan) that nearly the entire world shall become undone and desolated! Before these events will occur, certain strange birds will cry in the air, "Today! Today!", and after awhile will disappear.[115]

56) After this has endured awhile there will be (almost renewed) another reign of Saturn, a golden age.[116] Upon hearing the affliction of His people, God the Creator will command Satan to be hurled downward, and bound in the deep abyss. Then a universal peace between God, and men, will commence. Satan will be bound for a thousand years, then unleashed again.

57) All these figures have been justly integrated between the Sacred Scriptures and the visible celestial bodies, namely by Saturn, Jupiter, and Mars (as well as other planets in conjunction with them), as can be seen more at large in some of my quatrains. I would have calculated them a bit deeper (and coordinated one with the other), but realizing, O most serene King, the fact that some people who are given to censure would raise difficulties (standing ready to censure me). Thus now I choose to retire my pen and seek my nocturnal repose.

58) *Many things (events), O most powerful king of them all, of the most incredible sort, are soon to transpire, yet I could neither (nor would) list them all into this epistle. Yet in order to comprehend various (certain) facts, a few horrible destinies (or realities) must be set forth. Your humanity, towards all men, is so great, and your piety towards the gods, that you alone seem worthy of the great title of the most Christian King, and to whom the highest authority in all religion should be deferred.*

---

[110]Possibly suggesting Rome (the present seat of the Vatican).

[111]After the restoration of the Catholic Church, a pope will return to Rome only to discover that paganism is flourishing.

[112]Apparently an allusion to the third Antichrist.

[113]A reference to Satan.

[114]A particular period of history regarded in some way as remarkable or memorable.

[115]This is an interesting passage yet its meaning is unclear.

[116]Nostradamus foresees a golden (and harmonious) period of 1000 years following the gloomy period of future international war with the yet-to-arrive third Antichrist).

59) But I shall only beseech (implore) you, O most clement King, by your singular and prudent goodness, to understand the desire of my heart, and the sovereign desire I have to obey your excellent Majesty, since my eyes approached your splendor, than the grandeur of my activities can attain to, or acquire.

Michel Nostradamus from Salon, this 27th of June, 1558.

IN CONCLUSION

It was not the author's goal to create a pessimistic, or paranoid sense of the future in this book. Hopefully the future holds an abundance of good times for all of us. Yet somewhere between optimism and pessimism, perhaps reality can be found.

But what if Nostradamus was right? What if the future was actually laid out for us in his quatrains? Then what? One Nostradamus commentator suggested that simply being aware of possible negative events in the future might provide two-thirds of the cure necessary to effectively deal with them.

Was Nostradamus attempting to "shock" the people of our time into a path of lucid behavior, allowing us the opportunity to correct certain trends before it is too late to correct them? Or is it too late? Careful analysis of both on-going environmental changes and international events appears to be the call of duty to both the people of our time, and of the near future. By accurately monitoring international events, hopefully we can design effective contingency plans as a means to avoid, or contend with, some of the negative events which Nostradamus foresaw.

Though it defies our understanding of physics and logic, could it have been possible for one man to transcend the planes of space and time in a manner that allowed him to accurately foresee future events?

If it is possible that one person was able to accomplish this feat, should it be considered a miracle, or could this ability be more feasible than what we have convinced ourselves to believe is possible? The answer remains unclear. However, we should not exclude the remote possibility that Nostradamus somehow succeeded in this task.

So what are we to think about Michel de Nostre-Dame, the time-traveling voyeur of Renaissance France? What conclusions should we, as modern men and women, draw from the quatrains and other writings of Nostradamus?

Do you, the reader, see a similarity between history and some of the events prophesied in the quatrains? Did Nostradamus hit the nail on the head on some predictions, while others appear ambiguous or non-specific?

The majority of readers will probably find a correlation between the quatrains and past history, as well as between certain quatrains and the near future, based on current events, as they unfurl themselves before us.

Could a case be made for the likelihood of the future appearance of a third Antichrist, based upon the accuracy of the quatrains dealing with Napoleon and Hitler? Will wars, plagues, and famines manifest themselves around the change of the millennium? Will earthquakes, floods, and other natural disasters continue to occur as Nostradamus predicted? What about all the other events Nostradamus foresaw in the future? Rather than the author aiming the readers towards predetermined answers to these questions, readers should make their own deductions based upon the information presented herein.

The sense of the future perceived through Nostradamus is not what most of us would like to envision. Since Nostradamus, a mortal man, could not override "the will of God," all he could do as one individual was describe what he saw (and felt) in his visions, and hope that his writings would affect the collective free-will of his future readers in a manner that would maximize the odds of the most desirable outcome for humanity. This is the author's perception of his message. What is yours? Your perceptions may parallel mine, or they may be quite different.

If Nostradamus is correct, and if the author's personal interpretations of his prophecies are also correct and accurate, then the challenge to change our fate has just begun. According to legend it is rumored that Nostradamus suggested during his lifetime that it might be possible to change or alter his predictions of the future. Maybe that is possible, or maybe it is not. For our sake, and the sake of our children and their children, let's hope that's the case!

So what is the bottom line regarding our future? Is "reality" the collective sum of every individual's exertion of personal free will, or is so-called "reality" predetermined by the will of an all-powerful spiritual entity? Could "reality" consist of a combination of both collective free will and spiritual predestination? Again, the answer remains unclear, however, remember the future, remember the future, and never give up on it!

ADDENDUM

As stated in a previous chapter, this book is an unbiased examination of the writings of Michel de Nostredamus. The author neither advocates nor denounces Nostradamus as a prophet, and this book should never be confused with the spiritual prophecies contained in the Holy Bible or any other books of religion.

Readers should remember that Nostradamus never claimed to be a savior, or anything of the sort. He never claimed to be perfect, and when he died, he passed on like every other mortal man. So if anyone ever suggests that Nostradamus considered himself to be a spiritual demi-god or the originator of some new religion, they are absolutely incorrect!

Furthermore, anyone who considers the academic examination of Nostradamus' writings to be a form of "worship" in some type of New Age religion, is also incorrect. Nostradamus never intended for anyone to "worship" him, or his writings, as one would worship God. In the opinion of the author, Nostradamus would express pity for any individual foolish enough to do otherwise, and as a Christian, he would probably pray for their spiritual enlightenment! Therefore, the concept of "worship" should not be applied to the study of Nostradamus' writings.

It was never Nostradamus' intention to compete with any religion and he never presented himself in that manner. In the Preface, Nostradamus clearly stated his position as a Christian and declared that his prophetic insight emanated directly from God.

With the arrival of the third millennium A.D., the subjects of religion and prophecy have been brought to the forefront of the minds of millions of people across the world. Due to this, and in light of the fact that Nostradamus was a Christian, it seems prudent to briefly address several of the many Scriptures from the Bible pertaining to the topic of prophecy. Consider them spiritual food for thought.

In the book of 1 Corinthians 12:10, there is a list of the Nine Gifts of the Spirit. Among these spiritual gifts, the sixth gift is the ability to prophesy. This scripture states "to another is given (the gift of) prophecy". If interpreted literally, this passage appears to suggest that the human ability to accurately prophesy Earthly events is actually a spiritual gift from God.

Deuteronomy 18:15 states "the Lord thy God will raise up a prophet from the midst of thee, of thy brethren like unto me; unto him ye shall harken". The word "brethren" as defined in ecclesiastical terms, suggests a member of a men's religious order who is not in holy orders, but engages in the work of the order. Considering that Nostradamus was a devout member of the Catholic Church and was a personal friend of Pope Pius IV, this would seem to easily qualify him as a member of Christ's brethren. To "harken" means to listen attentively; to give heed.

Deuteronomy 18:18 states "I will raise them up a prophet from among their brethren, like unto thee, and will put my words in his mouth; and he shall speak unto them all that I shall command him." The prophet (or prophets) referred to in this passage remain unnamed. Among many possibilities, would someone like Nostradamus qualify as a prophet according to this scripture?

Deuteronomy 18:22 states "when a prophet speaketh in the name of the Lord, if the thing follow not, nor come to pass, that is the thing which the Lord hath not spoken, but the prophet hath spoken it presumptuously -- thou shall not be afraid of him." This passage appears to state that if a prophet prophesies an Earthly event which does not come to pass, then the prophecy was not something which came from the mouth of God. Amos 3:7 states "for the Sovereign Lord Jehovah will not do a thing unless he has revealed his confidential matter to his servants the prophets." This is an interesting thought.

Matthew 7:15-20, warns us of false prophets and provides us with a standard by which to judge the works of prophets "...ye shall know them by their fruits" states verse 16. This seems to suggest that if a prophet's prophecy later becomes reality, then the prophecy "bore fruit". Thus, judge Nostradamus (or any prophet) by the "good fruit" of his successful prophecies. If the prophet's predictions bear good fruit, and if the prophet declares that his prophetic ability emanates from God, maybe we should consider what he has to say.

According to the writings of one Christian theologian, if a prophet arises who claims the ability to fix a calendar date for the Second Coming of Christ, that person should be considered a false prophet, for nowhere in the Scripture is a date given for that event (I Thess. 5:1-2, Matt. 24:42-44, Acts 1:6-7). And with this in mind, for what it may be worth, Nostradamus never attempted to predict a date for Jesus' return to this planet!

In the second chapter of the Book of Acts 2, verses 17-19, Peter quoted the words of the prophet Joel and declared "And it shall come to pass in the last days, saith God, I will pour out of my Spirit upon all flesh: and your sons and your daughters shall prophesy, and your young men shall see visions, and your old men shall dream dreams. And on my servants and handmaidens I will pour out in those days of my Spirit; and they shall prophesy and I will show wonders in heaven above, and signs in the Earth beneath." This passage appears to suggest that many prophets among the believers of Christianity will surface during the so-called "last days" and will speak the holy words poured into their souls by God.

This passage also states that during the "last days" (an undated period of time preceding the second coming of Christ), God will show us "wonders in heaven above (suggesting atmospheric or celestial events) and signs in the Earth beneath" (suggesting mighty earthquakes or shifts in the geological core of the earth).

In regard to the future global flood Nostradamus prophecied, one should consider the wisdom of Matt. 24:39. It states "And they did not understand until the flood came and swept them away."

How Nostradamus' prophecies compare to those contained in the Bible is a matter of great public interest. Some might say the two parallel each other at various points, others might be of the opinion that there is little or no correlation between the two. However, this topic remains an interesting area of on-going research and philosophical (and spiritual) debate.

INDEX TO THE QUATRAINS

Adria	156
Adriatic Sea	89, 94, 106
Aegean	133
Aegean Sea	115
Aenobarbe	65, 153
aerial fire	115
Africa	62, 63, 108, 173
agricultural famine	122
Aix	76
Alania	158
Alba	105, 107
Albanians	174
Algiers	77
Allied fleet	131
Alps	110, 126
ambassador	71, 82
ambush	45, 106, 123
America	155, 161
amphibious support	78
Anthony	136
Antichrist	155, 159, 161
Apennines	157
Aquarius	160, 174, 177
Aquilon	50, 90
Arab	106, 107
Arab Empire	102
Arab Language	94
Arab Prince	174
Arabia Felix	109
Arabs	134, 136, 138, 164
Arctic pole	117, 118
Ardennes	65
Arethusa	143, 187
Aries	151
Arles	51, 76
Armenia	158
army	56, 59, 106, 123, 139
Artemis	145
Asia	62, 63, 103, 162, 172, 189
Asia minor	95
assassinated	81
Athens	174
Auch	116, 175
Ausonne	152
Austria	59
Austrian Hungarians	107
Avignon	76, 99
Babel	157
babies	187
Balance	103
Balliensis	83
barbarian	76, 80, 99, 112, 128, 134
Barbarian blood	118
barbarian fleet	53
Barbarian hands	124
Barbarian league	112
Barbarian Satrap	111
Barcelona	77, 121, 124
bark (of St. Peter)	111
barrel of bees' honey	50
battle	54, 61, 75, 83, 88, 92, 125
battlefield	40
bear	120
bearded star	81, 153
bearer of a petition	147
Bible	112
bird of prey	53, 143
black	42, 130
black head-dress	134
black one	119
Black Sea	106, 158
Blois	104
blood	63, 72, 85, 95, 97, 102, 166
Blue Turban King	160, 177
bluish-greens	159
Bohemia	66, 114
Bordeaux	54, 92
Borne	127
Boulogne	66
breech	137
Bretons	92
Brindisi	48, 126
British Isles	67
British nation	151
Brittany	105
Brussels	56
bushels of wheat	188
Byzantine	102, 129
Byzantine leader	138
Byzantium	74, 112, 118, 131, 174
Cadiz	131
calamity	172, 188
Camel	110
Campania	89
Cancer	115, 175, 177
Canton of Lucerene	127
Capricorn	177
captive	43, 68, 143
captivity	93, 172, 188
Capua	48, 138
Carcassonne	96, 116
Carmania	98

Castor and Pollux	81
Celtic	88
Celtic nation	48
Celts	158
Chalice	165
chief adversary	46
Christian King	104
Church	49, 174
church buildings	164
church men	166
Church of God	164
circle	90
clergy	166
cloud	84, 113
coast	62, 80
Cock	42, 79, 110, 127, 128, 166
Cologne	66
combat	53, 75, 79, 92, 103
comet	87
common & social	101
communal law	101
confederated	79
conjunct	173
consecration	123
conversation	133
copse	149
Corinth	172, 189
Corsica	124
country	191
Cremona	143
Crescent Sea	152
Crete	43
crops	105
cruel	66, 70
crusaders	64, 95, 176
Cyclades	96, 114
cycle of the ages	84
Cyrrene Sea	96
Dacia	66, 67
Dalmatia	83, 89, 134
Danube	64, 68, 110
dead	46, 97
death	67, 79, 148, 163
deceive	112
defense	46
De Gaule	72
destruction	87
Diana (Artemis)	154
dictator	97
discord	73
disease	84
divine one	36, 103
divine splendour	36
Divine Spirit	37
divine word	37
drizzle	137, 152
drought	93, 172, 189
drowned	189
duels	151
Duke	67, 102, 105
Durance	49, 100
eagle	40, 45, 122, 128, 166
Earth	37, 47, 103, 138, 153, 175, 187, 190
earthquake	172, 189
East	85, 109, 118, 129
Easter	153
Ebro	189
Egypt	74, 89, 174
elected	163, 164
Empire	41, 49, 51, 70, 115
enemy	123, 163
England	66, 152, 155
English	92, 118, 133
English chief	153
English fleet	152
English prince	151
Euboea	80, 82
Europe	58, 82, 159, 162
evil	95, 124, 147
exiled	159
faith	76
false ashes	114
false trumpet	74
famine	60, 68, 76, 84, 90, 91, 93, 114, 117, 124, 187
Fez	159
Fiesole	125
fire	57, 63, 73, 76, 83, 87, 88, 90, 128, 137, 160, 161, 172, 175, 176, 188
first personnage	148
fish	81
fishing bark	40, 156
Flanders	66, 101
fleet	77, 81, 82, 89, 96, 108, 120, 121, 139, 173
Flemish	92, 118
flesh	61
fleur-de-lys	191
flood	73, 176
flooded	152
Florence	89, 125, 127
Foix	116, 160, 177
foreign nation	126
foreign tongue	89
fortress	61, 136
forty-eighth degree	115
France	59, 76, 77, 79, 88, 94, 100, 118, 123, 124, 157, 158, 163, 166, 176
Franco	71
fraud	124
freeman	112
French	42, 44, 53, 67, 68, 73, 94, 131
French army	126

Frenchman	51, 133
friends	90
frogs	134
gall bladder	151
Gallic	68
Gallic citizens	44
Gallic fleet	85
games of slaughter	142
Ganges	85
Garonne	175, 189
Gaul	44, 45, 51, 59, 123, 133, 157, 158
Geneva	113, 133
Genoa	45, 50, 80, 122, 126, 138
German	56, 151
Germany	57, 66, 72, 120
Ghent	56, 66, 101
Gibraltar	42
God	55
God and the Saints	190
Gods of Hannibal	157
gold	37, 68
good omen	43
governor	93
Grand Mover	84
Great Britian	152
great brothers	91
great ditch	63
great empire	155
great Empire	41, 65
great golden one	93
great King of Terror	140
great legislator	47
great man	149
great plague	93
Great Po	44
great pod	97
great pontiff	68, 84
great revelation	38
great seventh number	142
great star	84
great troop	58, 159
greatest army	59
Greece	102, 107, 118
greedy dog	60
Greeks	77
grief	68, 166
gulf	71, 131
Gulf of Arabia	120
Gulf of Quarnero	131
hail	175, 177
half pig man	75
Hannibal	99
hawk-nosed one	65
heat	80
heaven	37, 40, 84
hemisphere	117
herald	89
Hercules	72, 191
Hermes	162
Hesse	116
Hister	56, 62, 64
Hitler	56, 62, 64
hollow mountains	146
holy insurrections	114
holy laws	103
Holy Seat	163, 167
homocide	
human flesh	64
Hungarians	108
Hungary	59, 72, 114, 128, 131, 138
hunger	55, 58, 87, 93, 128
Illyria	131
incendiary	116
infidel	190
Insubria	45, 101
intelligence	127
interdict	81
invincible army	82
Ionian harbour	96
Iran	76, 106, 174
Iranian leader	113
Iranians	77
Iraq	95, 100
isles	156
Isles	69
Ismaël	134
Italian	62, 66, 88, 104, 131, 164
Italy	41, 42, 50, 72, 88, 97, 104, 118, 120, 152, 172, 188
Jordan	85
Judea	99
Jupiter	173, 175-177
King	67, 72, 102, 104, 122, 158, 175
Kingdom of the East	58
King of the Islands	154
King of the Mongols	140
King Reb	155, 161
kings	72, 162
King's daughter	158
kingship	154
lakes of Geneva	122, 189
land	57, 60, 73, 89, 98, 101, 148, 155, 159, 190, 191
Langres	105
La Rochelle	87, 92, 133
Latins	77
Latin shore	81
latitude	97
law	56, 95, 98, 108, 173
leader of France	54
leadership	70
league	162

Legate	134
legion	59
Leo	174, 175
Leon	77
Leopard	40, 165
Lerida	78
liars	174
liberty	64, 79, 121
Libra	53, 88
Libyan fleet	156
Libyan prince	94
Liége	101
Ligurian	62, 76, 109, 131
Ligurian Sea	94
Lion	42, 44, 48, 79
Lisbon	134
Loire	78, 85, 110
Lombardy	172, 188
London	56, 147
London chief	155, 161
Lucca	93
Luna	135
Lusitanian	134, 155
Lycia	95
Lyons	54, 99
Mabus	87
Macedonia	91, 136
Macedonian	133
Mahomet	94, 109
Mahometan	89
Malta	62, 138, 156
man from the East	157
Mantua	57, 143
marine	113
marine city	128
marine tower	76
marine tributary city	48
marine arts	120
Mars	57, 77, 79, 87, 140, 151, 160, 166 172-177, 189
Marseilles	50, 54, 76, 124, 131, 142
Memphis	191
Mercury	160, 172, 176, 177, 188, 189, 191
Mesopotamia	95, 100, 130
Messiah's	108
Milan	45, 48, 67, 122, 127
military hand	119
milk	83, 84
millennium	142
million men	174
moderate	42, 76
Mohammedan	73, 96
Monaco	45, 80, 93, 138
monarch	40, 72, 76, 81, 121, 156
monster	83, 120, 166
Moon	99, 172, 189
mortals	78
Moselle	78
mountains	42, 45
mule	85
Mysia	95
mystic deed	37
Mytilene	106
Naples	56, 73, 124, 128
Narbonne	54, 85, 133
nautical fog	115
naval	92
naval battle	57, 83, 137
naval victory	124
neglect	102
negligence	73, 77
negligent folly	97
Negrepont	82
Neptune	42, 85, 92
new alliance	66
new bark	51
New City	143, 146, 187
new law	99
new league	152
new trick	137
Nice	98, 138
Nicopolis	136
night	75
Nimes	153
noise	75
Norican mountains	59
Norman	131
North wind	44
Norway	67
Ocean	92, 98
Ogmios	112, 120, 136
oil and wheat	60
old British chief	48
old man	62, 70
omen	44, 53
one hundred leagues	117
one hundred thousand rubies	68
one million	54
Orient	156, 162
Orléans	62, 114
Palermo	56, 124, 128
Palestine	99
Pannonians	59
papacy	40, 163
Paris	99
Parma	106
Parthia	96
Pau	49, 97
Pavia	122, 127
peace	40, 74, 121, 160
peace and truce	121
Peloponnesus	114

peninsula	97, 114, 136
Pennine Alps	123
Perinthus	114, 136
Persia	76, 91, 106, 174
Persian leader	96
pestilence	176
pestilent	117
phalanx	48, 82, 126
Pharos	64, 106
Philip	131, 136
pillars of Hercules	66
Pisa	76, 81, 138
Pisces	176
plague	55, 97, 114, 124, 128, 136, 147, 163, 172, 188
planets	173
Po	189
poisoned	146
Poland	59, 66
poles	164
Polish	151
politics	117
Pontiff	64
pope	163, 165
populated lands	74
populated places	91
port	55, 79, 131
port of Marseilles	73
Portugal	123, 134
Portuguese	155
powerful one of Asia	159
Prelate	67
prince	41, 93, 94
promontory	42
prudent man	60
Punic faith	85
Punic heart	156
Punic ships	88
Pyrenees	96, 123
quarter of a million	44
Queen	102
rain	76
Rainbow	120
rare bird	188
Ravenna	83, 134
RAYPOZ	133
rear guard	46
rebellious	47
Red adversary	92
red fleet	45
red gulfs	125
Republic of Venice	64
reverse side metaled	102
Rhine	59, 62, 110
Rhodes	64, 80, 107, 118
Rhodians	102
Rhône	85, 91, 110, 166, 176, 189
Riviera	71
roads	191
Roanne	92
Rocheval	42
rod	157, 158
Roman	67, 73, 122, 125, 157, 163, 164
Roman land	44
Rome	48, 72, 82, 105, 106, 107, 109, 128, 139, 165
Romulus	156
Rouen	62, 92, 101
Royal blood	118
Rubicon	88
sacred pomp	47
Sagittarius	172, 188
Salona	138
Samarobryn	117
Samothrace	102
Sardina	88, 124
satrapy	48
Saturn	63, 77, 109, 133, 160, 172-174, 177, 188
Satyr	98
Saul	119
Savona	128, 138
Savoyards	126
Saxons	116
Saxony	120
scandal	135
scepter	41, 175
Scotland	155, 161
scourges	55, 74
sea	42, 57, 60, 63, 73, 93, 98, 101, 108, 115, 121, 123, 129, 134, 137, 139, 142, 148, 155, 157, 159, 191
secret study	36
Seine	78, 127
Selin	79, 104, 120-122
Seville	77
sex	125
sextons	61
ship	73, 81, 137, 172, 188
shorelines	101
Sicily	56, 73, 80, 124, 131
Siena	73, 89, 121, 138
signs	133
skies	56, 103
sky	78, 88, 116, 133, 140, 157, 175, 190
slaughter	56, 77, 87
Slavonia	83, 138
sloping park	172, 188
soul	37
sovereignty	148
Spain	42, 79, 96, 97, 109, 118, 153, 163
Spaniards	76

Spanish	66, 78	troops	54
Sparta	114	Tunis	77
spirit	37, 167	Turbans	123
squadrons	106	Turin	48, 81
St. Mark	72	Turk	107, 129
St. Paul-de-Mausole	166	Turkey	74, 112, 113, 118, 131, 158, 174
St. George	153	Turkish	104, 160, 177
strange land	135	Tuscan	77, 104
strange nation	77	Tuscany	57, 58, 89, 147
submerged island	82	twin alliance	173
suburbs	80	two great chiefs	189
Sun	40, 63, 75, 80, 84, 104, 106, 108, 109, 121, 160, 173-175, 177, 190	two great masters	90
		two great rocks	143, 187
sunrise	40, 90	tyrant	56, 79
surrendering	89	Tyrrhenian Sea	115
Susa	56	uninhabitable	91
Swiss	113	united brothers	67
sword	68, 73, 76	universal	187
Syracuse	56	unparalleled realm	112
Syria	99	unripe fruits	135
Tagus	85, 189	Vatican	118
Tartary	158	Venetians	77
Taurus	53, 177, 191	vengeance	69
temple	125, 153	Venice	69, 128, 131
temporal kings	167	Venus	62, 63, 108, 173, 174, 177
ten thousand men	126	Verona	69, 97
terror	79, 118, 122	vessels	165
Thames	87	Vestals	105
the cross	159	vex	47, 88
the fleet	85	Victor	105
the great light horses	125	victory	46, 61, 122, 137, 143
the great market	174	Vienna	66
the great one	49, 56, 152	Virgo	177
the great theater	190	volcanic fire	143, 187
the Islands	122	Vulcan	154
the Isles	121	war	72, 74, 76, 78, 79, 98, 105, 109, 113, 124, 151-153, 159, 175, 176
the Lands of the West	102, 103, 158, 172, 188		
the league	69	water	68, 113, 138, 160
the red ones	160	waters	161
the Papacy	156	wave	117
the Pillar	129	weak brain	73
the See	164	weak party	53
the three brothers	128, 166	weapon	90, 91, 97, 106
the unique one	127	West	129
the West	94, 109, 137, 176	Western fleet	53
the year 1999	140	wheat	58
Thessaly	43, 136	white territory	46
Tiber	189	White Turbin King	160, 177
Tobruk	53		
travel by air	74		
Trebizond	106		
tremble	89, 138, 191		
trembling	177, 191		
tremors	187		
trident	85, 109		
Trojan blood	87		

BIBLIOGRAPHY

1. Napoleon Self Revealed, edited by J. M. Thompson, Haughton Mifflin Co., 1934.
2. Napoleon, A Sketch of His Life, Character, Struggles and Achievements, Thomas E. Watson, Dodd, Mead and Co., New York, 1926.
3. Oracles of Nostradamus, Charles Ward, Dandom House, New York, 1940.
4. Nostradamus, The Future Foretold, The Peter Pauper Press, New York, 1983.
5. The Complete Prophecies of Nostradamus, Revised Edition, Henry C. Roberts, Nostradamus Company, New York, 1982 (footnotes in the Preface).
6. The Classic Myths in English Literature and in Art, Charles Gayley, Ginn and Company, Boston, 1939.
7. Holy Bible, (New International Version), International Bible Society, Brunswick, New Jersey, 1988.
8. Napoleon, Emil Ludwig, Garden City Publishing Co., New York, 1926,
9. Global Warming, Are We Entering the Greenhouse Century?, Stephen H. Schneider, Sierra Club Books, San Francisco, 1989.
10. After 1984, Nostradamus, Spike James, GAL Incorporated, Hampon, Virginia, 1984 (glossary terms in the Epistle).
11. Nostradamus, The Man Who Saw Through Time, Lee McCan, Wings Books, New York, 1941, 1991.
12. Prophecies on World Events By Nostradamus, Stewart Robb, Liveright Publishing Corporation, New York, 1961.
13. Scorched Earth, by the editors of Time-Life, Time-Life Books, Alexandria, Virginia, 1991.
14. Afrikakorps, by the editors of Time-Life, Time-Life Books, Alexandria, Virginia, 1991.
15. The Battle of the Atlantic - World War II, by the editors of Time-Life, Time-Life Books, Alexandria, Virginia, 1977.
16. The Bunker, The History of the Reich Chancellery Group, James P. O'Donnell, Haughton Mifflin Co., Boston, 1978.
17. Nostradamus and His Prophecies, Edgar Leoni, Bell Publishing Company, New York, 1982.
18. The Prophecies of Nostradamus, Erika Cheetham, Perigee Books, New York, 1973.
19. AION, Researches into the Phenomenology of the Self, C. G. Jung, Princeton University Press, 1959.
20. Planets in Transit, Robert Hand, Para Research, Rockport, Massachusetts, 1976.
21. The Final Prophecies of Nostradamus, Erika Cheetham, Perigee Books, New York, 1989.
22. La Premiere Face du Janus Francois, Jean-Aime de Chavigny, Pierre Roussin, Lyons, France, 1594.
23. Nostradamus, The Man Who Saw Tomorrow, Warner Bros., 1981, 88 minutes.

24. The Life, Prophecies, and Mystique of Nostradamus, American Video Corp., 1988, 102 minutes.
25. Nostradamus, Visions of the Future, J.H. Brennan, Aquarian/Thorsons, London, 1992.
26. My Life and Prophecies, Jeane Dixon, William Morrow and Co., New York, 1969.
27. Burnham's Celestial Handbook, Robert Burnham, Jr., Dover Publications, Inc., New York, 1978.
28. Alchemy, The Medieval Alchemists and their Royal Art, Johannes Fabricius, Diamond Books, London, 1994.
29. Nostradamus 2, Into the Twenty First Century, Jean-Charles de Gontbrune, Henry Holt and Company, New York, 1984.
30. "A Global Warning", by Ross Gelbspan, The American Prospect (March-April 1997), Cambridge, Massachusetts.
31. Catholic Prophecy, Yves Dupont, Tan Books, Rockford, Illinois, 1973.
32. The Discovery of Neptune, Morton Grosser, Dover Publications, New York, 1979.
33. Stars and Planets, Giorgio Abetti, American Elsevier Publishing Co., New York, 1966.

PHOTO AND ART ACKNOWLEDGEMENTS

1. NASA, 1. Lunar buggy and astronauts, 2. The Space Station.
2. The Department of Defense, 1. General Colin Powell 2. The U.S.S. San Jacinto.
3. The National Archives, 1. President John F. Kennedy 2. Nuclear Test.
4. Dallas City Archives, 1. Lee Harvey Oswald 2. Deely Plaza 3. Jack Rubey.
5. The New York Convention and Visitors Bureau Inc., Skyline of Manhattan Island.
6. Lockheed Corporation, 1. F-16 in flight over Europe, 2. Jet pilot in cockpit.
7. The Spanish Embassy, photo of General Francisco Franco.
8. The French Embassy, photo of Charles De Gaulle.
9. The Grassy Knoll, photo by Michael Ivey.
10. Adolph Hitler, #HU5234, The Trustees of the Imperial War Museum, London.
11. Mr. Sun image by S. Jackson and Stuart Reid.
12. Illustration for the "Hermes Bird" in Thomas Norton's Ordinal of Alchemy (written in 1477, published in 1652).
13. "The Climbing of Jacob's Ladder", from a popular alchemy book from the Middle Ages.